Psychoanalysis and Eco Edge of Chaos

This book argues that psychoanalysis has a unique role to play in the climate change debate through its placing emphasis on the unconscious dimensions of our mental and social lives. Exploring contributions from Freudian, Kleinian, Object Relations, Self Psychology, Jungian, and Lacanian traditions, the book discusses how psychoanalysis can help to unmask the anxieties, deficits, conflicts, phantasies and defences crucial in understanding the human dimension of the ecological crisis.

Yet despite being essential to studying environmentalism and its discontents, psychoanalysis still remains largely a 'psychology without ecology'. The philosophy of Deleuze and Guattari, combined with new developments in the sciences of complexity, help us to build upon the best of these perspectives, providing a framework able to integrate Guattari's 'three ecologies' of mind, nature and society. This book thus constitutes a timely attempt to contribute towards a critical dialogue between psychoanalysis and ecology.

Further topics of discussion include:

- ecopsychology and the greening of psychotherapy
- our ambivalent relationship to nature and the non-human
- complexity theory in psychoanalysis and ecology
- defence mechanisms against eco-anxiety and eco-grief
- Deleuze|Guattari and the three ecologies
- becoming-animal in horror and eco-apocalypse in science fiction films
- nonlinear ecopsychoanalysis.

In our era of anxiety, denial, paranoia, apathy, guilt, hope, and despair in the face of climate change, this book offers a fresh and insightful psychoanalytic perspective on the ecological crisis. As such this book will be of great interest to all those in the fields of psychoanalysis, psychology, philosophy, and ecology, as well as all who are concerned with the global environmental challenges affecting our planet's future.

Joseph Dodds lectures in various courses in psychology and psychoanalysis at the University of New York in Prague and at Charles University's CIEE Study Center. He is a candidate member of the Czech Psychoanalytical Society (IPA) and works as a psychotherapist at Terapie.Info and in private practice.

Psychoanalysis and Ecology at the Edge of Chaos

Complexity Theory, Deleuze|Guattari and Psychoanalysis for a Climate in Crisis

Joseph Dodds

Foreword by Martin Jordan

Routledge
Taylor & Francis Group

LONDON AND NEW YORK

First published 2011
by Routledge
27 Church Road, Hove, East Sussex BN3 2FA

Simultaneously published in the USA and Canada
by Routledge
711 Third Avenue, New York NY 10017

Routledge is an imprint of the Taylor & Francis Group, an Informa business

British Library Cataloguing in Publication Data
A catalogue record for this book is available from the British Library

Library of Congress Cataloging-in-Publication Data
Dodds, Joseph, 1978-
   Psychoanalysis and ecology at the edge of chaos : complexity theory,
deleuze|guattari and psychoanalysis for a climate in crisis / Joseph Dodds.
        p. cm.
   Includes bibliographical references and index.
   ISBN 978-0-415-66611-4 (hardback) – ISBN 978-0-415-66612-1 (pbk.) –
ISBN (invalid) 978-0-203-00000-0 (ebk.) 1. Climatic changes–Psychological
aspects. 2. Environmental psychology. 3. Psychoanalysis. I. Title.
   BF353.5.C55D63 2011
   150.19'5–dc22

                                                              2011008853

ISBN: 978-0-415-66611-4 (hbk)
ISBN: 978-0-415-66612-1 (pbk)
ISBN: 978-0-203-15766-4 (ebk)

Typeset in Times by Garfield Morgan, Swansea, West Glamorgan
Paperback cover design by Andrew Ward
Printed and bound in Great Britain by TJ International, Padstow, Cornwall

Contents

Figures and illustrations

Figures

Illustrations

Filmography

The Age of Stupid (Armstrong 2009)
An American Werewolf in London (Landon 1981)
Alien (Scott 1979)
Alien Resurrection (Jeunet 1997)
Avatar (Cameron 2009)
The Blair Witch Project (Myrick & Sanchez 1999)
Cat People (Schrader 1982)
The Day After Tomorrow (Emmerich 2004)
The Day the Earth Stood Still (Derrickson 2008)
The Day the Earth Stood Still (Wise 1951)
Examined Life (Astra 2008)
The Fly (Cronenberg 1986)
Franz Kafka Inaka Isha/Franz Kafka's A Country Doctor (Yamamura 2007)
The Happening (Shyamalan 2008)
The Haunting (Wise 1963)
The Lord of the Rings: The Two Towers (Jackson 2002)
The Matrix (Wachowski & Wachowski 1999)
The Metamorphosis of Mr. Samsa (Leaf 1977)
Natural Born Killers (Stone 1994)
The Others (Amenabar 2001)
Psycho (Hitchcock 1960)
Sex, Lies, and Videotape (Soderbergh 1989)
Suspiria (Argento 1977)
Wall-E (Stanton 2008)
Willard (Mann 1971)
The Wolfman (Johnson 2010)

Preface

> . . . we are not outside the ecology for which we plan – we are always and
> inevitably a part of it. Herein lies the charm and the terror of ecology
>
> (Bateson 2000: 512)

Climate change is increasingly recognized as perhaps the single biggest
threat to have faced our species, but existing approaches constitute an
'ecology without psychology', and psychoanalysis is required to unmask the
anxieties, deficits, conflicts, phantasies and defences crucial in understanding the human dimension of the ecological crisis, the phantasy of ecology.
Psychology is the missing link in the climate change debate, and this book
argues that psychoanalysis has a unique role to play, with its emphasis on
the unconscious dimensions of our mental and social lives.

This investigation begins by reviewing the important contributions of
various psychological approaches to the problem of climate change, including cognitive psychology, evolutionary psychology, consumer psychology,
environmental psychology, and social learning theory. While acknowledging
the need for all these areas of psychological research into the common crisis,
this book follows a predominantly psychoanalytic approach. Starting from
Freudian approaches to eco-anxiety and defence, and to our civilization's
highly ambivalent relation to the other-than-human world, the book moves
on to the potential contributions of object relations theory in this area,
which offers us a more ecological and relational approach to human
subjectivity and takes us further towards a truly ecopsychoanalytic model.

However, despite being essential to studying environmentalism and its
discontents, psychoanalysis still remains, thus far at least, largely a 'psychology without ecology'. Ecopsychology attempts to move beyond anthropocentrism by combining insights from both ecology and psychology,
offering an ecology of phantasy stressing the importance of the non-human
environment in human development and offering a broader understanding
of the role of 'nature' in psychotherapy. However, while invaluable in
correcting certain psychoanalytic blind spots, ecopsychology runs the risk of

idealizing and mystifying 'Nature', a danger Lacanian and postmodern approaches aim to deconstruct through an 'ecology without nature'. Taken too far, however, this leads to nature dissolving entirely into the human, all too human, realm of the signifier.

Ultimately all these approaches are unable to integrate the different levels of analysis required to effectively deal with and conceptualize climate change. The philosophy of Deleuze and Guattari, combined with new developments in the sciences of complexity, help us to build on the best of these perspectives, while avoiding many of the pitfalls. They provide a framework, or rather a 'meshwork', able to integrate Guattari's 'three ecologies' of mind, nature and society, not as a Hegelian or even Gaian 'totality', but, through a morphogenetic study of processes such as self-organization and emergence, building up assemblages on all levels, from the bottom up.

This book builds upon research undertaken for an MPhil in Psycho-analytic Studies (Dodds 2010) at Sheffield University's School for Health and Related Research (ScHARR), and on 15 years of engagement with both psychoanalysis and the ecological movement, which I increasingly came to see as more intimately related than either field generally realized, outside of the work of a few ecopsychological pioneers. The work consti-tutes an attempt to contribute towards a critical dialogue between psycho-analysis and ecology. In our era of anxiety, denial, paranoia, apathy, guilt, hope, and despair in the face of climate change, this seems more urgent now than ever.

As such it is hoped that the book will be of interest to those in the fields of psychoanalysis, psychology and psychotherapy, as well as to wider communities in social theory, philosophy, and ecology, and all who are concerned with the global environmental challenges affecting our planet's future. This book therefore explores the possibility of a nonlinear eco-psychoanalysis (Dodds 2011c) with which to respond to the crisis of a climate at the edge of chaos, in the hope that it will be possible to construct a new alpha function (Bion 1962a) capable of dreaming at the precipice.

Foreword

Ecopsychoanalysis represents a major step forward in attempting to think about the relationship between psychoanalysis, ecology, 'the natural' and the problem of climate change. It is our very embeddedness in a matrix of relationships between mind, nature and society that makes it so difficult to see what we are doing and to feel its consequences, so that to think in ecological terms becomes very problematic.

Psychoanalysis has always subverted dominant notions of a coherent, ordered, known and conscious self. In the same way climate change tells us that nature can be manipulated, disordered and attacking, rather than a benign and stable backdrop to our lives. The very ground of our existence is troubling us deeply, even persecuting us for our desires and behaviours. What does psychoanalysis have to say about climate change? How can it shed light on our response, or lack of response, to the threat? Can eco-activism itself be seen as an unreflective acting out of unexamined desires and prejudices? Psychoanalysis at its best holds up a mirror to the self and the society around it. Harold Searles (1960, 1972) pioneered psychoanalytic approaches in this area with his seminal work on the non-human environment. Dodds contemporizes psychoanalysis by placing it within a complex, nonlinear web, part of a much broader set of ecological relationships and ideas.

Showing himself to be a 'nomadic scholar' of the highest order Dodds both draws on relevant psychoanalytic ideas to explore the ecological terrain, and points out its limitations in remaining, in spite of all its advantages, fundamentally a psychology without ecology. By drawing upon the geophilosophy of Deleuze and Guattari and current thinking in complexity theory, he puts together an exciting and very interesting argument (or arguments in a rhizomatic form) for how we may approach this current crisis. He doesn't shy away from the problems inherent in a romanticization of nature which if left unchecked threatens to turn it into a Disney theme park. He asks, as others have started to do in the field of ecocriticism (Morton 2007), whether we need an ecology without the idea and projections of an idealised 'Nature'.

No one group will be completely comfortable with his ideas. The growing field of ecopsychology will be reluctant to give up on long-held notions of nature and indigenous wisdom. Since humans first manipulated their environment they have been making species extinct, yet the current human-driven mass extinction is not going to be answered by linguistic games or by imagining a benevolent Gaia which can be pacified through ritual. We need new forms of thinking and being. Many psychoanalysts will also be unhappy giving up their love of structure and the linear, although the inherent non-linearities in psychoanalytic practice and theory would find a much more appropriate home in these new ideas than the outdated nineteenth-century models of science it still so often clings to. Scholars of Deleuze and Guattari will argue that they oppose psychoanalysis on nearly every point so may be deeply sceptical of any project which involves bringing these two fields together, although, as Dodds writes, in many ways this move may be necessary to more fully develop Guattari's ideas of 'schizoanalysis', especially as applied to the clinic.

Deleuze and Guattari clearly felt psychoanalysis was important enough to require a detailed and often productive critique, and they certainly knew a lot more about psychoanalysis than many contemporary Deleuzians. Thus, in a manoeuvre some may find disorienting, he takes the important things psychoanalysis brings to the table, making psychoanalysis strange to itself, but in ways which in the long term will help it become more vital, more alive, and less weighed down with the authority that has dogged it since Freud's radical vision emerged at the turn of the twentieth century. Dodds attempts to play with what each approach has to offer in the sense of a multiplicitous heterogeneity, an assemblage of ideas and processes mirroring the interlocking complexity and chaos of climate change itself and thereby opening up new spaces for thought. What could be more Deleuzian, or rather Deleuzo-Guattarian, than that?

An ecological psychoanalysis also helps us to begin to reimagine therapeutic practice so that we can start to create spaces for thought that links to the earth. Deleuze and Guattari's ideas, such as assemblage, immanence, the rhizome and the body without organs, do not invoke static theoretical concept-objects in the traditional sense so much as a tool kit, itself both pragmatic and ephemeral, taking lines of flight and thought and in so doing deterritorializing the toolkit into thought/earth spaces which are then again reterritorialized into different forms and processes. Good psychotherapy is all about process, not about 'Truth' and rigidified thought, as demonstrated in Bion's use of Keat's theory of negative capability to develop an attitude of bearing uncertainty while conducting psychoanalysis without memory or desire, and Winnicott's conception of psychotherapy as a highly specialized form of playing. Ecopsychoanalysis takes seriously the challenge of ecopsychology and its call for us to move beyond the narcissism of anthropocentrism in our thought and therapeutic practice.

The problem with traditional ideas of ecology as it is defined within positivistic parameters is that it seeks the linear and structured processes of known causal relations between things. The complexity of the natural world, its unpredictable, fractal and vital nature is sterilized under a lens; the gaze of the scientist is allowed only to see in particular ways, hence the need for nonlinear approaches has been most strongly felt in the field of ecology. Couple this up with the quasi science of mainstream psychology, which deadens off subjectivity and affectivity in all sorts of ways in order for it to become known and understood, and we have an unfolding disaster of thinking.

Bateson told us that we are making Lake Erie insane with our thinking (Bateson 2000), and that we need a new way to envisage the ecology of mind. Hence the central claim of the field of ecopsychology, which Dodds engages with constructively even while criticizing its unreflective assumptions and idealizations, that 'ecology needs psychology, psychology needs ecology' (Roszak, Gomes & Kanner 1995). This linking of thought to the Earth is strongly present in the work of Bateson, as well as Deleuze and Guattari. Here, earth and mind are intertwined, folding back on one another in a multiplicity of assemblages, becomings and lines of flight. Nature becomes something both reassuring and terrifying, that ambivalent, uncanny terrain that psychoanalysis, despite all its faults, has made its own.

In Dodds' strange ecology, thought and earth move together, become destabilized together, flow and erupt. Thought becomes multiplicity and is heterogeneous. By conjoining geophilosophy with complexity theory, Dodds helps to develop the potentials in both, providing the philosophy we need to help us to think through the implications of this new form of nomadic nonlinear science, and the science to develop the intuitive leaps generated by philosophy. This creates the conceptual framework Dodds needs to dislocate psychoanalysis, providing a new *unheimlich* home in which psychoanalysis can think through what Dodds calls the ecology of phantasy.

The next ten years are central to moving forward towards new forms of interdisciplinary writing and research, and ultimately new forms of relatedness to the earth. The complex interdependent web that climate change sets up between the three ecologies of mind, nature and society demands that we start to be able to think, feel and act in more ecologically complex forms. Ecopsychoanalysis calls on us to start thinking at the precipice. We need to start being able to bear ecological thought and revision the world and ourselves in nonlinear ways, mirroring the strange ecology that swirls around us and threatens to destroy us, but which, with all its beautiful complexity and chaos, can, just perhaps, show us the way out.

Martin Jordan, Senior lecturer in counselling and psychotherapy,
Ecopsychology and European Journal of Ecopsychology, editorial board
member; HPC and UKCP registered

Part I

Climate change: A psychological problem

The principle task of civilization, its actual raison d'être is to defend us against nature ... But no one is under the illusion that nature has already been vanquished; and few dare hope that she will ever be entirely subjected to man. There are the elements which seem to mock at all human control; the earth which quakes and is torn apart and buries all human life and its works; water, which deluges and drowns everything in turmoil; storms, which blow everything before them ... With these forces nature rises up against us, majestic, cruel and inexorable; she brings to our mind once more our weakness and helplessness, which we thought to escape through the work of civilization.

(Freud 1927: 15–16)

We make no distinction between man and nature ... man and nature are not like two opposite terms confronting each other ... rather they are one and the same essential reality, the producer-product.

(Deleuze & Guattari 2000: 4–5)

Chapter 1

Climate crisis

Psychoanalysis and the ecology of ideas

> The ecological crisis is the greatest threat mankind collectively has ever faced . . . [*which*] with rapidly accelerating intensity threatens our whole planet. If so staggering a problem is to be met, the efforts of scientists of all clearly relevant disciplines will surely be required . . . psychoanalysts, with our interest in the unconscious processes which so powerfully influence man's behavior, should provide our fellow men with some enlightenment in this common struggle.
>
> (Searles 1972: 361)

The planetary crisis

The Fourth Assessment Report of the International Panel on Climate Change (IPCC 2007: 5) concluded that human activities are affecting the Earth on a planetary level, with 'atmospheric concentrations of carbon dioxide, methane, and nitrous oxide' now far exceeding anything 'over the past 650,000 years', including a rise in greenhouse gas emissions of '70% between 1970 and 2004'. Fourteen of the 15 warmest years on record occurred in the last 14 years (the other was 1990, which was warmer than 1996) (Brohan *et al.* 2006, from the UK Met Office, 2009), and the first decade of the twenty-first century, 2000–2009, was the warmest decade ever recorded (Voiland 2010), with the 2001–2010 period being even hotter (World Meteorological Organization 2011). The scientific consensus is now overwhelming, with no major scientific body disputing the seriousness of the situation.

> Warming of the climate system is unequivocal, as is now evident from observations of increases in global average air and ocean temperatures, widespread melting of snow and ice and rising global average sea level . . . evidence from all continents and most oceans shows that many natural systems are being affected . . . Most of the observed increase in

... temperatures since the mid 20th century is very likely due to the observed increase in anthropogenic (human) greenhouse gas concentrations ... The probability that this is caused by natural climatic processes alone is less than 5% ... temperatures could rise by between 1.1 and 6.4 °C ... during the 21st century ... Sea levels will probably rise by 18 to 59 cm ... [P]ast and future anthropogenic carbon dioxide emissions will ... contribute to warming and sea level rise for more than a millennium ... [but] the likely amount ... varies greatly depending on the intensity of human activity during the next century.

(IPCC 2007: 2–5)

We have so altered the physical processes of the Earth that future geologists, should they still exist, will be able to identify a clearly distinct period of the Earth's history for which a new term was introduced at the start of this millennium, the 'anthropocene' (Crutzen & Stoermer 2000; Zalasiewicz *et al.* 2008; Revkin 1992). Between 20,000 and 2 million species became extinct during the twentieth century, and the rate is now up to 140,000 per year in what is labelled the sixth major extinction event to have occurred in the last 540 million years (Morell & Lanting 1999), the first to be caused by the activities of a single species. Harvard biologist E. O. Wilson, in *The Future of Life* (2003) warns that half of all known species could be extinct by the end of the century. The 2010 UN Convention on Biological Diversity (CBD), held in Japan, increased the number of officially endangered species on the 'Red List' to now include one fifth of all animal and plant species (including 41 per cent of amphibians). Major extinction events should also not be seen as linear processes, as beyond certain critical thresholds entire ecosystems can be brought to a state of collapse, and can take ten million years to recover (Science Daily 2011; Whiteside & Ward 2011).

We are taking part in a planetary pyramid scheme, getting into an ecological debt from which there can be no bail outs. Yet somehow this just doesn't hit home, our behaviour doesn't match our knowledge. Why? In what we might call a 'deficit' account of our inactivity, George Marshall (2005, 2001) claims we have a faulty 'risk-thermostat' and so are unable to grasp the abstractness of the issue. To try to get more of a handle on what global temperature rises might do, George Monbiot (2005) makes it more concrete:

We know what these figures mean ... but it is very hard to make any sense of them. It just sounds like an alteration in your bath water ... The last time we had a six degree rise in temperature ... around 251 million years ago in the Permian Era, it pretty well brought life on earth to an end. It wiped out 90% of all known species ... Virtually everything in the sea from plankton to sharks simply died. Coral reefs were completely eliminated not to reappear on earth for ten million years . . . On land, the ground turned to rubble . . . vegetation died off very quickly, and it no longer held the soil together . . . [which] washed . . . into the sea . . . creating anoxic environments at the bottom of the ocean . . . [There was a] drop in total biological production of around 95% . . . Only two quadrupeds survived . . . We are facing the end of human existence . . . this is a very, very hard thing for people to face.

Here we are on more psychoanalytically interesting (if emotionally terrifying) territory, suggesting an 'anxiety-defence' understanding of inactivity. Monbiot (ibid.) continues, asking why we can accept the threat of terrorism and the related changes to our lives, but not the far greater threat of climate change. There has been a marked shift over the past decade. In public statements, politicians and major business groups are increasingly united on the importance of the issue (if not its policy implications). Yet despite growing consensus, little is actually being done. Years of positive speeches by the UK government, for example, and claims of substantial – even 'world-leading' – reductions disguise the fact that CO_2 emissions from overall British economic activity have actually continued to rise, due in part to growing consumer demand. In addition, many of the claimed 'reductions' have come more from structural changes in global economic production (including so-called 'carbon outsourcing') than from actual efficiency savings.

This has been dramatically demonstrated by Baiocchi & Minx (2010: 1177; see *Figure 1*), who applied structural decomposition analysis (SDA) to a global multiregional input-output model (MRIO) of changes in UK CO_2 emissions between 1992 and 2004. They found that while 'improvements from domestic changes in efficiency and production structure led to a 148 Mt reduction in CO_2 emissions' this 'only partially offsets emission increases of 217 Mt from changes in the global supply chain' including from the phenomenon of carbon outsourcing, and 'from growing consumer demand' (ibid.).

The 2009 Copenhagen Summit, billed as the epoch-making turning point when the world would come together to save the planet – it was even dubbed 'hopenhagen' (Brownsell 2009) – was all but a complete failure (Vidal 2009). Even the Kyoto Protocol, seen as a more successful agreement, has not led to any actual reductions in global carbon emission rates, which grew by 24 per cent between the 1997 agreement and 2005 (World Bank 2010: 233). In the context of climate change, the gap between knowledge and action does not seem to be narrowing, and it is becoming increasingly clear that what is most needed is *psychological* research, for it is ultimately in human thinking, feeling and behaviour that the problem is generated, and can potentially be solved.

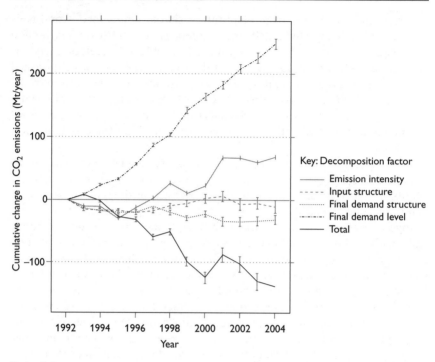

Figure 1 Decomposition of annual changes in the UK's carbon footprint for the 1992–2004 period in millions of tonnes of CO_2 per year

Source: Baicchi & Minx 2010, 1179

Psychological approaches to environmental problems

Psychology is now waking up to the fact that it offers the 'missing link' in climate change science (Schmuck & Vlek 2003; Oppenheimer & Todorov 2006; Reser 2007). This book offers primarily a psychoanalytic approach, which is particularly sensitive to dealing with issues around emotion, anxiety, and defences, as well as subtle psychological processes not easily captured on survey questions. In other words it emphasizes the unconscious psychological dimension of our individual, group, and social lives. However, it is important to emphasize that all areas of psychology have something important to offer towards this effort, and indeed the crisis is so acute that no one approach will be enough in the face of the immensity of the task at hand (Winter & Koger 2004). All need to participate in the wider ecology of ideas. Psychoanalysis, with its focus on the unconscious aspects of behaviour, needs to have a prominent place in this important work.

What are some of the non-psychoanalytic psychological approaches to climate change and environmental problems? Schmuck and Vlek's (2003) review of the literature explores various areas where psychology can play an important role. One approach is to study environment problems as dilemmas of the commons (Hardin 1968; Ostrom 1990; Vlek 1996), sometimes referred to as social dilemmas (Dawes 1980; Dawes & Messick 2000; Osbaldiston & Sheldon 2002). These are situations involving a conflict between collective interests, or the aggregate interests of a large number of people (including potentially future generations of people as yet not born), and short-term individual interests.

This area is continuing to be developed in more focused work on the environment, for example Van Vugt's (2009) 'Averting the Tragedy of the Commons: Using Social Psychological Science to Protect the Environment'. Evolutionary psychology (Buss 2004, 2005; Barkow 2006; Tooby & Cosmides 2005) argues that in such situations while it may be in the interest of each individual for everyone else to follow the rules which benefit the group as a whole, it is not necessarily in the individual's own interest to do so themselves (Ridley 1997; Axelrod 1984). In addition, while many individuals may discount the importance of their own negative impact on the common physical or social environment, the cumulative effect of many such small impacts leads to significant environmental problems.

Given that over-consumption of the Earth's resources is a key root of the ecological crisis, consumer psychology also has much to offer. Traditionally, consumer psychology has studied consumers wants and needs, and has understandably been used to help businesses to better predict, satisfy and – crucially – produce consumer demand for their products. Clearly, this is an area where psychology has been part of the problem, in that it has aided the effort to encourage the over-consumption which is so threatening the planet today. However, it has also developed a body of knowledge and techniques which its exponents suggest can now be turned to the task of developing pro-environmental behaviour. In addition, consumer psychological research has shown that increased consumption (beyond a minimum level) has no positive correlation with increased happiness (Csikszentmihalyi 1999; Durning 1995). On the contrary, according to Schmuck and Vlek (2003), evidence suggests that 'self-centered consumer values, life goals, and behaviors' have been 'associated with detrimental effects for individual well-being' (Cohen & Cohen 2001; Schmuck & Sheldon 2001).

Turning to cognitive psychology, studies of cognitive biases (Haselton, Nettle & Andrews 2005; Finucane et al. 2000) suggest that individuals tend naturally to focus on short-term gains rather than long-term goals, especially under situations of uncertainty (Kahneman, Slovic & Tver 1982), an area where effective action in the face of climate change is obviously relevant (Yudkow 2006; Pawlik 1991). Given these obstacles to action, how can psychology engage with these biases and help towards individual and social change?

Albert Bandura applied social learning theory and social cognitive theory (Bandura 1986, 2002) to an intervention designed to decrease population growth, ultimately one of the key drivers of many of the environmental problems we face. Social learning theory suggests that our behaviour is affected not only by direct reinforcers or punishments or behaviour shaping, as explored in classical and operative conditioning in the behaviourist tradition (Skinner 1969, 1981; Watson 1970; Baum 2005), but also indirectly by observing others (modelling, observational learning) and the rewards or punishments they receive (vicarious reinforcement). This is, after all, how advertising works. We are often shown people who are beautiful, happy and successful (in terms of love and wealth) following purchase of the item concerned.

Based upon these concepts, Bandura arranged a series of broadcasts in several regions with high population growth rates which showed the advantages of small families and the disadvantages of large families. Controlled studies demonstrated that these interventions led to an increased preference for small families, an increased use of contraception, and a clear drop in birth rates. Discussing this successful psychological campaign, Bandura writes:

> One of the central themes . . . is aimed at raising the status of women so they have equitable access to educational and social opportunities, a voice in family decisions and child bearing, and serve as active partners in their familial and social lives. This involves raising men's understanding of the legitimacy of women making decisions regarding their reproductive health and family life.
>
> (Bandura 2002: 222)

Environmental psychology (Gifford 2007) and the psychology of human–environment interactions have traditionally focused on the built environment with less emphasis on the natural environment and ecology (Scull 1999). However, this is now beginning to change. Stern (2000) suggests that many psychological theories have clear applications to the environmental crisis, some of which have already been applied. These include cognitive dissonance theory (e.g. Katzev & Johnson 1983, 1987), norm-activation theory (e.g. Black, Stern & Elworth 1985; Stern et al. 1999; Kalof 1993; Widegren 1998), and the theory of reasoned action or the theory of planned behaviour (e.g. Bamberg & Schmidt 1999; Jones 1990).

Stern (2000, 2004) has attempted to integrate much of this research into a more detailed understanding of pro-environmental behaviour. He suggests that given the urgency of the situation, psychological research and interventions should be targeted on areas likely to have the biggest impact, for example in decisions related to purchases of environmentally impactful items such as houses, domestic heating and cooling equipment, and cars. According to Stern (2000: 527) 'one-time decisions can have environmental effects for decades because of the long life of the equipment (Gardner & Stern 1996; Stern & Gardner 1981).'

One crucial area where psychological research can inform environmentalists is research on the effects of traditional environmental campaigns which use fear to frighten us into action. Stern (2005: 5) points out, however, that much of the research into the effect of such appeals in general has been far from supportive of this approach (Finckenauer 1982; Higbee 1969; Johnson & Tver 1983; Weinstein, Grubb & Vautier 1986), arguing that:

> The best evidence suggests that fear appeals may lead people either to take constructive action or to minimize or ignore a problem, depending on various factors, such as whether they believe they are vulnerable to the threat, their judgment of its severity, their awareness of positive actions to take in response, and the belief that they can actually take those actions at an acceptable cost.
>
> (Stern 2005: 5; see also Gardner & Stern 1996)

In fact, generally, adaptive coping is most likely to occur when 'threats are perceived to be severe and personal and when cost-effective responses are known and available', while high levels of threat 'without the perceived ability to cope leads to maladaptive responses such as minimizing the danger or unfocused emotionality' (Stern 2004: 4). This book shall argue that the fear and anxiety elicited not only by environmental campaigns but also by the actual existing threats to the environment plays an important role in our current psychological situation. Here, psychoanalysis has something important to offer us through its deep theorization and clinical experience about the ways – at times very strange ways – that humans respond to anxiety (Lertzman 2008).

From a broader perspective, Oskamp (2000: 496) suggests that psychology is crucial in the current ecological crisis, a crisis which threatens 'to make Earth nearly uninhabitable for future generations' as a result of human behavioural patterns, 'particularly overpopulation and over-consumption'. For Oskamp (ibid.), 'urgent changes to human lifestyles and cultural practices are required for the world to escape ecological disaster' and therefore 'psychologists should lead the way in helping people adopt sustainable patterns of living.' Oskamp goes on to describes some of the areas in which psychology has already contributed towards developing a more sustainable future for humanity and the Earth. These include energy conservation methods (Katzev & Johnson 1987) and recycling and resource conservation (Oskamp 1995a, 1995b). However, faced with the task at hand, and the risk of a future uninhabitable Earth, this is as yet nowhere near enough. The changes required in human behaviour are immense.

> Achieving a sustainable society will require basic changes in the behavior of most of the world's peoples, and aiding those changes is an

important task for psychologists . . . Social scientists need to work on
changing institutions and organizations in ways that will strongly
encourage pro-environmental options and behavior. Such changes in
society's organizational and institutional patterns will need to be motivated and supported through changes in some basic values.

(Oskamp 2000: 506)

The idea of the importance of changes to our overall value systems from
extrinsic to intrinsic values (Zimmerman 2007; Monbiot 2010; Crompton
2010; Kluckholn & Strodtback 1961) is increasingly being discussed in the
field and in recent psychoanalytic interventions (Weintrobe 2011a, 2011b).
Oskamp (2000) suggests that as well as considering the level of individual
choice (Elgin 1993; Brower & Leon 1999) and group and social norms and
activities (Olson 1995), we need to focus on a 'superordinate goal that all
nations and peoples can share (Sherif et al. 1961)'. For this kind of worldwide shift in values he draws on William James's (1911) concept of a 'moral
equivalent of war', in this case involving 'a war against the common enemy
of an uninhabitable Earth.' This, he argues, is crucial 'for mobilizing the
widespread public support needed to accomplish the huge changes necessary for a sustainable society . . . Environmentalists need nothing less than
this level of fervor if they are to change worldwide patterns in time to
forestall environmental disaster' (Oskamp 2000: 505).

At his 2010 British Academy/British Psychological Society Annual
Lecture on psychology and climate change, environmental psychologist
David Uzzell (2010) supported this proposal. Uzzell (2010: 881) emphasizes
however that the attitudes and values that drive environmentally harmful or
sustainable behaviour 'are not formed in a social and political vacuum' but
are closely connected with our sense of identity, and are 'embedded and
nurtured in and emerge from a social context, such as class, gender, ethni-
city and environmental settings, all of which lead to the development of
everyday cultures and practices.' Uzzell (2010: 883) concludes that psychologists could help to reframe sustainable society so that we come to see it
'not as a threat or a sacrifice but as an opportunity.' There is therefore a
need for what Deborah Du Nann Winter (1996: 299) called a vision of a
sustainable world worth fighting for.

An excellent overview of this topic, which tries to bring together the
contributions of different areas of psychology to the environmental crisis, is
found in Winter & Koger's (2004) book, *The Psychology of Environmental
Problems*, which includes crucial sections on psychoanalysis that will be
explored in more detail below. They argue that:

In order to endure, we will need a robust psychology to help us make
crucial changes in our behaviours, thoughts, feeling, and values. How

to sustain human existence on the planet could become psychology's core question, offering an intellectual coherence to a discipline fragmented by diverse concerns.

(Winter & Koger 2004: 211–212)

After discussing the varied contributions of psychoanalysis, behaviourism, cognitive psychology, social psychology, health and physiological psychology, gestalt, ecopsychology and transpersonal psychology, Winter and Koger (2004: 215) conclude that all areas of psychology are needed, and that the long history of conflict between the psychological schools is counterproductive, especially at this crucial moment in history.

We believe the question of 'which psychology is best?' is problematic for a number of reasons. First, human behaviour is so complex no one approach can capture everything . . . Environmental behaviour is multiply determined, as Hallin (1995) showed . . . Second, the debate about which approach is better can distract us from solving our problems . . . Ecosystems will not care if we spend our time debating the relative merits of behavioural or cognitive theory, nor which theory wins the most followers. Ecosystems will collapse whether or not we win our intellectual debates. Only changing our behaviour will make any difference to the outcome of our crisis . . . The third reason . . . is that . . . choosing to change one element of our functioning will in turn change others . . . it does not matter which theory you choose to act on; the more important point is that you choose to act.

(Winter & Koger 2004: 215–216)

To conclude this section on psychology's contribution, we can turn to the American Psychological Association's (2010) task force on climate change which recently published a major report identifying key research areas which current and future psychological research needs to focus on. These include *perceptions of risk* 'including people's tendency to discount the likelihood of future and remote events'; *psychosocial drivers* of climate change; *psychosocial impacts* 'including stress, anxiety, apathy, and guilt'; 'ethical and social justice implications'; *psychological barriers* to 'individual and collective action' and the *development of empirically based interventions* 'to promote coping, adaptation and healthy responses' (APA 2010: 6–8). Psychoanalysis, with its long tradition of engagement with social, cultural and group analysis, as well as its rich clinical approach to human subjectivity, can potentially contribute to each of the key areas the APA describes, and needs to take its place among the community of sciences if we are going to have a chance of dealing with the ecological crisis before it is too late.

Why psychoanalysis?

The perspective used here builds mainly on the psychoanalytic tradition, but in the spirit of Winter & Koger, it does not seek to disparage alternative approaches. However, a detailed study of all psychological contributions to solving the environmental crisis, beyond the overview above, is beyond the scope of this book. But I will argue that for psychoanalytic interventions in this area to bear the most fruit, they need to learn from other perspectives, including in particular ecopsychology, the sciences of ecology and complexity theory, and the philosophy of Deleuze and Guattari (Bell 2006). These areas of thought, and their relation to psychoanalysis and the ecological crisis, will be explored in more detail in later chapters, once the contributions that psychoanalysis itself can make have become clear.

The long and productive history of psychoanalytic engagements with critical social theory and research into social and cultural phenomenon includes, for example, Freud's studies of groups and civilization, the cultural school of the neo-Freudians, the Frankfurt School of Critical Theory, Kleinian Group Analysis, the systemic psychodynamic group relations of the Tavistock Institute, feminist and Marxist psychoanalytic critique, and Lacanian postmodernism (see Frosh 2010; Elliot 1999; Freud 1913a, 1915, 1921, 1927, 1930; Marcuse 1998; Fromm 1992, 2001, 2006; Clarke 2003; Clarke & Hoggett 2009; Dalal 2002; Young 2002; Bell 2007; Lawrence 1997; Žižek 2009; Chodorow 1991; Irigaray 1985; Adorno & Horkeimer 2002; Stacey 2003; Hinshelwood 1989). For a useful review of the history of psychoanalysis and social theory from Freud to Kristeva, see Elliot (1999).

In his recent book, *Psychoanalysis Outside the Clinic: Interventions in Psychosocial Studies*, Frosh (2010) reviews the potential benefits and pitfalls of psychoanalytic work outside the consulting room, and in the social sciences in particular. He argues that despite the very real dangers of psychological reductionism, pathography, and 'wild analysis' (Freud 1910)

> psychoanalysis holds something significant for all the other disciplines
> – specifically a capacity to theorize subjectivity in a way that is provocative and unique, through reference to the unconscious. In addition, the fertility of its applications reflects back on psychoanalysis itself. Some of the most important critical work applied to psychoanalysis has come from outside the clinical situation, as if the freedom to think without being concerned with the requirements of therapy is a necessary condition for theoretical development.
>
> (Frosh 2010: 36)

One of the most recent incarnations of this approach is psychosocial studies, which attempts to form an interlinked understanding of affect, psyche, society, and socio-political systems and structures, in a way which refuses to break them down into the separate entities traditionally studied by psychology or sociology. With its emphasis on psychoanalytic under-standings of subjectivity and its interweaving with the social, psychosocial studies draws on various social sciences, critical social theory, gender studies and philosophy. Its aim is to explore the interpellation of inner and outer worlds, of object relations and social relations (Clarke & Hoggett 2008), to the point where terms such as internal and external, inside and outside, psyche and society, lose some of their simple binary character without abandoning the specificity of each domain.

However, until recently, the almost total lack of engagement with ecology or environmental issues from psychoanalytic researchers (beyond the 'environment' of the family) remains a glaring lacuna in psychoanalytic theory (both as an applied social science and as a clinical field). This virtual absence would be striking enough on its own but in the context of an increasingly urgent planetary crisis, it becomes almost perverse. This is now thankfully beginning to change, as we shall see in particular in Part II and Part III of this book, with a growing interest in environmental issues emerging among psychodynamic researchers and therapists. The time for opening out psychoanalytic social theory into a more fully eco-psycho-social perspective is therefore ripe. It is a major task of this present work to seek to begin to correct this historical blind spot, and it is the exploration of the psychodynamics of this terrain, or we might say its ecology, which will be a key focus of this book.

Chapter 2

Theoretical crisis

Complexity as meta-theory

We are in the middle of a paradigm turn, the so-called complexity turn.
(Qvortrup 2006: 345)

Eighteenth-century science, following the Newtonian revolution, has been characterized as developing the sciences of organized simplicity, nineteenth-century science, via statistical mechanics, as focusing on disorganized complexity, and twentieth and twenty-first-century science as confronting organized complexity.
(Kauffman 1993: 173)

Alpha function and the failure of theory

The current crisis is not only an ecological crisis, but a crisis of theory, which, according to Doppelt (2008), represents 'the greatest failure of thought in human history', a failure characterized by 'systems blindness'. This causes tremendous problems for potential responses to the environmental threat and for effective social or psychological research. Our fields of knowledge have long been divided into manifold disciplines and sub-disciplines, continuing to fragment into ever more narrowly defined subjects where specialists often have little understanding of even closely adjacent subfields, causing serious barriers to comprehensive research.

The reality of a changing climate and endangered biosphere undercuts many of these disciplines' basic assumptions, none of which have adequate tools for the job, including psychoanalysis itself. To deal with the crisis, this state of affairs is not enough and it is time to follow Deleuze and Guattari's (2003a: 372–373) call for a more 'nomadic' science. Mandelbrot, the pioneer of fractal geometry (who sadly died during the completion of this book), wrote that 'science would be ruined by withdrawing entirely into narrowly defined specialities. The rare scholars who are nomad-by-choice are essential to the intellectual welfare of the settled disciplines' (cited in Mackay 1991: 163).

Climate change embodies a world of unpredictable, multiple-level, highly complex, nonlinear interlocking systems, and to fully grasp the threat on a psychological, group, community, national and global level, and the resulting interactions with local, regional and planetary ecology, is more than any one intellectual field can encompass. Psychoanalysis has an important role to play as part of a wider ecology of ideas, but there is a need for a kind of meta-perspective or meta-theory able to integrate the many disparate strands (disparate in terms of our arbitrary divisions, not in terms of how the world really works). This should be understood not as the kind of 'master-theory' so distrusted by postmodernists (Bertens 1995; Lyotard 1997), but a way to connect or link different strands of knowledge together. What is required is therefore not a fixed theoretical grid to impose a single meaning on all data, but perhaps something more akin to what the British psychoanalyst Wilfred Bion (1959) calls the work of linking, which he connects with the alpha function and dreamwork (Bion 1989).

In Bion's theory of thinking and psychosis (Bion 1962a, 1962b, 1965), he describes the building of links between mental objects, and the attack on linking characteristic of the psychotic state of mind, leading to the 'bizarre objects' of schizophrenic hallucination (Bion 1957, 1958). These links operate within the mind but also function within groups (Bion 1961), and, without the process Bion termed 'alpha function', they remain undigested fragments of experience, 'beta-elements' not capable of being weaved into the tapestry of our dreams or thoughts. For Bion 'knowledge is not a thing we have, but a link between ourselves and what we know . . . +K is being willing to know but not insisting on knowledge' (Parsons 2000: pp. 67 and 48).

At the same time, avoiding the trap of imposing meaning on the new through rigid preconceptions, Bion (2007) supported Keats' concept of 'negative capability', which Keats described as being 'capable of being in uncertainties, mysteries, doubts, without any irritable reaching after fact and reason' (Scott 2002; Dewey 2005). Bion (1967) therefore called on the analyst to be without memory or desire, in order to be most open to the truth that the psychoanalytic session unfolds, leading to what he called 'transformations in O' (Bion 1965), a capacity he connects with the mother's 'reverie' with her infant.

From this perspective we could describe academia as having divided human thought into a schizoid fragmented space. Therefore, the kind of theory I am calling for is one of linking in Bion's sense, an 'alpha function' helping to connect diverse elements together without each losing their own identity, specificity, and importance. In other words, we need a way to help us think about how something new emerges from a heterogenous swarm of interconnecting, interdependent, complex, nonlinear relationships. In this sense it is perhaps closer to DeLanda's (2005: 93) concept, derived from Deleuze and Guattari, of a 'meshwork', rather than the rigid grid of a frame.

This book argues that here we need the new sciences of complexity and nonlinear dynamical systems theory, and the philosophy most suited to deal with this often counterintuitive way of thinking: that of Deleuze and Guattari. We will attempt to plug into various aspects of these 'machines', to see which tools can form productive symbioses. As Deleuze and Guattari (2003a: 90) write, 'tools exist only in relation to the interminglings they make possible or that make them possible.'

The nonlinear revolution

A variety of commentators have claimed we are in the midst of an epistemological revolution (Goujon 2006), a paradigm shift (Kuhn 1996) leading us to a stranger and more complex world. According to Stewart:

> So docile are linear equations that the classical mathematicians were willing to compromise their physics to get them . . . if you decide that only linear equations are worth thinking, self-censorship sets in. Your textbooks fill with the triumphs of linear analysis, its failures buried so deep that the graves go unmarked and the existence of the graves goes unremarked.
>
> (Stewart 1989: 83)

Katherine Hayles (1991) argues that the new sciences of complexity and chaos have transformed the nature of science and the 'epistemic ground' of Western culture, shifting the previously clear boundaries between order and chaos. This has important implications for psychoanalysis itself, as we shall see in Chapter 12. Insights from ecology and complexity theory provide psychoanalysis with a more adequate scientific framework than the linear nineteenth-century hydraulic models embedded in Freudian thought (Spruiell 1993; Piers, Muller & Brent 2007), allowing new approaches to studying such phenomena as the psychoanalytic process (Palombo 1999; Boston Change Process Study Group 2008), group analysis (Stacey 2003), and social dynamics (Lemieux 1994; Dodds 2008).

Manuel DeLanda (2005), whose articulation of Deleuze and Guattari's thought with complexity theory parallels to some extent my own, writes that:

> Prigogine revolutionized thermodynamics in the 1960s by showing that the classical results were valid only for closed systems . . . If one allows an intense flow of energy in and out of a system . . . [pushing] it far from equilibrium . . . [i]nstead of a unique and simple form of stability, we now have multiple coexisting forms of varying complexity (static, periodic, and chaotic attractors) . . . at a critical point called a bifurcation . . . minor fluctuations may play a crucial role . . . Attractors and bifurcations are features of any system in which the dynamics are

not only far from equilibrium but also nonlinear, that is, in which there are strong mutual interactions (or feedback) between components. Whether the system in question is composed of molecules or of living creatures, it will exhibit endogenously generated stable states, as well as sharp transitions between states, as long as there is feedback and an intense flow of energy coursing through the system.

(DeLanda 2005: 14)

DeLanda claims that 'the move away from energetic equilibrium and linear causality has re-injected the natural sciences with historical concerns' (ibid.), as we shall see in Chapter 11. One example is *hysteresis* (Sole & Goodwin 2000; Nicolis & Prigogine 1989), by which the precise point of a bifurcation (e.g. water moving between liquid and gas, a horse switching between a walk and a gallop) depends on the *direction* of change so that as in the social sciences and psychoanalysis, *history matters*. With the shift in sciences towards historical concerns, DeLanda calls for 'a similar move in the social sciences' towards 'a nonlinear and non-equilibrium history' (ibid.). Deleuze and Guattari's powerful attack on established psychoanalysis could be seen as a call for just such a transformation within Freud's science, akin to what Donald Meltzer (1994: 526) may have meant when he appealed to psychoanalysts 'to people mental space with a new kind of psychology, akin to the revolution in mathematics by the invention of negative numbers or non-Euclidean geometry.'

This is especially clear with Felix Guattari (himself a psychoanalyst, albeit a highly unorthodox one), where in his book *Chaosmosis* (1995) he calls for 'a science of ecosystems . . . a generalized ecology – or ecosophy.' This was to be understood as a 'generalized machinics' with 'resonances, alliances and feedback loops between various regimes, signifying and non-signifying, human and non-human, natural and cultural, material and representational' (Guattari 1995: 91; cited in Herzogenrath 2009: 2). This book therefore argues that there is as much a need to bring nonlinear and ecological thinking into psychoanalysis as for a psychoanalytic approach to ecology, taking seriously the possibility of thinking in terms of what Guattari (2000) called in his final book, *The Three Ecologies* of mind, nature and society.

Chapter 3

Ecology at the edge of chaos

The atmosphere is a self-organized system . . . [with] well-defined large scale structures . . . The tornado is a sort of runaway convection current . . . We can see it, photograph it, watch it destroy houses. Yet . . . it is nothing more than a collection of atmospheric molecules that have organized themselves to circulate rapidly in a spiral formation . . . At equilibrium each molecule behaves as essentially independent entities. They ignore each other. We would . . . call them 'hypnons', sleep walkers . . . non-equilibrium wakes them up and introduces a coherence quite foreign to equilibrium.

(Prigogine & Stengers 1984: 80–81)

The long-term good health of populations depends on the continued stability and functioning of the biosphere's ecological and physical systems . . . We ignore this long-established historical truth at our peril: yet it is all too easy to overlook this dependency, particularly at a time when the human species is becoming increasingly urbanized and distanced from these natural systems. The world's climate system is an integral part of this complex of life-supporting processes, one of many large natural systems that are now coming under pressure from the increasing weight of human numbers and economic activities.

(McMichael 2003; cited in American Psychological Association 2010: 13)

Complexity theory and ecosystemic collapse

Trying to think about the sheer range and levels of the ecological crisis can be overwhelming. Climate change operates globally with effects at all scales, from psychological to planetary. However, one principle is clear: we live on a finite planet but have an economic system predicated on unending growth. Whether we make the conscious choice to live sustainably or not, this will come to an end one way or another. We are like infants unwilling to accept that the breast is not a source of infinitely increasing nourishment. In the present context, any suggestion of weaning, however gentle, is still heresy.

Scientists estimate that human demand may 'have exceeded the biosphere's regenerative capacity since the 1980s', and already reached 120 per cent by 1999 and this demand is still rapidly increasing (Wackernagel *et al.* 2002: 926; Norgaard & Randers 2002). Schmuck and Vlek (2003: 71) warn that 'without fundamental changes in population growth, consumption patterns, and environmentally harmful technologies, modern industrial human beings are likely to leave a gradually worn-out earth to future generations.'

How is the complexity approach relevant here? Science has grown up largely working with the concept of linear systems where x input = x output in predictable, stable ways. Increasingly, science realises that these linear relationships represent merely a special minority case in an otherwise fairly nonlinear world. Systems theory (Bertalanffy 1968) and cybernetics (Francois 1999) focused in their early stages on *negative feedback* processes, which allow systems to self-regulate within certain parameters, like the thermostat which responds to fluctuations in temperature by initiating a process to bring it back to a fixed point. Increasingly in science today there is an emphasis on the study of nonlinearities driven by *positive feedback* where an increase in a variable feeds back recursively producing catas-trophic runaway increases if not reined in eventually by negative feedback.

We can think about this using the concept of *attractors* which are points towards which a system tends to converge. Wherever you place a marble in a washbasin the marble will roll towards the 'plug hole attractor'. Like a black hole, any variation in starting point within the *basin of attraction* is cancelled out by the powerful pull of the attractor. Within limits as our body or global climate temperature increases, negative feedback processes act to draw the system back to a more central point. This is known as a *point attractor* (other more complex attractors include 'periodic' attractors and 'strange' or 'chaotic' attractors). However, when the marble is moved to the edge of the basin, the slightest movement or air vibration can move it either back into the basin (of attraction) or into a completely different attractor (falling out and rolling on the floor). At these *bifurcation* points, nonlinearities rule as the slightest difference in starting conditions or the tiniest fluctuation causes a radical shift, a *phase transition* to a new attractor or set of attractors (Guastello 2004).

Climate scientists suggest that our climate may well be approaching such a tipping point, with potentially lethal positive feedback processes which are no longer capable of being damped out by the various negative feedback mechanisms in the system. An example from ecology would be the popu-lation explosion. In a natural state, rabbits and foxes form a *coevolving system* (Thompson 1994; Barbosa & Castellanos 2004), keeping each other's populations in check through negative feedback. If the foxes are removed and the rabbits also discover new spaces the result is an explosive exponen-tial population growth. Eventually when they surpass the carrying capacity (as we have already done on our planet) there will be a crash in population numbers once all resources are depleted. Such crashes can in the worst case lead to the population concerned being wiped out, an experience which is unfortunately all to familiar from the history of human societies.

The latter is explored in Jared Diamond's (2006) timely book *Collapse: How Societies Choose to Fail or Survive*, where he applies a five-point framework in understanding how human societies have been brought to states of collapse, sometimes total. These key factors include environmental damage and resource depletion, climate change, hostile neighbours, decreased support from friendly neighbours, and the society's response to its problems. Historically, each of the factors have interacted in complex (often nonlinear) ways to cause the collapse of civilizations such as the Mayan cities in Central America, Easter Island in the Pacific Ocean, the Anasazi in North America, Norse Greenland, Mycenean Greece and Minoan Crete in Europe, and the Khmer Angkor Wat and Harappan Indus Valley cities in Asia.

Will our own civilization follow its predecessors? Were this to occur the collapse might well be more total and more global than anything previously seen. In his chapter on Easter Island, Diamond (2006: 119) points out that they were as isolated and lonely in the pacific as the Earth is in space, so when their collapse came, there was literally nowhere for them to run, and no help to expect from outside. According to Diamond, much depends for us on the fifth criterion, how we respond to the crisis of the first two factors – environmental damage and climate change.

Positive feedback and climate change

A nonlinear perspective is crucial not only for climate science, for under-standing and modelling sustainable and unsustainable patterns of devel-opment (Jacobsen 2010; Dore 2010), and for understanding social and civilizational collapses (Sole & Goodwin 2000: 302), but also for the psy-chology of risk perception. Our familiar, linear ways of thinking imagine there must be a linear relationship between CO_2 emissions and warming. Within certain conditions (a particular basin of attraction) this may approxi-mate the truth. However, at a given point a phase transition occurs and the system rapidly shifts to a new basin of attraction. The previous 'regime' rapidly collapses to be replaced by a new system of effects. It is hard for us to mentally grasp this fact as we continue to imagine that if we keep going at this rate, warming will happen at a measured pace, and there will always be time later to turn it around, at some unspecified point in the future.

Due to the fact that it ignores the potential of explosive positive feedback loops leading to runaway climate change, including not only meteorological and ecological, but also social, psychological and behavioural loops, this involves a fundamental failure of thought. There are multiple potential tipping points and unfortunately we do not know how close we are, or whether we have already started to cross them. However, science is providing increasing evidence that this is already the case. Recent simulations based on the Canadian Earth Systems Model suggest that even if all CO_2 emissions were to be somehow eliminated by the year 2100, the warming of the oceans that has already been triggered by existing causes is set to continue until the end of the millennium, leading to the collapse of the West Antarctic Ice Sheet and the flooding of Hong Kong, New York, and other coastal cities (Gillet et al. 2011).

So what are the possible positive feedback loops involved in runaway climate change? The first loop concerns *tropical forest fires*, which become more common as temperatures increase, emitting more CO_2 and 'fixing' less (Lashof & DeAngelo 1997) while the land also becomes hotter due to a reduction of cooling forest cover and a decreased ability to reflect heat. A second loop involves frozen *ocean methane* (Sawaya 2010; Soden & Held 2006), billions of tons of which are locked away as gas hydrate which is only stable under specific conditions of high pressure and low temperatures. This can be released suddenly and dramatically when temperatures cross a threshold. A third loop involves the melting of *tundra permafrost*, which contains a third of the world's soil-bound carbon, releasing further CO_2 (Anisimov 2007). In Alaska, for example, 'in the 1970s the tundra was a carbon sink, but today, it is a carbon source' (Oechel et al. 1993: 520). A fourth loop involves the *melting of polar ice* which results in more heat being absorbed rather than reflected, ice having a higher 'albedo' or reflection rate (Lawrence Berkeley National Laboratory 2006). Further positive feedback loops include increased *methane production from bogs/peatland* as a result of warming (White et al. 2008) and *decreased ocean solubility of CO_2* following increased temperatures, turning current regional ocean carbon sinks into sources (Friedlingstein et al. 2001).

Complicating the situation further are positive feedback cycles which in addition to their own effect on the climate system also interact with and amplify the warming effect of other feedback loops. For example, *atmospheric water vapour* (itself an important greenhouse gas) has increased by 0.41 kg/m^2 per decade since 1988 (Lynas 2008; Cess 2005) due to the fact that at higher temperatures the atmosphere can hold more water vapour (Gillett 2007). Thus, as well as forming another important feedback cycle in itself by amplifying the warming effect of CO_2 following temperature rises (Hansen 2008; Desslet, Zhang & Yang 2008), it also exacerbates the effects of other loops, for example those involving ice albedo or clouds. In fact, as a result of these complex effects, the IPCC (2007) considers water vapour the single largest feedback-affecting climate sensitivity, causing as much as 3.5 times as much warming compared to the situation where water vapour concentrations remain unchanged (Hall & Manabe 1999, 2000).

There are additional positive feedback loops believed to be involved in climate change but the ones listed above are sufficient for our purposes, apart from a final category which is more directly related to the theme of this book: *human behavioural* positive feedback loops (Sawaya 2010). One example is that climate change is likely to lead to an increased use of energy and fuel to run more air conditioning, to farm more effectively and in more difficult conditions, or to rebuild areas devastated by extreme weather. Other possible behavioural positive feedback loops are more irrational, and move into more psychoanalytic territory. 'We're already seeing signs of destructive consumptive behaviour,' writes Marshall (2005), 'and we can probably expect an ever faster spiral into destructive consumptive behaviour as things get worse – what psychoanalysts would call reaction formation.'

Whether 'rational' or not, all these feedback loops lead to an increased emission rate and therefore further temperature rises. Of course there are negative feedback loops too, such as the spread of *desertification* (Wenshou 2008) reflecting more heat and leading to an increased *radiative cooling effect* (increased temperatures result in greater heat radiation into space, see IPCC 2007) and a possible mass die-off of human and animal life (reducing greenhouse gas emissions, including methane emissions from cattle and other livestock as well as CO_2 emissions). *Figure 2* illustrates this effect by comparing CO_2 levels and mass extinction events over time, with mass extinctions following increased CO_2 levels and then leading to a reduction in these levels following the mass extinction (see also Glikson 2010).

However, both the spread of desertification and mass extinction are obviously preferably avoided, even if they result in lower temperatures and lower atmospheric greenhouse gas concentrations, especially as in this case the extinction event concerned may potentially include ourselves. In the end the Earth will probably survive and new life can begin again, as after previous extinctions (although it may take ten million years to build up to comparable levels, see Whiteside & Ward 2011), but that is more than can be said for humans (and other species) whose future is far from sure. Yet even this is not certain, as a runaway greenhouse effect could in the worst case leave the earth uninhabitable, like Venus, which seems to have gone through a process such as this in the distant past (Rasool, De Bergh & De Bergh 1970; Kasting 1988), where positive feedback eventually led to its oceans boiling away (Hansen 2008).

At this point the consensus is that this nightmare scenario is unlikely (IPCC 2009), however, scientists are increasingly acknowledging that the proliferation of known positive feedback processes, with natural negative feedback loops nowhere near powerful enough to counteract their effects, are a cause for serious concern (Kerr & Kintisch 2010). As Rachel Sawaya writes:

> There are many potential positive feedback loops in climate change, and unfortunately few negative feedback . . . mechanisms which might keep them in check . . . These mechanisms could quickly grow out of

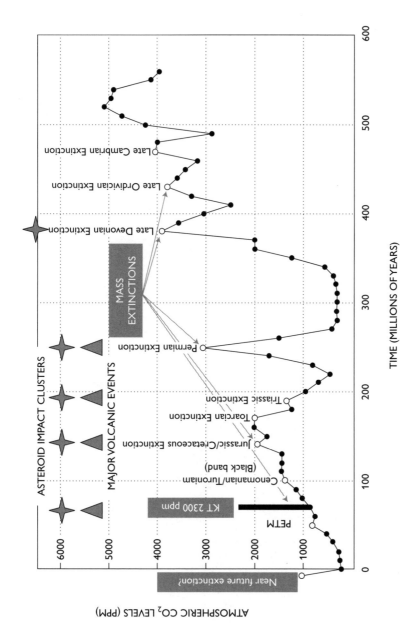

Figure 2 CO_2 and mass extinction of species through time

Source: Ward 2007: 135

control, causing some of the more . . . frightening doomsday scenarios that scientists have put forth . . . most of these mechanisms are not thought to be at a tipping point yet. Potentially, people have time to take action before disaster strikes.

(Sawaya 2010: 1)

Part II

The phantasy of ecology
Psychoanalysis of climate change

Psychology as much as science will thus determine the planet's fate, because action depends on overcoming denial, among the most paralyzing of human responses.

(Postel 1992: 4)

Chapter 4

Classical psychoanalysis

We psychoanalysts must make some real contribution, along with our brothers in other fields of science, toward meeting the ecological crisis.

(Searles 1972: 373)

Environmentalism and its discontents

Why psychoanalysis? On the face of it, it seems frankly irrelevant. Surely it is the basic sciences of geology, ecology, biology, and climatology that we need, combined with various hi-tech engineering? Yes and no. The science informing us of the risks and possible technical solutions has run far ahead of our psychological state. We are not yet at the point emotionally of being able to clearly grasp the threat, and act accordingly. We need to ask why this issue, despite its current prominence, fails to ignite people's motivation for the major changes science tells us is necessary. This concerns not only the 'public' but the academy and the psychoanalytic community. In spite of the fact that Harold Searles was already writing in 1960 that psychoanalysts need to acknowledge the psychological importance of the non-human environment, until very recently his colleagues have almost entirely ignored him.

In this section we explore some of the theories with which we may be able to construct a psychoanalysis of ecology. Fuller elaboration will involve incorporating approaches from the sciences of complexity and ecology, and Deleuze and Guattari's 'geophilosophy' or 'ecosophy', which itself emerged in critical dialogue with psychoanalysis and complexity theory. However, we first need to explore the ecological potential within psychoanalysis itself, as without the latter's methods and theories for unmasking hidden motivations and phantasies, this investigation will not be able to proceed.

Renee Lertzman (2008), one of the first psychoanalytically informed social scientists to engage with the ecological crisis, describes a common surreal aspect of our everyday responses to 'eco-anxiety', the experience of flipping through a newspaper and being suddenly confronted with:

the stop-dead-in-your-tracks, bone-chilling kind of ecological travesties taking place around our planet today . . . declining honey bees, melting glaciers, plastics in the sea, or the rate of coal plants being built in China each second. But how many of us actually do stop dead in our tracks? Have we become numb? . . . if so, how can we become more awake and engaged to what is happening?

Environmental campaigners have become increasingly frustrated and pessimistic. Even as their messages spread further and further, and as scientists unite around their core concerns, there is an alarming gap between increasingly firm evidence and public response. The fact that oil companies donate millions to climate 'sceptic' groups doesn't help (Vidal 2010). Nor does the fact that eight European companies which are together responsible for 5–10 per cent of the emissions covered in the EU emissions trading system (Bayet, BASF, BP, GDF Suez, ArcelorMittal, Lafarge, E.ON, and Solvay) gave $306,100 to senatorial candidates in the 2010 United States midterm elections who either outright deny climate change ($107,200) or pledge they will block all climate change legislation ($240,200), with the most flagrant deniers getting the most funds (Goldenberg 2010; Climate Action Network 2010). These are the same companies that campaign against EU targets of 30 per cent reductions in emissions using current inaction in the United States as a justification, while claiming their official policy is that climate change is a major threat and they are committed to doing all they can to help in the common cause of dealing with the danger (for the full report see Climate Action Network 2010).

Recent opinion polls show climate scepticism is on the rise in the UK as well. In February 2010 a BBC-commissioned poll by Populus (BBC 2010a, 2010b) of 1,001 adults found that 25 per cent didn't think global warming was happening, a rise of 8 per cent since a similar poll in November 2009. Belief that climate change was real fell from 83 per cent to 75 per cent, while only 26 per cent believed climate change was established as largely man-made compared with 41 per cent in November. A third of those agreeing climate change was real felt consequences had been exaggerated (up from a fifth) while the number of those who felt risks had been understated fell from 38 per cent to 25 per cent (see *Figure 3*). According to Populus director M. Simmonds, 'it is very unusual . . . to see such a dramatic shift in opinion in such a short period . . . The British public are sceptical about man's contribution to climate change and becoming more so' (BBC 2010a).

Most remarkable here is the discrepancy between public and expert opinion. According to the chief scientific advisor at the Department for the Environment, Food and Rural Affairs, Professor Robert Watson: 'Action is urgently needed . . . We need the public to understand that climate change is serious so they will change their habits and help us move towards a low-carbon economy.' Why this shift? Whilst the poll took place with the

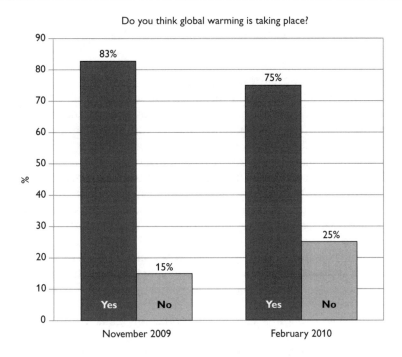

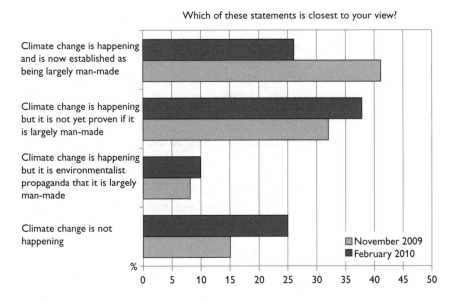

Figure 3 Climate 'scepticism' on the rise?

Sources: Based on data from BBC 2010a, 2010b

background of heavy snow and blizzards in the UK, always a convenient backdrop to climate sceptic jokes, the BBC (2010a) article focused on a high-profile story concerning stolen emails alleging scientific malpractice at the University of East Anglia (UEA). While this was a very serious accusation, no mainstream scientific body seriously imagines it changes in any real way the overall science, and yet this is not how the public perceived it.

Subsequently, the UK Parliament's Commons Science and Technology Committee completed its investigation into the case (BBC 2010c). The MPs' committee concluded there was no evidence that UEA's Professor Phil Jones had manipulated data, or tried 'to subvert the peer review process' and that 'his reputation, and that of his climate research unit, remained intact' (BBC 2010c). The report noted that 'it is not standard practice in climate science to publish the raw data and the computer code in academic papers' and that 'much of the data that critics claimed Prof Jones has hidden, was in fact already publicly available' (BBC 2010c) but called strongly for a greater culture of transparency in science. The report concluded that it 'found no reason in this unfortunate episode to challenge the scientific consensus that global warming is happening and is induced by human activity' (BBC 2010c).

This story was followed closely by another in January 2010 when the IPCC admitted a mistake concerning the timetable of Himalayan glacial melting. In such a lengthy report of over 3 000 pages, produced from the combined efforts of the world scientific community on a topic with as many variables as climate change, it is unsurprising some estimates need revising. Undoubtably there will be more revisions in the future, some major. It is important to emphasize that for the world's scientists the overall picture has not been affected, but public perception is completely different, with triumphant claims of proof 'it is all made up'. No doubt many sceptics will use the Parliamentary committee's report as further evidence of an institutional cover-up.

The important psychological point is that people are ready for such events, indeed eager for it – the psychosocial equivalent of a sandpile in a state of self-organized criticality (Palombo 1999; Bak 1994), when a single grain can cause a major avalanche cascading through the whole system. Understanding such subtle shifts, and the often unconscious motivations behind them, is where psychoanalysis perhaps more than any other discipline has a lot to offer. As Lertzman (2008) writes:

> What if the core issue is more about how humans respond to anxiety? . . . [E]nvironmental problems . . . conjure up anxieties that . . . we are done for, and nothing can really be done . . . To help me understand more, I turn to Freud . . . because I have found few others who speak as eloquently, and sensitively about what humans do when faced with anxiety or anxiety-provoking news.

Freud, civilization, nature and the dialectic of the Enlightenment

Is Freud really relevant to understanding our current crisis? While he was very much engaged in relating psychology to social issues, from war to racism, group psychology and the discontents of civilization (Freud 1913a, 1915, 1921, 1927, 1930), he was writing during a period when the possibility that human activities could bring the Earth's ecosystems to the brink of collapse would have been hard to contemplate. Romanticism may have complained about 'unweaving rainbows' and industry's 'dark satanic mills', but by Freud's day this could be seen as Luddite anti-progress talk, especially for those working within the *Weltangschung* of science and the Enlightenment to which Freud (1933) pinned his psychoanalytic flag. However, much of our current bewildering situation can be understood as rooted in part in a world view that was at its zenith during Freud's day and, as Lertzman (2008) suggests, in our responses to anxiety. In addition, Freud did offer us some crucial reflections on our relationship with nature:

> The principle task of civilization, its actual *raison d'être*, is to defend us against nature. We all know that in many ways civilization does this fairly well already, and clearly as time goes on it will do it much better. But no one is under the illusion that nature has already been vanquished; and few dare hope that she will ever be entirely subdued to man.
>
> (Freud 1927: 51)

Here we can see an interesting ambivalence in Freud's rhetorical style, which perhaps unwittingly captures two crucial aspects of our civilization's relationship to 'Nature' and thus begins to open up a psychoanalytic approach to ecology. First, he depicts a series of binary oppositions typical for his era, and not so different in our own: human versus nature, man versus woman and (more implicitly) order versus chaos. Here we find the classic tropes of the Enlightenment, modernity, patriarchy, industrialism and capitalism, which Jungian ecopsychologist Mary-Jane Rust (2008) calls the myths we live by. The myths she is referring to in particular are the 'myth of progress' and the 'myth of the Fall'. She argues that in order to create a sustainable future, or indeed any future, we need to find other stories, other myths, through which to live our lives, to rethink how we have fallen and what it means to progress. Freud's work suggests that Western culture views civilization as a defence against nature, and against wildness, inner and outer, but as Rust (2008: 5) writes, at 'this critical point in human history we most urgently need a myth to live by which is about living with nature, rather than fighting it.' Thus, according to Rust,

> we find ourselves . . . between stories (Berry 1999), in a transitional space . . . of great turbulence, with little to hold onto save the ground

of our own experience. Our therapeutic task . . . is to understand how these myths still shape our internal worlds, our language, and our defences . . . [S]omewhere in the midst of 'sustainability' . . . lies an inspiring vision of transformation . . . We need to dig deep, to re-read our own myths as well as find inspiration from the stories of others.

(ibid.)

The myth of progress enters the climate change debate in calls for geo-engineering and utopian techno-fixes such as putting thousands of mirrors in space, and in the dismissal of even gentle questioning of current economic models of unlimited growth. We will later look at Harold Searles' (1972) approach to our fascination with technology and its role in the current crisis. Returning to Freud, however, there is, as always, another side, an implicit awareness that the feeling of mastery civilization gives us is in many ways a dangerous illusion. Behind our need for mastery lies our fear and trembling in the face of the awesome power of mother nature.

There are the elements which seem to mock at all human control: the earth, which quakes and is torn apart and buries all human life and its works; water, which deluges and drowns everything in turmoil; storms, which blow everything before them . . . With these forces nature rises up against us, majestic, cruel and inexorable; she brings to our mind once more our weakness and helplessness, which we thought to escape through the work of civilization.

(Freud 1927: 15–16)

Here is the other side of Freud's writing on the relation between 'Nature' and 'Civilization', with humanity portrayed as a weak and helpless infant in awe and fear of a mighty and terrible mother. The lure and horror of matriarchy lie behind the defensive constructs of patriarchal civilization, just as Klein's paranoid-schizoid fears of fragmentation, engulfment, and annihilation lie behind later castration threats (Hinshelwood 1991). With each new earthquake or flood, nature erupts into culture – similar to Kristeva's (1982) description of the eruption of the 'semiotic' into the 'symbolic' – and we are thrown back into a state of terror. The 'illusion' in the title of Freud's 1927 essay *The Future of an Illusion* was meant to refer to how religion arose to deal with these anxieties. However, the structural function of the myth of progress, while undoubtably more successful in terms of practical benefits, can also be included here. In these words of Freud we have already a deep understanding, albeit largely implicit, of our own current crisis: a relationship to nature based on a master–slave system of absolute binaries, and an attempt to maintain an illusory autonomy and control in the face of chaos.

There is often a tension in Freud, between the celebration of Enlightenment values found in works such as *The Future of an Illusion* (1927) and the more Romantic Freud who won the Goethe prize and constantly emphasized the elements Enlightenment rationality leaves out such as jokes, dreams, slips and psychological symptoms. Thus, as well as being a perfect example of the Enlightenment with its call to make the unconscious conscious and give the 'rational' ego greater power over the wilds of the id, psychoanalysis also provides a serious challenge to this way of thinking. There will always be something beyond our control. We are not, and never can be, masters in our own house, and the core of who we are is irrational, and often frightening. Marcuse (1998) touched on a similar tension when declaring Freud's (1930) *Civilization and Its Discontents* both the most radical critique of Western culture and its most trenchant defence. Psychoanalysis, as always, is exquisitely ambivalent.

Ultimately, for Freud, both the natural world and our inner nature are untamable and the most we can hope for are temporary, fragile, anxious compromises between competing forces (Winter & Koger 2004). The chaos of nature we defend against is also the chaos of our inner nature, the wildness in the depths of our psyche. Civilization does not only domesticate livestock but also humanity itself (Freud & Einstein 1933: 214). However, attempts to eliminate the risk have in many ways dangerously backfired, comparable to the ways that the historical programmes aiming to eliminate forest fires in the United States have led to far bigger and more uncontrollable fires taking the place of previously smaller and more manageable ones (Diamond 2006: 43–47).

The control promised by the Enlightenment, the power of the intellect to overcome chaos (environmental and emotional), is therefore at least partly a defensive and at times dangerous illusion. In our age of anxiety, with the destruction of civilization threatened by nuclear holocaust, ecosystemic collapse, bioweapons and dirty bombs, Freud's warning is more relevant than ever:

> Men have gained control over the forces of nature to such an extent that with their help they would have no difficulty in exterminating one another to the last man . . . hence comes a large part of their current unrest, their unhappiness and their mood of anxiety.
>
> (Freud 1930: 135)

Freud's binaries 'masculine/Enlightenment/control/autonomy' versus 'feminine/nature/chaos/dependency' also lead us to consider what Gregory Bateson (2000: 95) called the 'bipolar characteristic' of Western thought, which even tries 'to impose a binary pattern upon phenomena which are not dual in nature: youth versus age, labor versus capital, mind versus matter – and, in general, lack[s] the organizational devices for handling triangular systems.' In such a culture, as with the child struggling to come to terms with the Oedipal situation, 'any "third" party is always regarded . . . as a threat' (ibid.).

Deleuze and Guattari describe such dualistic forms of thinking using the ecological metaphor of the tree with its fork-branch patterns (although they would not use the term metaphor): 'Arborescent systems are hierarchical systems with centers of signifiance and subjectification . . . an element only receives information from a higher unit, and only receives a subjective affection along preestablished paths' (Deleuze & Guattari 2003a: 16). However, Freud's 'arborescent' system of binaries can also show us the way out, capturing the psychological bind we are now in. As Deleuze and Guattari (2003a: 277) write: 'The only way to get outside the dualisms is . . . to pass between, the intermezzo.' Deconstructing these dualisms allows us to think about how our destructive urge to dominate and control is connected to our fear of acknowledging dependency on this largest of 'holding environments', the ultimate 'environment mother' (Winnicott 1999, 1987).

This thesis is remarkably consistent with Adorno and Horkheimer's (2002) discussion of 'memesis' in *Dialectic of Enlightenment*. In this work, they argue that the natural tendency or defence to become like nature, to blend in with our surroundings, through camouflage, becomes perverted in the development of civilization into a fear of becoming like nature that is expressed as an urge to dominate and control initially 'external' nature, and later our psychological and social selves. For Adorno and Horkheimer (2002) this problem lies at the heart of civilization, leading to the terrible 'symptoms' of Fascism. However, as Deleuze and Guattari (2003b: 122) write, there is always a 'line of flight' which escapes: 'The most closed system still has a thread that rises toward the virtual, and down which the spider descends.' Similarly for Freud (1930: 89): 'We shall never completely subdue nature; our body, too, is an organism, itself a part of nature, and will always contain the seeds of dissolution, with its limited powers of adaptation and achievement.'

Using a related theoretical framework, Erich Fromm, former Frankfurt School colleague of Adorno and Horkheimer, came to a similar position with his concept of the fear of freedom. Fromm (2001) suggests that the human project is one of gradually winning greater freedom from external oppression but at the cost of a sense of isolation and aloneness, including disconnection/isolation from nature. Humans are cast out of the garden after eating from the tree of knowledge, a knowledge which condemns us to be free, alone with our desires. He identified various 'mechanisms of escape' through which we try to avoid the conflict, such as *automaton-conformity*, *authoritarianism* and *destructiveness*, and defensive personality structures and 'social characters', such as the 'marketing personality', each with their associated 'social unconscious' (Fromm 2006) and all of which are relevant to understanding our current ecological crisis (Fisher 2009).

Fromm's fear of freedom combines an intense anxiety/fear of becoming like nature with a simultaneous longing for merger and (re)connection.

Fromm's solution is that there is no way back to the garden (as some contemporary 'primitivists' and ecopsychologists seem to suggest). Instead we must reconnect with the world on a higher level (a higher synthesis), continuing the path of human emancipation which will allow us to return in moments of love and empathy to a freely given connection with the wider world, including the non-human environment, in what he calls a positive 'freedom to'. Interestingly, a term Fromm frequently uses to describe this love of nature, humanity and life, in contrast to its opposite, 'necrophilia', is a term ecopsychology, drawing on Wilson (2003), is especially fond of: the term 'biophilia' (Fromm 1964). Whether or not Fromm's Hegelian optimism, with his belief in a higher synthesis between humanity and the world, can bear fruit, we would do well to reflect on Gregory Bateson's warning:

> The materialistic philosophy which sees 'man' as pitted against his environment is rapidly breaking down as technological man becomes more and more able to oppose the largest systems. Every battle that he wins brings a threat of disaster. The unit of survival . . . in ethics or in evolution . . . is not the organism or the species but the largest system or 'power' within which the creature lives. If the creature destroys its environment, it destroys itself.
>
> (Bateson 2000: 332)

This engagement of 'critical theory' with ecology is long overdue according to some writers. Ley (2008) calls for a psychoanalytic critical ecology, conceiving of 'sustainability' as a concept with relevance to the internal world, requiring a more creative balance between ego and id, and between human culture and the wilds of our 'internal' and 'external' nature. Fisher (2009) similarly argues that ecopsychology requires a more nuanced political perspective, which he suggests can be gained through a critical engagement with the work of the Frankfurt School to provide a model of how to integrate psychological and social concerns, while taking the further step of including the ecological. This book suggests that to achieve this latter step we need to engage with the work of Gilles Deleuze and Felix Guattari, and in this case in particular Guattari's (2000) idea of the three ecologies of mind, nature and society.

Eros and Thanatos

> From the Freudian perspective, our planet is populated by a species systematically destroying its own habitat. Although they think of them-selves as intelligent and rational, the creatures, driven by Eros, are destroying themselves through over-consumption and overpopulation. Rushing through existence in order to procure more and more appetitive

satisfaction, the animals instead enjoy less and less. Filled with Thanatos, they unconsciously destroy their environment, at the same time building weapons of mass destruction that threaten to destroy the whole of their species.

(Winter & Koger 2004: 31–32)

Winter and Koger's (2004) *The Psychology of Environmental Problems* is one of the first books to think psychoanalytically about the environmental crisis (although this mainly occupies just the first chapter) and it therefore provides a good starting point for exploring this area. The authors apply Freud's second drive theory of Eros and Thanatos, showing that Freud's 'eternal adversaries' are unfortunately unlikely bedfellows in their destructive effects on nature.

Both aspects of Thanatos can feed into our destructivity: the active destructive desires and the more 'silent' desires for non-existence and annihilation which Freud felt lay beneath this. The latter are also visible in the rhetoric of the environmental movement which often includes apocalyptic themes, sometimes as warnings but at times with almost utopian yearning. This is also evident in recent 'eco-disaster' films, as discussed in the following section. Deep Ecology's call to move from an 'anthropocentrist' to an 'ecocentrist' position sometimes masks a highly misanthropic – or at least potentially fascist – position. We may also see the 'nirvana principle' (Freud 1920) in the virtual indifference with which we face the world's sixth great mass extinction, from which there is no reason to assume we will be spared. This indifference to such staggering loss stands in stark contrast to the reaction we are likely to make following the death of our (Oedipal, or rather Oedipalized) pet (Deleuze & Guattari 2003a: 240).

In addition, Eros, through over-consumption and overpopulation, also unwittingly works towards the potential collapse of the ability of the biosphere to sustain our complex civilization. In her paper 'When Drives are Dangerous: Drive Theory and Resource Over-Consumption' Frances Bigda-Peyton (2004: 251) argues that harmful over-consumption 'occurs when psychic structures dominated by destructive instincts succeed in overpowering life-sustaining impulses' and that over-consumption 'also functions as a defense against the awareness of death wishes.' In addition, she claims that 'narcissistic fixations keep individuals and groups from maturing to the point of recognizing that they must give to the environment in order to be provided for in a sustainable way.' Evidence that denial and projection are involved here comes from Schor's (1998) study which showed that the majority regard *other* people as more materialistic and more motivated to consume for social status than themselves.

Following Wachtel (2003), Bigda-Peyton (2004) suggests the need to look at structural aspects of 'pathological consumption', related not only to an id that is chronically over-stimulated by advertising, but also our culture's consumerist ego-ideal. In the form of 'biophilia' (Wilson 2003; Kellert & Wilson 1993) Eros could, however, also work to reinvigorate our love of nature, as ecopsychology is keen on suggesting. Sally Weintrobe (2011a: 1–2), for example, suggests that our 'love of nature includes the erotic, that free play of sensual pleasure of all the senses.' This will be crucial if we are to turn back from the brink. As Freud (1930: 145) writes: 'It is to be expected that the other of the two "Heavenly Powers", eternal Eros, will make an effort to assert himself in the struggle with his equally immortal adversary. But who can foresee with what success and with what result?'

The rise of the eco-disaster film

> I came to save the Earth . . . If the Earth dies, you die. If you die, the Earth survives – Klaatu, in *The Day the Earth Stood Still*.
>
> (Derrickson 2008)

Eco-disaster films seem to be on the rise today. Movies such as *The Day the Earth Stood Still* (Derrickson 2008), *The Day After Tomorrow* (Emmerich 2004), *Avatar* (Cameron 2009), *Wall-E* (Stanton 2008) and *The Age of Stupid* (Armstrong 2009) are interesting for a psychoanalytic ecology because of their themes, the fact that they are appearing now, and the contradictory responses they have generated.

> *The Day the Earth Stood Still* . . . touch[es] on timeless mythic themes: destruction and redemption, death and resurrection, mortality and immortality, individual liberty and group unity, national sovereignty and global community, and, of course, scientists playing God and technology run amok. Myths, whether in written or visual form, serve a vital role of asking unanswerable questions and providing unquestionable answers. Most of us . . . have a low tolerance for ambiguity and uncertainty. We want to reduce the cognitive dissonance of not knowing by filling the gaps with answers. Traditionally, religious myths have served that role, but today – in the age of science – science fiction is our mythology.
>
> (Shermer 2008)

Sci-Fi often deals with social anxieties. The original version of this film dealt with the cold war while the update revolves around whether humans deserve extermination for endangering the planet or if they should get another chance. This lead to it being attacked in some quarters for it's perceived misanthropy. Self-proclaimed climate 'sceptic' Wesley Smith (2008a, 2008b) argues that the film 'pushes the mantra of deepest ecology':

> Today's Hollywood reflects the cultural views of the left . . . [which] has gone insanely anti-human. This misanthropic nihilism is usually implied between the lines, but it is the unequivocal and explicit message of *The Day the Earth Stood Still* . . . In the original film from the 1950s [Wise 1951], aliens threatened to destroy us because of our warlike ways . . . now, we are apparently to be destroyed for *Gaia*.

Similar anti-environmental hostility met previous eco-disaster films, such as *The Day After Tomorrow* (Emmerich 2004), about which Holleran (2004) writes, adding a dash of racism into the mix:

> *Day After* dramatizes its faith that Earth is better off without man; we have it coming. The German-born director also depicts the end of the United States of America with relish . . . [It] is a homily brought forth by true believers with its deity revealed in the screen's final image. That the masses are already on their knees in the Church of Environmentalism doesn't make its first major motion picture any less monstrous.

Turning to *Avatar* (Cameron 2009), many have hailed it for its pro-environmental themes. Harold Linde (2010), for example, writes that it is 'without a doubt the most epic piece of environmental advocacy ever captured on celluloid'. He continues:

> The film hits all the important environmental talking-points – virgin rain forests threatened by wanton exploitation, indigenous peoples who have much to teach the developed world, a planet which functions as a collective, interconnected Gaia-istic organism, and evil corporate interests that are trying to destroy it all.

The director, James Cameron, has also explicitly discussed the film's environmental message, claiming it represents 'a fictionalized fantasy version of what our world was like before we started to pave it and build malls, and shopping centers . . . an evocation of the world we used to have' (Cameron, cited in Poorie 2010). In another interview (Cameron 2010) he said that 'we are going to go through a lot of pain and heartache if we don't acknowledge our stewardship responsibilities to nature.'

However, Slavoj Žižek (2010) argues that 'beneath the idealism and political correctness . . . lie brutal racist undertones' combined with the traditional Hollywood Oedipal narrative of the 'resigned white hero who has to go among the savages to find a proper sexual partner . . . marrying the aboriginal princess and becoming king.' Ian Parker (2010) also warns us to look below the 'radical' surface of *Avatar*:

We also need to ask how it is that an ecological message gets recuperated, neutralised and absorbed, so that instead of operating as a radical political critique it comes to be an ideologically potent part of the spectacle. There is a motif of 'connection' at three levels in the film, and this makes it a very appealing fantasy machine . . . Even if the film is radical in some respects, we need to notice how it sets the conditions for us to believe it is radical, how it incites us to enjoy those radical moments all the more firmly to keep us inside the limits of those conditions (for that is what fantasy, ideological fantasy, is).

However, Rupert Read (2010) has attempted to take on and rebut the various criticisms of the film (in particular, the accusations of sentimentalization, disability prejudice, anti-Americanism, covert imperialism, pro-violence and an unrealistic ending) and maintains support for *Avatar's* potential for a radical anthropology, and by extension ecopsychology.

Whatever our ideological position, how should we view the increasing number of such films and the reactions they have engendered? Do they provide a medium where our anxieties and hopes can be explored, where we can think about otherwise unthinkable scenarios while being challenged towards real change? Or do they rather present a caricature of ecology, making it easier to attack and dismiss, creating viewing that is at times as uncomfortable for 'green' spectators as for anti-green or 'magenta' spectators (magenta is the purple-pink 'after-effect' that studies of perception have shown that you are left with when you stare at green for too long; see Shimojo, Kamitani & Nishida 2001). Does the way eco-disaster films convey their 'green' message lead to a kind of backlash, an 'after-effect' of people seeing magenta? Or do such films challenge certain half-thought-out aspects of ecology itself? Is there a hidden misanthropy and apocalyptic thinking embedded in environmental rhetoric?

There is a suicide motif (Searles 1972) in these films where we might discern the silent call of Thanatos. *Age of Stupid* (Armstrong 2009) centres on the question of why humanity's last act was an act of suicide, while *The Happening* (Shyamalan 2008) depicts plants which rebel against human oppression by releasing a pheromone that causes people to commit mass suicide. Destruction in *The Day the Earth Stood Still* (Derrickson 2008) comes from swarms of cyborg 'insects' stripping everything in their path, drawing on fears of genetic and nano engineering and introducing a strange hybrid 'eco-techno' agent that will bring about our demise. Meanwhile, extra-terrestrial globes appear all over the planet, arks collecting every species except humans to repopulate the world once humanity has been wiped out. Apart from the discomfort ecologists feel when their ideas are connected to such anti-humanism, it is important to think about their appeal.

> Apocalypticism . . . is one of humanity's most powerful ideas . . . It is a
> very ancient pattern of human thought . . . [concerning] the ultimate
> struggle between the forces of order and chaos. It is deeply appealing at
> a psychological level because the idea of meaninglessness is deeply
> threatening. Human societies have always tried to create some kind of
> framework of meaning to give history and our own personal lives some
> kind of significance.
>
> (Paul Boyer, cited in Rohrer 2008)

The green apocalypse is certainly one of its current forms. The fact that it
is not 'only' a fantasy does not make its deep psychological appeal any less
powerful (if the apocalypse didn't exist, we would need to invent it). We are
haunted and enthralled by the idea of a 'world without us' (Weisman 2007).
Freud said we cannot really imagine our own death; when we try to do so
we are still present, as spectator to our own funeral. Similarly, in most
imagined end of the world or end of humanity scenarios, we implicitly
count ourselves among the few survivors, able perhaps to finally build the
ecotopian dream.

> We, humans, are reduced to a pure disembodied gaze observing our
> own absence. As Lacan pointed out, this is the fundamental subjective
> position of fantasy . . . like the fantasy of witnessing the act of one's
> own conception . . . or the act of witnessing one's own burial . . . 'The
> world without us' is thus fantasy at its purest: witnessing the Earth
> itself retaining its pre-castrated state of innocence, before we humans
> spoiled it with our hubris.
>
> (Žižek 2007)

Annalee Newitz (2008) suggests four reasons for the current popularity of
this theme. First, *environmental guilt*, where people 'overwhelmed with a
sense of hopelessness . . . yearn for stories about a world where humans
aren't around anymore to muck things up.' Second, *future ennui*, whereby
we are liberated from the constant exhaustion of planning for the future by
removing ourselves from it. Third, *fear of extinction*, where, according to
Newitz, 'we're also scared shitless that the future will smack us on the head
and wipe us all out . . . We imagine the world without ourselves as a coping
mechanism, a way to accustom ourselves to the idea that no matter how
much we plan, we still may not make it as a species.' Finally, *evolution
degree zero* reverses time and undoes all human mistakes, leaving open the
possibility that we might evolve again, better the second time. Psychoanalysis can prove useful in unmasking the depths of human phantasy and
motivation in such themes, where we can detect complex forms of anxiety,
and defence.

Chapter 5

Eco-anxiety and defence

Becoming aware of our environmental problems does not mean that we can easily stop ourselves from ruining our habitat. Freud posited that if we became aware of our unconscious sexual and aggressive motivations, we would be greatly disturbed. Instead, our psyches expend energy to keep impulses below the surface so that we can fool ourselves into thinking that we behave for rational or moral reasons, when in fact much of our behaviour is driven by subversive needs, wishes, fears, and impulses.

(Winter & Koger 2004: 32)

Into the climate kettle

Psychoanalysts have long known that defences need to be tackled carefully. Perhaps green campaigns, as worthy and as truthful as they may be, might at times have caused more harm than good, representing a 'sledgehammer' approach to tackling eco-defences. The shift following the 'email scandal' which, almost inevitably, was quickly labelled 'climategate' by the media (Jonsson 2010) is indicative of how powerfully our motivations influence our perception of events, leading us to seize on any opportunity to refuse the anxiety-provoking situation. As Lertzman (2008) writes, we 'have a way to go . . . before we can fully appreciate the impact environmental issues have on our mental and emotional health.' She argues that 'those working in communication arts . . . [should] look at what psychoanalysts have to say about the nature of anxiety; we may find a whole new approach to getting our messages across that may inspire fight, rather than flight.' A good place to start is Marshall's (2001) description of his reactions on first hearing about the climate threat:

My first real exposure to the issue of climate change was reading a newspaper article in the *Sydney Morning Herald* in 1988, by a leading Australian climatologist. Climate change, he said, had the potential to destroy our society and even threatened our continued survival as a species. I was deeply moved . . . A highly qualified scientist had calmly and credibly outlined a process which, were it to be believed, made all other news in the paper marginal if not irrelevant. Yet the story . . . sunk without a trace. I could see only two explanations; either it was a hoax, which seemed unlikely, or it was so conjectural that no one could seriously accept it. Either way, my immediate instinctive drive to do something was squashed.

(Marshall 2001)

Only much later did he consider a third more psychoanalytic explanation, 'that people can accept the truth of what is said without accepting the implications' (ibid.). Here we have an example of what psychoanalysis calls denial. In the classic scenario, Freud (1925) suggested that the fetish covers over a lack that is simultaneously accepted and denied; in the textbook case of the maternal phallus this translates as 'I know very well that mummy does not have a penis, nevertheless I do not really accept it.' Are we dealing here with a kind of mass denial of the castration of Mother Earth?

Freud's great insight in his topographical model is that we are not only looking at two different psychological *levels* (conscious and unconscious) but also two different *forms* of mental functioning (Freud 1911), embodied in the primary and secondary process for which there is now some empirical support from experimental psychology and neuroscience (e.g. Shevrin 1996). These ideas have also received a more rigorous mathematical-logical formulation in Matte-Blanco's (1998) 'bi-logic', which uses set theory to describe the unconscious as 'infinite sets' and as functioning according to the principle of 'symmetry' opposed to the 'asymmetric' logic of consciousness. The understanding that conscious and unconscious refer not only to two different levels of functioning, but also to two different 'logics' is crucial to looking at unconscious defensive and affective responses to the threat of climate change.

One of the characteristics Freud (1911) attributed to the functioning of the unconscious mind is that it can tolerate mutual contradictions without difficulty – Matte-Blanco's (1998) 'symmetric' logic – while consciousness experiences what we now call 'cognitive dissonance' (Cooper 2007). This can be illustrated using Freud's (1905: 62) 'borrowed kettle' joke. A man is told that he should replace a pot he has borrowed and returned damaged. He refuses, claiming: 1. When I gave it back it was fine; 2. The hole was there when you gave it to me; 3. I never borrowed it in the first place! These three mutually contradictory answers alert us to the presence of unconscious processes, which in this case are united by the underlying *motivation* or *desire* to be found innocent, to remove the blame, to prevent the need for any action or effort to remedy the situation (see also the 'Irma injection' dream in Freud 1900a: 106–121).

This joke is particularly useful in our context because of its structure (mutual contradictions united by a common motivation), the fact that a kettle is, like our climate, a container that can be broken when heated up beyond a certain limit, and because the joke's formula corresponds well to the many arguments against action on climate change (often argued by the same person simultaneously). For the purposes of simplification these can be summarized in three positions, progressively accepting more of the reality of the ecological crisis but all resulting in inaction: 1. Its not happening; 2. Its not my fault; 3. There's nothing we can do about it (so I can just get on with my life as usual). What phantasies, anxieties and defences are expressed within these positions?

1. There's nothing wrong with the climate kettle

The first set of phantasies behind this position are basically paranoid in structure (e.g. a conspiracy by Al Gore, the UN or communists trying to take away our freedom, or capitalists trying to stop third world countries from developing so they remain exploitable, etc.). The second set of ideas claims that 'the evidence is not conclusive', the implication being that we need 100 per cent certainty to take the action scientists suggest is required (the IPCC's 'unequivocal' is just not unequivocal enough). At first this appears more logical, but when compared with other evaluations of risk its irrationality becomes more apparent. Few would agree to play Russian roulette (without some suicidal inclination) even with a 90 per cent certainty of not getting the bullet, yet the scientific consensus is that we are all playing Russian roulette with the entire planet with far, far worse odds.

2. There was a hole in the planet when you gave it to me

Here there are two main contradictory claims (often argued simultaneously): 'It is just a regular pattern of climate variation, or it's due to sunspots, or the earth is shrinking, it is not our (humanity's) fault.' Alternatively, 'It is caused by *other* people (India, China), not me, so there's nothing I can (or should) do, so I may as well just ignore it.' Both contradictory beliefs (not human-caused and caused by *other* humans) support the unconscious deflection of guilt onto the 'not-me'. However, even if one were true, the deflection of guilt does nothing to stop the disastrous consequences of climate change so we would still need to take urgent action. One psychoanalytically interesting conclusion from this is that at least at times people can fear guilt more than their own, or even everyone's, destruction.

3. There is nothing we can do about it

'All the king's horses and all the king's men can't put the climate back together again, so why should we bother?' This is also found in many pessimistic, burnt-out environmentalists filled with overwhelming feelings of despair and disempowerment.

The different arguments over the planetary kettle boil down (pun intended) to defences against specific anxieties. To use Kleinian terminology: *Its not happening* (the kettle is fine) involves psychotic defences against paranoid-schizoid anxiety (destruction, fragmentation and annihilation); *Its not our/ my fault* involves neurotic defences against depressive anxiety (difficulty in acknowledging human culpability and guilt); *It is happening and it is our fault, but there's nothing I/we can do about it* is closest to recognizing and engaging with the problem. But without a realistic chance for reparation the individual is stuck with the despair and pain of the depressive position without hope (the non-manic hope that reparation is possible, as opposed to the manic hope leading to short-term activism which collapses when change is not rapid enough). More primitive defences, such as splitting, may then need to be employed.

Media as symptom and the role of humour

> On no previous occasion have we ever witnessed such internal contradictions in the media as we see every day on climate change . . . a minor reflection of a far wider, more profound and sustained disconnection at all levels of society between the seriousness of the threat of climate change and the action that we take in response.
>
> (Marshall 2005)

The media influences our mind and beliefs but also reflects them. At a conference on the psychology of climate change at the University of the West of England in 2009, George Marshall provided some interesting examples. *The Independent* newspaper from 24 January 2005 included a major article titled 'Countdown to global catastrophe' warning that 'a point of no return may be reached in ten years, beyond which the world would be irretrievably committed to disastrous changes' including 'widespread agricultural failure, water shortages and major droughts, increased disease, sea level rise and the death of forests – with the added possibility of abrupt catastrophic events such as "runaway" greenhouse global warming, the melting of the Greenland ice sheet, or the switching off of the Gulf Stream' (cited in Marshall 2009). Right next to this article was the advert 'British Airways sale is now on' with flights for 'as little as £10' (ibid.). Another example came from a competition on the *Guardian* newspaper's website which called for innovative solutions to climate change with the prize of a holiday to Dubai, while an article on the importance of the contributions of transport to climate change appeared next to a huge advertisement for a 4×4 (ibid.).

These contradictions are brought into sharp focus in two parallel surveys. A WWF poll from 2001 (WWF 2001) showed that 90 per cent of people favoured government action to reduce greenhouse emissions, while in a MORI poll the same year 80 per cent thought they would travel more frequently in the future, and a 2004 BBC survey found that only 37 per cent would agree to pay more for petrol (Marshall 2005). We don't usually notice such contradictions even when they are staring us in the face. When we do, our response might be: 'This would be funny if it wasn't so serious.' In fact, psychoanalytically, it is perhaps more accurate to say that it is funny precisely because it is so serious. Freud (1905) taught us to take jokes seriously and that laughter is connected not only with joy but also anxiety. How can we understand the role of humour here? Is it a form of denial, escapism or trivialization, or can comedy help to counter the preachiness many people associate with environmentalism? To gain further illumination, let's turn to some climate jokes.

Jay Leno (Kurtzman 2010) joked: 'According to a new UN report, the global warming outlook is much worse than originally predicted. Which is pretty bad when they originally predicted it would destroy the planet.' Out of context it looks not funny but positively frightening, with laughter perhaps the only emotional response we can produce other than terror. On the more ridiculous side Jimmy Kimmel quipped: 'President Bush has a plan. He says that if we need to, we can lower the temperature dramatically just by switching from Fahrenheit to Celsius' (ibid.). As well as finding a relatively easy target to make fun of, always an effective way to squeeze out a joke (Freud 1905), this also connects with a powerful wish inside all of us that a simple solution will be found, that perhaps if we only look at the problem from the right angle, it will simply disappear.

Perhaps my favourite joke is from George Monbiot who quoted an email he received: 'Thank you for your excellent work in bringing the dangers of climate change to the attention of people. If we do not do something at once, the whole world will be turned into a dessert.' Monbiot replied: 'Although this is an appealing prospect, unfortunately the science does not support it' (Hickman 2008). But comedy cuts both ways, as winter snow-drifts provide an endless source of amusement for climate sceptics even though, as we all know, climate change is snow joke (Coren 2010). *South Park* chose as its target the perceived self-righteousness of the environmentalists through a pun where the 'smug' emitted by hybrid car owners becomes so great that people are forced to return to their SUVs (Butler 2008). Freud's lesson that jokes are in fact very serious things should be a message taken on board by climate campaigners, as perhaps a more comic method might reach parts that the tyrannical green superego (Randall 2005) just cannot reach.

Conflict or deficit: Death anxiety or failed risk-thermostat?

> The unique quality of climate change . . . is that it combines every single quality that we find it hardest to engage with . . . [Like] deadly diseases . . . perfectly formed to bypass our immune system, climate change is perfectly formed to confound our problem-solving skills.
>
> (Marshall 2005)

In general it seems that we have evolved to deal optimally with threats which are immediate, clear, visible, with simple causation, caused by a clearly identifiable 'enemy', and with obvious direct personal consequences. Unfortunately climate change is invisible, highly complex, highly uncertain in its impacts, and caused by *all* of us. It thus can also be seen as an example of the ultimate bystander effect with its associated diffusion of responsibility (Hudson & Bruckman 2004; Darley & Latané 1968).

To illustrate the unique ability of climate change to bypass our 'risk-thermostat' Marshall compares it with other potential or real threats. For example, the Y2K computer bug was complex, caused by no one identifiable enemy, with highly uncertain effects, but its immediate and known deadline led to 'a high level of public concern (in some cases virtual panic) and a rapid global response involving the investment of $60 billion in mitigation measures' (Marshall 2005). Or, to consider a potential future threat (and climate change already affects us now):

> Let us imagine that astronomers discover that we are due to collide in fifty years with a meteorite so large that an impact would provoke massive destruction and a permanent alteration in the world's weather patterns . . . we could be reasonably confident that there would be a sustained global mobilization . . . There are a lot of rockets in the world, and a lot of people who would very much like to play with them . . . even though the impacts would be the same as climate change, action was enabled by the presence of a clear [and simple] external cause.
>
> (ibid.)

If the cause became an identifiable enemy human group (e.g. North Korea using chemical weapons to alter the world's climate) we would find a predictably greater response. On this model, climate change is unique and almost perfectly designed to miss our usual buttons, in that 'every single one of its aspects, unfortunately and tragically, lines up with the areas in which we are least psychologically enabled to take action' (ibid.). But is this the whole story? Is a deficit model enough to account for our inaction on climate change? Bigda-Peyton asks:

> Do people strike out against the natural world because the inevitability of death is so evident in nature? . . . If individuals treat natural resources as limitless, then they can maintain the illusion of their own limitlessness. Destroying nature is preferable to becoming aware of death and the wish for it.
>
> (Bigda-Peyton 2004: 261)

As psychoanalysts have long pointed out, even where there is a clear deficit, we need also to look at how the mind dynamically adapts and deals with the deficit, an insight more recently applied by neuropsychoanalysts to working with patients with focal brain lesions (Kaplan-Solms and Solms 2000). In the case of climate change, this means that we need to think about our anxieties and phantasies around death. Marshall (2005) writes:

> I am also struck by the observation, drawn from my own emotional response . . . that climate change correlates uncomfortably well with the one area in which denial is a psychological strength; our response to our own mortality. Like death, climate change entails permanent and irreversible loss. It means that the world as we currently experience it is no more than a passing dream and is doomed as surely as we are ourselves. When I look out of my window and I think all this will be gone – that if we don't stop this thing, then this world will never exist again except in fading memories or photographs – it touches the same part of me as the thought of my own passing.

It actually touches something even more fundamental. Terror Management Theory (TMT), drawing on the work of the cultural anthropologist Ernest Becker (1973), has demonstrated empirically (e.g. Greenberg et al. 2000) that attachments to our world views become more absolute and rigid, with less tolerance of dissent and outsiders, when we are confronted with considering our own death. TMT argues that one important function of our world view is as a cultural-symbolic defence against death anxiety which would otherwise paralyze us as the only species able to contemplate (with certainty) its own death. World views, and the civilizations they are a part of, provide symbolic immortality either through promises of a life after death, or the knowledge that your culture/world view will continue after your own passing.

From a TMT perspective, the ecological threat would lead us to cling even more tightly to our world view. But the latter is also threatened by climate change, either directly by climate chaos or by the ecologists and scientists who point out that we need to change in radical ways, leading to greater levels of death anxiety as this major defence seems less solid. We thus have another potentially catastrophic positive feedback loop. It is always difficult for us to let go of our way of life, but it is especially difficult now when it is most required. Here, splitting in various forms becomes a common defence, including in our politics.

> Our prime minister tells us that climate change is 'a challenge so far-reaching in its impact and irreversible in its destructive power, that it alters radically human existence.' His chief scientific advisor says it is the most severe problem we face . . . And yet, nothing in the government's response reflects this rhetoric. Its work on climate change is incoherent, underfunded, and constantly undermined by the support . . . [of] high emitting industries.
>
> (Marshall 2005)

This brings up a fundamental question for ecopsychoanalytic research. Is the 'deficit' or the 'anxiety-defence' model more appropriate for our current situation? In other words, is our inaction due to anxiety and subsequent defence mechanisms (individual and social) or the abstractness of the issue, which our evolved minds are unable to grasp? The answer determines which strategies are likely to be effective and which will backfire. Should environmental campaigners increase the emotional impact of their message and the sense of urgency to allow people to connect viscerally to an otherwise abstract issue? Or is the 'ecology of fear' (Žižek 2007) counterproductive as defences against anxiety become ever more rigid and extreme?

In the latter case a more effective strategy would be to try to identify and deal with the underlying anxieties to enable us to move beyond our current stuck position, although the time for working though is unfortunately limited, especially on the global scale required. The likely answer is that the two explanations interact. The very abstraction of climate change is a paramount example of what Timothy Morton (2010c) calls 'hyper-objects', objects which are 'massively distributed in time and space such that any particular (local) manifestation never reveals the totality of the hyper-object' (for more on hyper-objects see Chapter 8). Perhaps these characteristics provide the ideal opportunity for the various defences, such as splitting, denial and intellectualization, to be so easily and effectively employed. However, the relative contribution of each will have major consequences when determining strategy from the point of view of psychoanalytically enlightened ecological politics.

Defence mechanisms in the face of eco-anxiety

> Wouldn't splitting our awareness be an ingenious solution, allowing us to both maintain our behavior and still retain our knowledge of reality? This is precisely the state that most of us live in – a split-off, fragmented,

dissonant state in which we continue on with our destructive behaviours while paying some, although not full, heed to the mounting threats to our ecosystem.

(Winter & Koger 2004: 34)

Recently, psychologists have begun to talk about *climate denial* (American Psychological Association 2010; Marshall 2001). Stanley Cohen (2001) suggests that when societies are confronted with collective moral responsibility for mass human rights abuses they almost always enter into collective denial, structured around an unspoken compact that certain topics will not be discussed and/or are not real. These mostly unconscious alliances (Kaes 2007) are created socially, through small interactions at all levels, without any one person having to consciously create it. In complexity theory this is an example of *self-organization* (Camazine *et al.* 2001; Piers, Muller & Brent 2007), or the formation of what Elliott Jaques (1955) calls *social phantasy systems* and Menzies-Lyth (1988) terms *transpersonal defence mechanisms*. These can be seen as arising from lower-level interactions between individual defence mechanisms forming higher-level structures embodying emergent properties. At this point let us return to Žižek (2007):

So, back to the prospect of ecological catastrophe, why do we not act? . . . One can learn . . . from the Rumsfeldian theory of knowledge . . . 'There are known knowns . . . things we know that we know. There are known unknowns . . . things that we know we don't know. But there are also unknown unknowns . . . things we don't know we don't know.' What he forgot to add was the crucial fourth term: the 'unknown knowns', things we don't know that we know . . . the Freudian unconscious, the 'knowledge which doesn't know itself', as Lacan used to say . . . In the case of ecology, these disavowed beliefs and suppositions are the ones which prevent us from really believing in the possibility of the catastrophe, and they combine with the 'unknown unknowns' . . . like that of the blind spot in our visual field: we do not see the gap, the picture appears continuous.

Cohen (2001) argues that mass denial occurs most often in situations with no cultural mechanism to deal with or accept the gravity of the problem. Using Bion's terms there is no 'thinker' to allow the thought to be born(e), no alpha function to allow the traumatic beta-element to enter the dream-fabric of our reality. Primo Levi (2010) suggests that the reason so few European Jews were able to accept the fact of their impending extermination was that they had the belief that 'things whose existence is not morally possible cannot exist'. According to Marshall (2005):

In the case of climate change . . . we can intellectually accept the evidence of climate change, but . . . find it extremely hard to accept our responsibility for a crime of such enormity . . . we are both bystanders and perpetrators, an internal conflict that can only intensify our denial. We can also draw on historical experience to anticipate which defenses we will adopt when . . . we are confronted by our grandchildren demanding to know why we did so little when we knew so much.

Lertzman (2009) points out that we should understand splitting as operating on social as well as psychological levels (and we might add the ecological level as well, to complete Guattari's three ecologies). In our everyday experience the ecological webs we are a part of are largely invisible. We get our food pre-wrapped in the supermarket, and though we may occasionally intellectually grasp the complex networks behind it, phenomenologically food is just there, appearing on the shelves and waiting for us to consume it. Ecological critiques of capitalism often focus on the need to reconnect with these webs, through farmers' markets, fair trade schemes and so on, just as 'anti-globalization' critiques highlight the role of child labour behind our favourite brands which disappears behind the low price tag and the shiny logos (Klein 2009).

We can also see the work of splitting in Sally Weintrobe's (2011a) writings on the connection between psychic landscapes and natural land-scapes, and the importance of such landscapes to sculpting the inner world of phantasy. Weintrobe (2011a) suggests that deregulated capitalism attacks the (bio)diversity of the inner landscape as well as the outer. It does so 'by promoting . . . a culture of splitting and idealization and by encouraging identification with superior entitled in-groups and increasing fear of being consigned to denigrated and non-entitled outgroups' (Weintrobe 2011a: 2–3). Through what she calls 'mind share', 'our relationships in . . . our various landscapes become narrowed down to being dominated by feeling superior and entitled to exploit and consume the other in the relationship without the psychic pain of guilt and responsibility' (Weintrobe 2011a: 3). An example of this is the case of the colonization of the internal landscape of a bird-lover.

> A person who loves birds and also loves walking . . . may be seduced away from loving birds into seeing him/herself as the owner of the most special binoculars, the best new walking poles and with a superior capacity to find the best and most exotic global locations in which to walk and see birds. The net result is an increased carbon footprint that will adversely affect birds. I suggest such a person has been both willingly and unwillingly colonized. What is particularly colonized and deformed is their love of nature.
>
> (ibid.)

The resulting split internal landscapes assign an inner spatio-temporal location of 'far away' or 'on the other side' for our concern for others, for nature, or the 'future'. Weintrobe suggests that such attempts to blunt our loving, empathic and concerned feelings for the natural world, and the resulting split internal landscapes, have even infiltrated wildlife nature documentaries (although here Weintrobe excludes David Attenborough's programmes). She describes a recent trend here 'to promote identification with idealized, superior and cut-off "hero" figures, while simultaneously blunting our feelings' (Weintrobe 2011a: 3). This is done through a kind of 'shock and awe' strategy, where the awe we are meant to feel refers not to nature but to the narrator-hero.

In such programmes, the natural sounds of wild spaces and animals are silenced, replaced with 'loud, often crass and anthropomorphizing music . . . sudden auditory flash noises and sudden visual shots that may include bloody body parts' (ibid.). The effect is to numb our sensitivity to pain and lead us to identify with the aggressor, but also to deaden 'more concerned depressive feelings' by 'promoting a blank state of mind, one that blanks the here and now of reality and seeks to replace it with the pumped up, self aggrandized, "here and now" state of the dream world of regressive wish fulfillment' (Weintrobe 2011a: 4).

This splitting or dissociation should not be understood as something only imposed from above, as we all collude in the process which blinds us to our interdependency. There is a part of us that longs to connect, but according to Lertzman (2009) when we do the experience can be 'shattering and traumatic'. Similarly, ecological campaigns which try to overcome this dissociation through aggressive guilt may be counterproductive. Lertzman asks:

> Is it ever OK for a parent to berate a child for misbehaving? Having known adults who were raised in such environments, my answer is no. Such individuals are plagued with a chronic sense of disempowerment, insecurity and self-loathing . . . Persecutory guilt plagues many newcomers to our current ecological mess, is reinforced by environmental media campaigns . . . and has been shown to rarely translate into good acts.
>
> (ibid.)

The psychoanalytic alternative, to listen and understand, rather than go on the attack, may seem weak and ineffective, especially given the urgency of the situation. But Lertzman argues the contrary: 'It's a powerful assertion of what is really happening, and a loving ability to face this straight on' (ibid.). She compares this to the Kleinian idea of moving towards the depressive position and the desire for reparation and positive change, inner and outer. Facing our 'losses and griefs and disappointments' will be difficult, and we will undoubtably 'be angry and frustrated and irritated, but it's not a place to dwell in' (ibid.).

The split can also take the form of an *intellectualization*, separating abstract awareness of the crisis from real emotional engagement (by writing a book on psychoanalysis and climate change or making a presentation to a conference on the ecological crisis, reached by flying on a low-cost airline). General principles are at times more easy to face emotionally than our personal contributions, the threats to *other* species easier to acknowledge than the threat to our own. Thus the abstractness of the issue that can be such a barrier to action can be partly artificially induced to protect us from feeling.

The affect refused in intellectualization can also be dealt with through *displacement* onto a different, less threatening target. Winter & Koger (2004: 36) suggest that environmental concern can be displaced in ineffective but more comfortable activities such as buying a T-shirt with a whale picture or 'reconnecting' with nature by going on carbon-emitting flights to exotic lands. On the other hand, eco-anxiety can be displaced onto other groups and scapegoats, exasperating existing hatred of immigrants or conflicts such as the War on Terror.

Scapegoating mechanisms are always around but they tend to increase during times of anxiety and uncertainty. A good example is the witch persecutions of the Early Modern Era, which became a focal point, a lightning rod for all kinds of anxieties (religious, existential, sexual, relational, social and psychological) connected to the transitional period from the medieval-religious to the modern-scientific world. (For psychoanalytic explorations of this history see Lyndal Roper's [1994] *Oedipus and the Devil: Witchcraft, Religion and Sexuality in Early Modern Europe* and Evelyn Heinemann's [2000] *Witches: A Psychoanalytic Exploration of the Killing of Women.*) Displacement can also result in 'blaming the ecological messenger', in a way comparable to how the unpalatable insights of psychoanalysis still provoke enough emotion for a whole 'Freud-burying' (Tallis 2009) industry (but like the undead, one burial never seems enough). As Marshall (2005) writes:

> Climate change is deeply threatening to anyone whose world view sees increasing personal consumption as a fair reward for a lifetime's dedication to the growth economy. We all feel small and powerless in the face of a huge and daunting problem and although we are not actively punished for speaking out against it, we are hardly well rewarded . . . Try bringing it up when a friend shows you their holiday tan and you will see what I mean.

One relevant example here is the Czech President Václav Klaus who not only denies outright the existence of anthropogenic climate change, but even compares environmentalism with Nazism, Fascism and Stalinism (Dujisin 2007). Others evoke the phrase 'ecofascist' to describe anyone with a vaguely green agenda. All these responses need to be explored by psychoanalytically informed social theorists and environmental researchers.

In terms of displacement, it is interesting also to consider Marshall's (2005) comments on certain New Age trends, which, while leading many to care deeply about ecology through a 'mother earth' spirituality, may provide space for defensive displacements. He relates the story of a manager of a chain of luxury hotels in Mauritius who said 'we take these environmental problems very seriously . . . we are the first company in Mauritius to open a Feng Shui hotel' where people 'can reconnect with the natural environment' including 'special Feng Shui meals' where 'everything is rounded to help the movement of the chi forces' (ibid.). Marshall sees this as emblematic of a certain response to ecological threat, shared by 'the tourists who identify with the New Age marketing and will pay a premium for the eco-theming of their air conditioned room' (ibid.). Furthermore, on visiting a large well-known bookshop he found that while they sold over 30 books on feng shui, they stocked not a single volume on home energy efficiency.

> In the face of a problem which 80% of people say is a major issue, vastly more people wish to control and manage the movement of chi energy around their house than the real energy going out through their windows . . . It is hard not to think of Feng Shui as the ideological equivalent of dioxins which occupy and block key receptors in the body which should be engaging with nutrients . . . We chose to replace the daunting and terrifying environmental problems . . . with manageable and entertaining pseudo-environmentalism.
>
> (ibid.)

Psychoanalysis cannot provide the answer to how we should respond, but it can help us to think about the difficult questions and to avoid overly simplistic and reassuring answers. It is important to study not only the defensive aspects of anti-environmentalist beliefs, phantasies and behaviours, but also those found in the green movement itself, including flights into superego moralism, reaching for comforting pseudo-solutions, or the collapse into despair. In whatever form they take, social phantasy systems are constructed incorporating differing individual and collective needs, anxieties, and defences.

Suppression is a conscious attempt to put the anxiety-provoking thought out of one's mind and is seen in the way we skip over disturbing articles in the news, or avoid contemplating the effects of driving. The conscious nature of suppression renders it less problematic but we might find that once we confront our use of suppression, it can open a path to dealing with deeper and more unconscious defensive processes, such as *repression*. Winter and Koger (2004: 37) give an example of the latter from their own lives, when Winter realised she had unconsciously repressed awareness of the nuclear waste problem just a few miles from her home, although the information had been in the news for decades, adding that 'governments and other aspects of the social system may support repression.'

Reaction formation is a particularly bizarre but unfortunately common defence. In classic reaction formation the person denies the impulse while giving intense expression to its opposite. There is a certain theme in 'climate sceptic' discourse involving a kind of perverse gloating over the amount of waste they produce, as though people become more wasteful to convince themselves that they don't believe and/or they don't care. Others (e.g. Rust 2008) have suggested that compulsive consumption might increase as a means of blotting out the ecological effects of compulsive consumption, involving another dangerous positive feedback loop. We may expect that reaction formation might surface in environmentalists too, such as in harshly condemnatory 'greener-than-thou' attitudes.

Environmentalists and anti-environmentalists might also be seen to live in a mutual set of *projections* and *reprojections*, embodying a split between good and bad (good environmentalists versus evil developers, good businessmen helping to drive economic growth in difficult times versus Luddite eco-terrorists, etc.). We should also consider how sea, land, air, water, animals, trees, earth and 'Nature' (whether or not a mother) can all act as containers for our projections, reaching at times mythical proportions. Similarly industry, technology, civilization, machines, etc. can also arouse and elicit different projections, and all structure our relation to the environment in complex ways.

Žižek (2007) has called, following Morton (2007), for an 'ecology without nature', which we can see as in part a call to take back the projections we have made onto a Romantic Nature. Similarly, Jordan (2009) warns against the dangerous splits embodied in our attachments to nature, warning against idealization as well as denigration. The non-active majority may also project their own environmental concern (and guilt) onto 'activists' who act so they don't have to, while the non-acting public is 'uncaring and selfish' so the activist doesn't have to be. Psychoanalytic social theory suggests projective processes are crucial for structuring social systems, and social responses to climate change are no exception.

Finally, in Freud's work *sublimation* was seen as the most mature defence, and occurs when we channel unconscious anxiety and drives into socially acceptable projects which contribute to society (and perhaps we might extend these contributions to the other-than-human world). In sublimation we don't deny or repress our feelings or act them out directly, but instead channel them into creative activities such as art and science, and perhaps also environmental concern and activities. Both sublimation and reaction formation may lead to pro-environmental behaviour but the latter, as Winter and Koger (2004) point out, will be accompanied by a certain level of hostility, anxiety, overly judgmental attitudes, and 'unintentional' behaviours which go against the conscious ideal, creating the danger of a backlash. Sublimation is closer than reaction formation to accepting the 'reality principle', but sticking to purely Freudian theories means that it is sometimes difficult to distinguish between them. Klein's reformulation of sublimation which led her to the concept of reparation in the depressive position (Hinshelwood 1991) can take us further, as we shall see below.

How to confront our defences

> We cannot begin the difficult problem of environmental clean-up until we allow ourselves to feel the anger, disgust, or guilt that confronting our waste sites might elicit . . . We must be willing to acknowledge dismay, sadness, and fear about our environmental predicament in order to free up the psychic energy now used by the defences to be used in more creative problem solving. From a psychoanalytic perspective, being willing to experience discomfort is the first step toward a solution to our problems.
>
> (Winter & Koger 2004: 39–40)

We need to confront our own 'dirt', including both the disavowed aspects of ourselves that we project outwards or otherwise defend against, and also the pollution and waste that physically embodies the 'shadow' side of our culture. This is also discussed in a different way by Slavoj Žižek, who in the film *Examined Life* (Astra 2008) choose to discuss ecology not by standing in a beautiful rainforest or by a pristine lake but in a rubbish dump, and he calls on ecologists to love such places, or at least to be able to bear them.

Winter and Koger (2004: 48–49) argue that 'the first step in solving environmental problems is to allow ourselves to *feel*.' However, as Mary-Jane Rust (2008: 6) writes, this is difficult because if we 'allow ourselves to feel, we might find a whole range of strong emotions, such as anxiety and fear about the future, despair at our lack of political will, grief for so many losses, guilt that we continue to be part of the cause, and more.' On the other hand, 'when we block out our feelings, we lose touch with the urgency of crisis' (ibid.). As painful as they are, these feelings 'are legitimate reactions to our situation' and without directly experiencing them 'part of our psyche must be allocated toward arranging a defence of them, thus robbing our full intelligence for finding creative solutions' (Winter & Koger 2004: 48).

How can we experience our feelings without being overwhelmed? Nicholsen (2003) argues that this needs to take place in the safety of 'holding environments', of loving relationships. This brings up the whole area of ecopsychology and ecotherapy such as Joanna Macy's (1995) 'despair and empowerment workshops' which will be looked at in Chapter 7. To conclude, I would argue that Freud's work provides a crucial first step to any psychoanalytic approach to ecology. However, his predominantly one-person drive psychology has its limitations which object relations theory tries to remedy through a more relational approach to the human mind. The relevance of object relations theory to the psychology of climate change and to understanding human relationships to nature will be the subject of the next chapter.

Chapter 6

Object relations theory

A more ecological approach to mind

> The child's first erotic object is the mother's breast that nourishes it . . .
> to begin with, the child does not distinguish between the breast and its
> own body . . . This first object is later completed into the person of the
> child's mother, who not only nourishes it, but also looks after it and thus
> arouses in it a number of other physical sensations, pleasurable and
> unpleasurable. By her care of the child's body she becomes its first
> seducer. In these two relations lies the root of a mother's importance,
> unique, without parallel, established unalterably for a whole lifetime as
> the first and strongest love-object . . . the prototype of all later love
> relations.
>
> (Freud 1938: 188)

'Mother nature' and the Earth-breast

Object relations theory, with its emphasis on the self as constituted in and
through relationships, can be seen as moving psychoanalysis in an 'ecological' direction. It built on the advances of Melanie Klein (1987), Ronald
Fairbairn (1992), Donald Winnicott (1987, 1999), Wilfred Bion (1989) and
others to develop Freud's initial ideas into complex theories of internal and
external object relations. Internal objects (Ogden 1983) are mental representations of external objects taken into the mind through psychological
processes such as introjection, incorporation and internalization, combined
with self-representations including the 'self-in-relation'. A psychoanalytic
'object' implies a relationship and usually, but not necessarily, a person.
Freud hinted at a more relational and even social approach in his *Group
Psychology and the Analysis of the Ego* (1921: 69), writing that 'a mind
without links to objects is not a human mind' so that 'from the very first
individual psychology . . . is at the same time social psychology as well.'

Object relations theory understands 'self' as constructed through interactions with others, particularly the (m)other of infancy, laying complex
affective self–other templates on which we organize and interpret later
experiences. The self is thus not a given, but a complicated psychological

project taking years to construct and which even in adulthood undergoes continuous, if usually less drastic, reconstruction and reworking, as we live out our various lives through varied and often intense relations with 'objects' of all kinds. The mind is therefore formed through, and exists in, complex relational webs. This perspective has obvious affinities with the science of ecology (Mishan 1996) which is above all the science of relationships, interactions, and interdependencies.

Empirical studies have validated the central claim that early attachment processes powerfully affect later life (Bowlby 1988; Green 2004), an insight which may help us to understand the phrase 'Mother Earth' as indicating that our experience with the planet relates or mirrors in some way our experience with our mother, which does not only involve feelings of love and being held. Kleinian object relations in particular might interpret this term as suggesting a phantasy of an infinitely giving Earth-breast we feel entitled to suck on with ever increasing intensity without limit. In this respect our current difficulties resemble the terrible struggles of early infancy described by Melanie Klein under the terms paranoid-schizoid and depressive positions. The infant generally does not always take kindly to weaning, or to mother's explanations, but often responds instead with rage, envy, hatred, and destructiveness (Klein 1987).

Feminist object relations theorist Nancy Chodorow (1991) argues that as a result of the fact that it is usually women who mother, the developmental process tends to result in a defensive devaluing of the feminine, in order to deny the (absolute) dependency we felt in infancy towards an all-powerful mother. This is more pronounced in boys partly due to socialization practices dominated by the cultural 'ego-ideal' of men achieving radical autonomy, separateness and independence. As this is an impossible ideal, defensive constructs can become more violent and extreme. Similarly, Mishan (1996: 59) suggests that when we defend against the 'recognition of our relationship to the natural world, the consequences . . . are manifest in the external world in continued environmental destruction, and in the internal world in the form of persecutory guilt.'

From a more Jungian perspective Mary-Jane Rust (2008: 9) points out that many of our culture's myths and stories concern 'young male heroes cutting their way out of webs', where the unfortunate 'result of this bid for freedom is the dissolution of webs . . . and now the very web of life is unravelling.' Following Fairbairn (1992), most object relations theorists would agree, at least approximately, to a model of development that involves moving from 'absolute dependence' (or 'symbiotic unity') to 'mature dependence' (Fairbairn's term is more 'ecological' than Mahler's 'separation-individuation'; see Mahler, Pine & Bergman 2000). Object relations' emphasis on interdependence suggests an ecological vision for a more mature culture, involving a recognition that the self is an inextricable part of its relations to other beings, to our ecological webs, and to the Earth.

The holding environment and the non-human world

Winnicott's (1987) important theory of the 'holding environment' followed logically from his distinction between the 'object mother' (object of libidinous needs and desires) and what he called the 'environment mother'. The holding environment refers not only to the physical act of holding but all phenomena resulting in feelings of being held, psychologically and emotionally as well as physically. Holding applies to the 'good-enough mother' expressing love for her infant, and to therapists treating patients, and is especially applicable for treating those in more regressed states. Winnicott suggested a line of development which connects the environment of the womb to the stimulus barrier (Freud 1920), the holding environment of the (m)other and family, and later social containers such as school, club or nation. Thus, the holding environment can eventually become extended to include complex cultural and political organizations which provide a sense of safety, of being looked after, held and protected, an idea with certain affinities with the terror management theory (TMT) approach to 'world views'.

Events such as 9/11 can be felt as rupturing the stimulus barrier and compromising the holding environment (Rodman 2002). If we link these ideas to TMT, such events are equivalent to the first realization that we will die, and force us to see that our civilization too may eventually die. We have no rock on which to lean. Today, the Earth's 'holding environment' is also threatened, a crisis of such enormity that full acknowledgement may lead to threats of psychological disintegration and collapse. This is the 'mother' of all holding environments which contains all the others.

Dealing psychologically with environmental catastrophe (even more than terrorism) may seem too apocalyptic, too difficult, and too painful to even contemplate. Instead we simplify, and resort to splitting, projection, and denial. Using Winnicott we can begin to understand the threatened trauma and may perhaps find more sensitive and effective ways of dealing with it. We need to contain, process, and work through these anxieties, to allow a process of mourning to take place, and to repair the damage and the deep splits in our social, psychological, and ecological worlds.

Winnicott brought the 'environment' into psychoanalytic consideration but Searles went further in his book *The Nonhuman Environment* (1960), where he argued that we need to open up our concept of transference beyond human object relations to include the non-human world, and to recognize the importance of these experiences for neurosis, psychosis, and for healthy contact with nature. Searles took the first steps towards a truly ecopsychoanalytic approach when he called for a psychoanalysis that 'takes into account not merely man in his human environment, but man in his total environment' (Searles, cited in Nelson 1961: 121), supporting the contention that internal and external (environmental) worlds are deeply connected (Mishan 1996; Weintrobe 2011a).

Only very recently, as psychoanalysts have begun waking up to the ecological crisis, have a number of writers referred to the prescience and importance of Searles' paper (see for example Jordan 2009). Referring to Mahler's concept of separation-individuation (Mahler, Pine & Begman 2000), Searles argues that this should be thought of as referring to breaking the 'symbiotic' bond not only with (m)other, but also with the non-human world, a process which takes place only gradually and never completely. It thus remains an important aspect of our lived experience. Searles suggests that the schizophrenic shares with the infant the difficulty in separating self not only from mother, but also from the wider world, and agues that there is a powerful potential for similar experiences of merger in all of us.

Nicholsen (2003), who draws on both Winnicott and Searles, suggests that our relation to nature is connected to our earliest experiences, and that nature provides a containing mental space. Furthermore, due to its connection with our developmental origins, much of our relationship with nature occurs beyond (or perhaps before) words. For Nicholsen, the preverbal nature of this relationship may add to our difficulty in speaking or thinking about our environmentally damaging behaviour. In nature we at times find a place to experience merger and envelopment, an experience both longed for and feared.

> I believe that we . . . have anxiety – usually at an unconscious level, and under extraordinary circumstances at a conscious level – not merely that we regress ontogenetically (to an infantile or an intrauterine state, for example) but also lest we regress further, phylogenetically as it were to an animal, vegetable or even inorganic state. Such anxiety is particularly intense, in my experience, in neurosis and psychosis – above all, in the latter.
>
> (Searles 1960: 179, cited in Brody 1962: 105)

Here we have a psychoanalytic approach through which we might view Deleuze and Guattari's striking idea of 'becoming-animal' (an idea discussed in Chapters 9 and 10). Searles (1972) takes this further in his powerful paper 'Unconscious Processes in Relation to the Environmental Crisis' where he postulates that:

> An ecologically healthy relatedness to our nonhuman environment is essential to the development and maintenance of our sense of being human and that such a relatedness has become so undermined, disrupted, and distorted, concomitant with the ecological deterioration, that it is inordinately difficult for us to integrate the feeling experiences, including the losses, inescapable to any full-fledged human living.
>
> (Searles 1971: 368)

Oedipal and phallic levels and the tyrannical green superego

There are various developmental levels which may intersect with our problematic relationship with nature. At the phallic-Oedipal level, Searles (1972: 364) identifies the phantasy of eliminating Oedipal rivals while the self remains unharmed, and the 'moralistic' spirit with which 'most communications about this subject are conveyed' with the speaker 'projecting his own Oedipal guilt upon us, that we have raped mother earth and now we are being duly strangled or poisoned . . . for our sin.' He points out that the first attempted murder in the Oedipus myth was not that of the son against the father, but rather the father against the son, with Laius leaving the infant Oedipus alone on the mountainside after piercing his foot following the prophet's warning.

Searles (1972: 364) claimed that 'Freud greatly underestimated how formidable an Oedipal rival the son or daughter remains to both the parents and how frequently it is the youthful contestant who becomes in essence the victor.' From this point of view environmental destruction and war can 'promise to extinguish an Oedipal rival one has never . . . finally conquered', showing our 'unconscious hatred of succeeding generations . . . our vengeful determination to destroy their birthright through its neglect, in revenge for the deprivations, in whatever developmental era, we suffered at our parents' hands' (ibid.).

In addition, in our culture, thanks to relentless advertising, possessions such as cars become a symbol of genital achievement. So much so that Margaret Thatcher even claimed, apparently, that a man who reaches 30 and finds himself on a bus must consider himself a failure (Randall 2005: 173). Relinquishing such symbols of (male) genital primacy feels like a castration. In our culture, cyclists who choose not to own a car are often seen as somehow 'not quite adult'. Randall argued that this occurs when the 'environment mother' is dealt with through 'the equation of maturity (particularly masculine maturity) with the ability to dominate and exploit her'. This in turn is connected with the desire 'to escape her control and influence' and the phantasy 'that she no longer matters and perhaps that she never did' (ibid.).

As Randall writes, once cars become a cultural and psychological icon of maturity and 'grown-up-ness', there is an equating of 'realism' with consumerist acquisitions, any other approach being viewed as 'idealistic', 'immature' and 'childish'. However, behind this devaluation 'lies contempt for the mother: it is a deeply narcissistic version of maturity which turns away from the real relationship to the natural world' (Randall 2005: 174). It is important to stress that it is not only men who feel this contempt. Many women may also feel that 'the mature and realistic position is to be too busy or important to worry about environmental concerns' leading to a 'relationship to the environment-mother . . . as troubled as their male counterparts' (ibid.).

Consumerism, addiction and the fragile self

> Psychoanalysts are well versed in working with individuals who make self-defeating choices . . . [and therefore] can shed light on the feelings, fantasies, defenses and conflicts underlying over-consumption . . . [O]bject relations critiques of child-rearing practices have environmental implications . . . [W]hen infants are made to spend time alone, separated from primary caregivers . . . given bottles rather than breast-fed and then given a world of playthings, they learn to seek security in material things instead of the reassurance that comes from cherished people . . . [O]ver-consumption . . . is both a repetition of damaged early attachments and a defense against longings.
>
> (Bigda-Peyton 2004: 267)

Various commentators have described our era of late capitalism or post-modernism as a 'culture of narcissism' (Lasch 1991; Vital-Brazil 2001). This is not the place to explore the wider concept, but it is useful in under-standing not only over-consumption but our general attitude to nature. Narcissism leads to a view of nature as only existing for our gratification, which is the crux of the ecopsychological critique of 'anthropocentrism'. Winter and Koger (2004: 45) write that by 'positing that we are "on top" of the biological spectrum, humans portray their immaturity and narcissism' which 'prevent recognition of our responsibilities to members of our own species' so that 'we live for the present and try to suppress fears about the well-being of the next generation.'

The self-psychological work of Kohut (1985) and the independent object relations approach of Winnicott (1987) both suggest that narcissistic dis-orders are related to a fragile sense of self. The objects of consumer society may therefore function as 'selfobjects' in Kohut's (1985) sense, which tem-porarily stave off the crisis, resulting in a cultural addiction to consumerism which becomes an obstacle to developing more fulfilling object relations and authentic psychological health, as well as being a major contributor to the ecological crisis. Wachtel (1989, cited in Bigda-Peyton 2004) argues that a social level of analysis is also required. The alienation and absence of community in the modern world, the fragmentation of friendship networks and job insecurity, among other things, all lead to a vacuum into which the corporations step, with major ecological and psychological consequences. In this context, Gomes and Kanner (1995b: 80–81) argue that 'First World consumer habits are one of the two most serious environmental issues the world faces', the other being the crisis of overpopulation.

Corporate advertising is likely the largest single psychological project ever undertaken by the human race, yet its stunning impact remains curiously ignored by mainstream Western psychology . . . [L]arge-scale advertising is one of the main factors in American society that creates and maintains a peculiar form of narcissism . . . [I]n the United States during the 1920s . . . desire for non-essential goods and products was so weak that it needed active and ongoing cultivation . . . Creating such false needs was not such an easy task . . . [T]oday, the drenching of the psychological and physical environment with commercial messages has become so complete that people are largely numb to it.

(ibid.)

From an ecopsycological perspective, Gomes and Kanner (1995b) link over-consumption to Winnicott's false-self, forming what they call the 'all-consuming self'. Winter and Koger (2004: 44) similarly argue that 'without a firmly rooted internal organization, we are likely to use external objects to express who we are', so that much 'of our over-consumption may be driven by a "false-self" system.' This needs to be understood developmentally. According to Bigda-Peyton (2004: 253), early in development children learn 'to substitute what they are told to want for what they truly want.'

By the time they reach adulthood, authentic feelings lie buried and individuals have only the vaguest sense that something is missing. The false self masks unacknowledged longings . . . Gruen (1995) writes that this alienation from personal experience may account for why there would be little empathy for the environment. How can there be true empathy for externals if there is no empathy for the self? Further, he suggests that individuals may create pain in the external world in order to know their own feelings of pain.

(ibid.)

Theodore Roszak's (2009) research on consumerism suggests that shopping can serve multiple psychological functions such as overcoming depression, providing a sense of control over one's life through the power to decide what to buy, a way to deal with painful relationship break-ups, and an addiction providing an experience to temporarily fill the void. He calls on environmentalists to look at ecologically destructive behaviour as 'not the behaviour of monsters, but of troubled human beings trying to cope with jobs and families while the world around them seems to be turning to dust and ashes' (Roszak 2009: 32). If indeed we are looking at something which functions in some sense like an addiction, the lesson from psychotherapy is that 'the worst thing to do with addicts is to shame them . . . making them feel more guilty may only make things worse . . . [like] scolding a pyromaniac for setting fires' (Roszak 2009: 33).

Ecopsychologists have long claimed that the roots of our psychological difficulties reflect our damaged relationship to the natural world, which Michael Cohen (1997) calls 'nature-deficit disorder'. This kind of discussion remains highly controversial within psychoanalysis. The traditional approach would be to analyze environmental concern as reflecting 'deeper' feelings relating to human 'objects', internal and external. However, might this not sometimes be the other way round? Should psychoanalysis rule out the possibility from the outset that an individual human conflict could be instead a displacement from anxiety concerning the environment? Psychoanalysts and psychotherapists are not used to thinking in these terms, but thankfully this is beginning to change.

Susan Bodnar (2008: 484) found that her patients' alcoholism and what she calls 'dissociative materialism' can sometimes be understood as 'enactments of a changing relationship between people and their ecosystems.' Thus not only can environmentally damaging behaviour be a form of addiction, but addictions can themselves arise to deal with anxiety concerning our damaged world. Psychoanalysts therefore need to recognize that engagement with ecology is not only a possible area of 'applied' psychoanalysis, but is also of crucial relevance to its core clinical domain. Bodnar (2008) therefore calls on psychoanalysts to expand their concept of object relatedness to include the natural environment itself, as Searles did before her.

Returning to the model of 'consumerism as addiction', Rosemary Randall (2005) argues that compulsive shopping can function as a denial that there is anything wrong, that environmental problems simply do not exist:

> Shopping, with its cornucopia of delights, its visual, tactile and auditory appeals to the senses, its promises of enjoyment and pleasure says symbolically – 'All is well . . .' There is collective comfort in the knowledge that everyone is doing the same thing . . . the overall experience provides a soothing protection . . . In Kleinian terms the market at the moment of purchase is an idealised breast, a huge part-object whose beneficence is never questioned. Just as the hungry infant does not ask how the breast has acquired the milk, so the traumatised public does not question how the market has acquired its goods, nor who or what may have been damaged in the process.
>
> (Randall 2005: 167–168)

As in other forms of denial, the underlying anxiety can reveal itself in the manic compulsive quality which develops or in 'periodic scares over safety and quality', and so for Randall (2005: 168) shopping 'expresses both the denial of anxiety and the periodic return of that anxiety as the defence fails to contain it.' Ironically, according to Rust (2008: 7), the 'very thing that is causing our crisis – over consumption – has become our palliative, to soothe away our anxieties about the damage we are doing to the world.' Thus we have the positive feedback loop, comparable to the vicious circle of addiction (Prentice 2003; Glendinning 1994; LaChance 1991; Gomes & Kanner 1995, all cited in Rust 2008).

> Some people liken this to the vicious circle of addiction. Does that mean we have a bit of an eating problem? Well, yes . . . we've trashed the family home and we've binged on all the reserves; oil and gas may well have peaked already, we overfish, clearcut forests, and extract everything that can be sold for profit. Then we throw it up, undigested, into landfill sites.
>
> (Rust 2008: 7)

The paranoid-schizoid position

> The world's current state of ecological deterioration is such as to evoke in us largely unconscious anxieties . . . the general apathy that I postulate is based upon largely unconscious ego defenses against these anxieties . . . Many aspects of the ecologically deteriorating world in which we live foster in us, at a largely unconscious level, the mode of experience seen in an openly crystalized form in paranoid schizophrenia . . . characterizing the most threatened moments of normal infancy before the establishment of a durable sense of individuality.
>
> (Searles 1972: 363–369)

Melanie Klein (1987) claims that we all move between two fundamental 'positions': the depressive position (D) and the paranoid-schizoid position (PS). These are not linear developmental stages but rather complex psychological/affective/self/object organizations with characteristic defences and anxieties which can be explored along a series of dimensions. These can also be correlated with Bion's 'basic assumption' theory of group behaviour, as described in *Figure 4*. We shall be returning to Bion's basic assumption theory in the context of nonlinear approaches to psychoanalysis and group analysis in Chapter 12.

From a complexity perspective, PS and D can be viewed as attractors helping to organize psychic life both normal and pathological. PS is characterized by part-object relationships (the infant relates to the breast rather than the whole mother who is not recognized as a separate complete person); paranoid, persecutory anxieties; and fears of destruction, disintegration, fragmentation, chaos and annihilation. It is dominated by the defences of splitting (e.g. into good/bad breast) and projective identification (Ogden 1992, Young 1994).

	Anxiety source	Affects	Object relations	Defences	Adaptive uses
PS	Persecution and destruction of ideal self/object	Anxiety, dread, primitive terror	Part-object, split object (e.g. good/bad breast)	Splitting, denial, projective identification	Order experience, health suspicion, ideals, ability to act
baF	Persecution by powerful enemies	Panic, fear, terror, anxiety	In group/outgroup split, group members fused identity	Splitting off and projecting intragroup aggression/ anxiety outwards, idealization of leader	Realistic action, loyalty and commitment, sensitivity to danger
D	Recognizing dependency, own aggression may destroy caretaker, leads to retaliation	Guilt, despair, envy, greed	Whole object and awareness of dependency	Reparation, manic denial of aggression then turned inwards, repression, inhibition	Creativity, symbol formation, impulse control, linking internal-external
baD	Dependency on leader, fear of retaliation/ abandonment	Helplessness, depression, childishness	Dependent/submissive/hier-archical relation with leader/authority	Idealization of and repression/denial of aggression towards leader, splitting (group 'believers' and 'non-believers')	Appropriate learning from authority, discriminating followership, gratitude
Oedipus complex	Being excluded, third, retaliation from one for love of other	Jealously, exclusion, deprivation, loneliness	Triangular/dyadic relations, competition with one parent for love of other	Identification with the aggressor, combined parent phantasy, regression	Capacity for mature love, passion, sexuality, desire, reproduction
baP	Fear of exclusion, recognition of separateness	Hope, libidinal excitement, vicarious pleasure	Mobilization of and identification with the pair, compete for position of favourite child	Preservation/idealization of and identification with the pair to maintain hope. Repression of rivalry with pair members and own sexuality	Realistic orientation to future, accept pair as source of creativity, change and renewal

Figure 4 Klein's developmental positions and Bion's basic assumption theory of groups (fight-flight, dependency, pairing)
Sources: Adapted from Gould (1997) and Dodds (2008)

Projective identification differs from projection as it involves projecting *into* rather that *onto* the object, subtly pressuring the object to behave in ways conforming to the projection. (The specific controversies as to whether this interaction is necessary for projective identification to occur is beyond the scope of this book; the definition used here is close to Ogden's [1992].) In projective identification, parts of the self are felt to reside *inside* the object and can include claustrophobic anxieties of being trapped, phantasies of controlling the object from within, or of evacuating the deadly poison inside. Bion (1959) and Jaques (1955) see projective identification as crucial to group dynamics. Robert Young (1994) has even claimed that projective identification 'is the most fruitful psychoanalytic concept since the discovery of the unconscious.'

We have already looked at Western civilization's basically paranoid approach to nature, and we have seen a number of paranoid conspiracies around the climate change issue which at least create a clearly identifiable enemy. In this situation the 'bad sadistic enemy is fought against, not in the solitary isolation of the unconscious inner world, but in co-operation with comrades-in-arms in real life', where 'objective fear may be more readily coped with than phantasy persecution' (Jaques 1955, cited in Klein, Heimann & Money-Kyrle 1955: 483). The 'apocalyptic' threat of climate change may lead to extremely primitive persecutory anxieties and therefore the employment of psychotic defences (splitting, disavowal, massive projective identification). According to Jordan:

> We are in a paranoid-schizoid place in relation to the environment in that we are not in relation to it. This is an attempt to preserve some desperately needed sense of invulnerability in the face of impending environmental catastrophe that can be experienced as potentially annihilating . . . Omnipotence is an attempt by the infant to bring things under its control, to exert total power. These defences can be seen in our attempts to dominate nature, in the sense of vulnerability we feel at times in the face of its indifference to us and our dependencies on it, which causes us to attempt to bring it under our total control.
>
> (Jordan 2009: 29)

Searles (1972: 369) points out that, ironically and terrifyingly, there is now a certain 'objectivity' to the paranoid threats. These are both from the threat of nuclear disaster which 'evokes, deep in us, the frozen immobility of the child whose parent (equivalent to such godlike, vague entities as the hydrogen bomb or the awesomely powerful military-industrial complex) chronically threatens violence' and the toxic poisoning we are subject to by unknown outside forces. This can lead to many people intuitively feeling that the warnings of ecologists are 'crazy' and we shouldn't listen to them, partly out of fear of contamination, and partly because they touch a 'crazy' part of all of us. As Martin (cited in Searles 1972: 373) said, 'psychiatrists are familiar with the fantasy met in the early stages of schizophrenia that the world is coming to an end . . . In the second half of this century, the actual presence of this destructive potential makes "psychotic" end-of-the-world fantasies not so obviously out of touch with reality.'

We can also see more primitive levels of the mind functioning in what Paul Hoggett (2009) describes as the increasingly perverse response to climate change. Drawing on Susan Long's (2008) theory that we are moving from a culture of narcissism (Lasch 1991) to a culture of perversion, Hoggett (2009) argues that perverse organizations emerge on all levels (intrapsychic to social) where instrumental relations dominate, as a result of capitalism's effect both on social relationships and our 'abusive relation' to the natural world. Perverse organizations lead to splitting, denial and collusion, with a particular emphasis on the role of the accomplice, a role we are all placed into by the structural aspects of climate change.

Hoggett connects various unconscious (and conscious) alliances and collusions around climate change with John Steiner's (1985) re-reading of the ur-myth of psychoanalysis, which argues that everyone knew what Oedipus was about to uncover, but there was a systematic collusion in not knowing. Here we find Bion's (1984) '-K', which seizes on any chance to attack the truth, becoming an active process of destructiveness in which thought itself is hated, as destructive parts of the self are harnessed in an attack on truth-loving parts (Rosenfeld 1971), a process Bell (2007) connects with Freud's Thanatos.

The crucial lesson of psychoanalysis here is that what is most perverse and destructive in human nature is not only found in the criminal, the madman, or the most flagrant climate deniers, but in all of us. Part of each of us is ready to be deceived, a phenomenon Hoggett (2009) links to 'virtualism', involving an 'as if' relation to reality. In terms of climate change this is captured well in a very apt phrase of Monbiot's: 'We wish our governments to pretend to act' (Monbiot, cited in Hoggett 2009).

The depressive position

> Mankind is collectively reacting to the real and urgent danger from environmental pollution much as does the psychotically depressed patient bent upon suicide by self-neglect – the patient who, oblivious to any urgent physical hunger, is letting himself starve to death or walks uncaring into the racing automobile traffic of a busy street.
>
> (Searles 1972: 365)

In Kleinian theory (Hinshelwood 1991), the depressive position (D) is characterized by whole-object relationships and the object is seen to contain both good and bad aspects. This conjunction, though painful, is tolerated. The object is now seen as separate and whole. Mourning is now possible both for loss of unity and for the realization that phantasized attacks on the 'bad' object also attacked the 'good' object, as they were in reality the same thing. An urge to repair the imagined damage then emerges and the self becomes more integrated. D involves deep psychological working through of mourning, loss, guilt and separation, and can also at least potentially lead to authentic feelings of joy, love, gratitude and concern, as well as genuine pain and sadness. Defences against depressive anxiety are developmentally more advanced and include manic defences. Bion (1989) emphasized the volatility of these positions and the way one can oscillate rapidly between them, especially in groups, by putting a double headed arrow between them (PS↔D).

In terms of ecology, anxieties related to Klein's depressive position involve mourning for the losses involved in environmental destruction, guilt for the damage done and a reparative drive to restore, repair and recreate the lost and damaged world (internal and external, the latter including the non-human environment, following Searles [1960]). The difficulties infants face in negotiating the depressive position may be seen in the difficulties in recognizing personal and human culpability for climate change, and the difficulty in accepting that the lifestyle and civilization we are so proud of are causing such damage to planetary ecosystems.

Reactions to the complexity and enormity of environmental problems can also lead to despair. Our trust in the world can be affected as we feel the threat of the destruction of our 'holding environment' (Winnicott 1999; Winter & Koger 2004). Punitive guilt feelings may then arise which are defended against with manic denials or manic reparation. At times, this may even lead to a suicidal tendency which we have already seen in the 'world without us' theme as explored in eco-disaster films. This can now be understood not only in terms of the 'nirvana principle' of Freud's Thanatos, but also as a depressive reaction to guilt, and in Searles' (1972) view because modern life can be so empty as to not feel worth living.

Despite the clear advantages that Klein's theories provide, Kleinian thought, relentlessly focused as it is on the internal world of phantasy (which is both its strength and its weakness – we cannot expect a microscope to function well as a telescope), is still not enough to encompass our external ecology as well as our internal world. However, it can provide the basis for such a new formulation.

Environmental despair and the techno-god

'We're completely fucked' . . . If many people are secretly thinking this, and I suspect they are, their motivation for taking action in the face of climate change will be zero. As therapists, we know that when we face our worst fears, and feel the effects, we stand a chance of moving through darkness into enormous creativity . . . The 'we're completely fucked' response is yet another layer of the defence system, which gives us licence to give up thinking . . . when the collective gets stuck like this we have a wipeout that becomes an apocalypse.

(Rust 2008: 10–11)

Searles (1972: 366) asks: 'Is not the general apathy in the face of pollution a statement that there is something so unfulfilling about the quality of human life that we react, essentially, as though our lives are not worth fighting to save?' Our deteriorating environment then becomes both the means to this end, and a defence allowing us to avoid acknowledging how deep our depression goes, so that 'instead of feeling isolated within emotional depression, one feels at one with everyone else in a "realistically" doomed world' (ibid.). Searles links ecological pollution with sexual pollution and its punishment, moral 'pollution' involving a nostalgia for the lost unsullied ego-ideal of our youth, and the externalization of all this into environmental destruction and degradation.

Pollution thus serves multiple psychological functions connected with hatred and envy of our Oedipal rivals (including our children and future generations), our mourning for our idealized lost world, and omnipotent attacks and spoiling of the earth-breast. The latter might also be effectively conceptualized using Donald Meltzer's (1967) concept of the 'toilet-breast', emphasizing that psychologically the breast is not only a provider of nutrition, but a place into which we expel unbearable states of mind. Searles (1972: 365–366) connects the power of this reaction with the deteriorating social conditions of modern society which 'has brought with it so reduced a capacity in us to cope with the losses a life must bring with it to be a truly human life that we become increasingly drawn into polluting our planet sufficiently to ensure that we shall have essentially nothing to lose in our eventual dying.'

Here there are echoes of Freud's (1916) idea of 'anticipatory mourning' and the associated attacks and spoiling that we will study below (see p. 72). However, for Searles the natural world is not just a space for externalizing our conflicts. Rather, a healthy relationship to the non-human environment is essential for human psychological well-being. Furthermore, one consequence of our alienation from nature is an omnipotent longing for fusion with our technology, and a powerful anxiety should this fully occur.

Over recent decades we have come from dwelling in an outer world in which the living works of nature either predominated or were near at hand, to dwelling in an environment dominated by a technology which is wondrously powerful and yet nonetheless dead . . . [T]his technology-dominated world [is] so alien, so complex, so awesome, and so over-whelming that we have been able to cope with it only by regressing, in our unconscious experience . . . to a degraded state of nondifferentia-tion from it . . . [T]his 'outer' reality is psychologically as much a part of us as its poisonous waste products are part of our physical selves.

(Searles 1972: 368)

The further we are alienated from nature, the more we are driven into primitive regressive identification and omnipotent fascination with our technology, a powerful positive feedback loop. The inner conflict between our human and non-human selves, and our animal and technological natures, is projected onto the environment, further rupturing the relationship and leading to a spiral of destructiveness as we 'project this conflict upon, and thus unconsciously foster, the war in external reality between the beleaguered remnants of ecologically balanced nature and man's technology which is ravaging them' (ibid.).

Here we are in Klein's paranoid-schizoid world, with a primitive ego unable to differentiate between good and bad mother. While ecologists portray a good eco-mummy doing battle with bad techno-mummy, things are not so simple. As we have seen, civilization (and its technology) is a defence, a 'good mother' to protect us from capricious and uncaring mother nature (Freud 1930), but, as Searles suggests, we are supposed to accept that 'our good mother is poisoning us' (Searles 1972: 369).

For Searles (1972), behind both nuclear danger and ecological catas-trophe lies the raw destructiveness Kleinians link to Thanatos, or what Erich Fromm (1992) understands in terms of necrophilia. Searles (1972: 370) argues that at this level of functioning we project 'our own pervasive, poorly differentiated and poorly integrated murderousness, born of our terror and deprivation and frustration, upon the hydrogen bomb, the military-industrial complex, technology.' We may find the slow, more con-trollable death from pollution preferable to 'sudden death from nuclear warfare' or we might yearn for the quick relief of a nuclear blast to the 'slow strangulation' of environmental devastation (Searles 1972: 370). Living with such apocalyptic threats leads to a kind of ultimate version of the defence Anna Freud (1936) described as *identification with the aggressor*.

At an unconscious level we powerfully identify with what we perceive as omnipotent and immortal technology, as a defense against intoler-able feelings of insignificance, of deprivation, of guilt, of fear of death . . . Since the constructive goal of saving the world can be achieved only by one's working, as but one largely anonymous individual among uncounted millions . . . it is more alluring to give oneself over to secret fantasies of omnipotent destructiveness, in identification with the forces that threaten to destroy the world. This serves to shield one from the

> recognition of one's own guilt-laden murderous urges, experienced as being within oneself, to destroy one's own intrapersonal and interpersonal world.
>
> (Searles 1972: 370)

In this view, we are seeing a kind of repetition on a planetary level of an early intrapsychic anxiety situation. In childhood 'a fantasied omnipotence protected us against the full intensity of our feelings of deprivation, and now it is dangerously easy to identify with seemingly limitless technology and to fail to cope with the life-threatening scarcity of usable air, food, and water on our planet' (ibid.). Unfortunately our technological powers have outstripped our emotional maturity, and the omnipotent phantasies of infancy now have a frightening objectivity. In place of a religion we no longer believe in, or hopes for future generations we no longer have meaningful contact with, we identify with our immortal, inanimate technology.

> In this realm of omnipotent fantasy . . . mother earth is equivalent to all of reality . . . a drag . . . to our yearnings for unfettered omnipotence . . . It may be not at all coincidental that our world today is threatened with extinction through environmental pollution, to which we are so strikingly apathetic, just when we seem on the threshold of technologically breaking the chains that have always bound our race to this planet of our origin. I suspect that we collectively quake lest our infantile omnipotent fantasies become fully actualized through man's becoming interplanetary and ceasing thereby to be man . . . [W]e are powerfully drawn to suicidally polluting our planet so as to ensure our dying upon it as men, rather than existing elsewhere as . . . gods or robots . . . [T]he greatest danger lies neither in the hydrogen bomb . . . nor in the more slowly lethal effect of pollution . . . [but] in the fact that the world is in such a state as to evoke our very earliest anxieties and at the same time to offer the delusional 'promise' . . . of assuaging these anxieties, effacing them, by fully externalizing and reifying our most primitive conflicts . . . In the pull upon us to become omnipotently free of human conflict, we are in danger of bringing about our extinction.
>
> (Searles 1972: 371–372)

Transience, anticipatory mourning, and reparation

The environmental crisis forces us to face the traumatic aspects of transience, the fact that nothing is permanent and everything, including our own civilization and even the wider natural system of the Earth, will eventually disappear. Freud (1915) dealt with this issue in his 'Thoughts for the Times on War and Death', written as the horror of the First World War was

sweeping the old world away in its destructive fury and bringing disillusionment in its wake, and in 'On Transience' (1916). In her discussion of
the latter work De Mijolla-Mellor (2005) pointed out that Freud subtly
introduces a new aspect of mourning which many have still not fully
grasped, *anticipatory mourning*. For Rilke, who many identify as the name-
less poet in Freud's essay (Schur 1972), knowledge that a flower is temporary, that it will fade, die, and rot, removes the beauty it still has while it
is alive, to which Freud (1916: 306) replied with an inspiring ecological
vision: 'A flower that blossoms only for a single night does not seem to us
on that account less lovely.'

In terms of Freud's economic model anticipatory mourning involves
withdrawing cathexis from the object *before* it is lost, as a narcissistic
defence to avoid the painful process of a mourning, while at the same time
partly going through the mourning process prematurely. In addition we can
see in the poet's reaction above disgust related to devaluation of the object,
connected to a sense of betrayal and combined with a revolt against the
reality principle, against time itself (timelessness being an important
characteristic of Freud's unconscious, see Matte-Blanco [1984]).

Bion (1961) similarly suggested that in the basic assumption group
anything bringing an awareness of time is hated and attacked. The lesson
for us now is that these complex psychological responses might help us to
understand the ways individuals and societies unconsciously deal with
climate change. The first involves adopting the position of consciously not
caring about the environment or even the survival of our species, as a
defence against the mourning yet to come. The second involves engaging in
premature 'anticipatory mourning', falling into a despair which prevents
the very action which might help to avoid the feared loss, during a time
when effective action may still be possible.

Freud (1916: 306) urges us to face with honesty and courage the fact that
'[a] time may indeed come when the pictures and statues which we admire
to-day will crumble to dust, or a race of men may follow us who no longer
understand the works of our poets and thinkers, or a geological epoch may
even arrive when all animate life upon the earth ceases.' In the face of the
enormous pain and fear the ecological crisis evokes, we need to find effective means of reparation, to restore and recreate the damaged world inside,
and out. Without a hope that meaningful, as opposed to manic, reparation
is possible, we have only the choice between denial, madness and despair.

Part III

The ecology of phantasy

As nature around us unfolds to reveal level upon level of structured complexity, we are coming to see that we inhabit a densely connected ecological universe where nothing is 'nothing but' a simple, disconnected, or isolated thing.

(Roszak 1995: 8)

Our present ego-feeling is, therefore, only a shrunken residue of a much more inclusive – indeed, an all-embracing – feeling which corresponded to a more intimate bond between the ego and the world about it. If we may assume that there are many people in whose mental life this primary ego-feeling has persisted to a greater or lesser degree, it would exist in them side by side with the narrower and more sharply demarcated ego-feeling of maturity . . . the ideational contents appropriate to it would be precisely those of limitlessness and of a bond with the universe . . . with which my friend elucidated the 'oceanic' feeling.

(Freud 1930: 68)

Part II

The ecology of phobias

Chapter 7

Ecopsychology and the greening of psychotherapy

Ecology needs psychology, psychology needs ecology. The context for defining sanity in our time has reached planetary magnitude.

(Roszak 1995: 5)

I know the argument is circular. I am depending on the length of the diameter.

(Bion 1963, cited in Meltzer 1994: 469)

Biophilia and biophobia

The search for an ecological psychoanalysis and a psychoanalytic ecology now enters the terrain of ecopsychology, from which it is partly inspired. While ecopsychology in its classic form is in danger of creating a new mysticism or a new religion, there is much of value within the tradition so we shall see what symbioses can occur in this ecology of ideas. Ecopsychology can be defined as the project of questioning the 'maturity' of settling for Freud's 'shrunken residue' in the quote which opened up this third section of the book, and instead rediscovering a 'more intimate bond between the ego and the world about it' (Freud 1930: 68) which might provide 'the raw material of a new reality principle' (Roszak 1995: 12). Where Freud saw the oceanic feeling as 'something like the restoration of the limitless narcissism', Roszak (ibid.) instead sees it as reclaiming the repressed of the ecological unconscious.

This is connected to what the zoologist E. O. Wilson calls 'biophilia', 'the innately emotional affiliation of human beings to other living organisms' (Kellert & Wilson 1993), a consequence of our long evolution and adaptation to the natural world and for Wilson (2003) a crucial force in countering the biodiversity crisis. While he is a biologist and not an 'ecopsychologist', it is worth pausing to discuss Wilson's biophilia hypothesis, as so many of the claims of ecopsychology depend on something like it being true. Wilson's actual claim is less global than his ecopsychological readers often assume. In particular, the innate preference we seem to have for natural environments refers specifically to certain *kinds* of natural environments, the predominantly savanna environments and ecology our species evolved to live within. It is therefore ultimately an argument underpinned by evolutionary theory:

> It should be no great surprise that human beings, a biological species dependent on certain natural environments until very recently in its evolutionary history, should retain an aesthetic preference for savannas and transitional woodland among an array of natural and artificial environments laid before them. In general, what we call aesthetics may be just the pleasurable sensations we get from the particular stimuli to which our brains are inherently adapted.
>
> (Wilson 2003: 137)

However, Wilson emphasizes that we should not understand this as hard-wiring, but rather that we are predisposed to find certain environments preferable to others: 'Psychologists who study mental development say that we are hereditarily *prepared* to learn certain behaviors and *counterprepared* to learn others' (ibid.). For example, the 'vast majority of humans . . . are prepared to learn the lyrics of a song but couterprepared to learn calculus' (ibid.). Crucially for psychoanalytic and ecopsychological perspectives, such preparedness usually involves 'sensitive periods during childhood and early maturity in which learning and distaste are most easily picked up' and where 'the timing varies among categories of behaviour' (ibid.).

Thus, Wilson's biophilia is something that can be learned, encouraged and developed. It refers not to a fixed instinct but an innate tendency towards a connection with the natural world which can be nurtured or not, especially during the crucial stages of child development which are of such interest to psychoanalysts. He goes on to describe the stages of the acquisition of biophilia (which could be interestingly compared to Freud's work on children's relations with animals, see Genosko [1993] and the discussion of animal phobias in Chapter 10).

It must be added that these findings are mostly the result of psychological research in Western (mainly American) culture, although an increasing number of transcultural studies are underway which so far seem to support the overall hypothesis. Interestingly, although Wilson does not say this, in some ways we could describe our culture as a whole as remaining stuck within the first stage of the development of biophilia.

> The critical states in the acquiring of biophilia have been worked out by psychologists during studies of childhood mental development. Under the age of six, children tend to be egocentric, self-serving, and domineering in their responses to animals and nature. They are also most prone to be uncaring or fearful of the natural world and of all but a few

familiar animals. Between six and nine, children become interested in wild creatures for the first time, and aware that animals can suffer pain and distress. From nine to twelve their knowledge and interest in the natural world rises sharply, and between thirteen and seventeen they readily acquire moral feeling toward animal welfare and species conservation.

(Wilson 2003: 137–138)

The timing of these stages obviously shows a fairly large variability among individuals so sticking rigidly to this scheme is potentially limiting. It is also worth exploring the developmental stages of children's relation to the environment as a whole. This research supports other findings we shall study below in the ecotherapy section of this chapter, when we will review the significant health benefits (psychological and physical) of living near green spaces, for both children and adults (Bird 2007). Studies show that children tend to move from confining themselves to the immediate vicinity of their home and the small creatures found there (around age four) to exploring 'nearby woods, fields, ditches, and other unclaimed spots they can claim as their own' (Wilson 2003: 138) between approximately the ages of 8 and 11. As Wilson writes, drawing on David Sobel's (2001) book *Children's Special Places*, here they 'often build some kind of shelter such as a tree house, fort, or cave where they can read magazines, eat lunch, conspire with a friend . . . play games, and spy on the world' (ibid.). If natural environments are not available, as for example in areas such as East Harlem, children will instead build forts 'in culverts, alleyways, basements, abandoned warehouses, railroad right-of-ways, and hedges' (ibid.). Crucially:

The secret places of childhood . . . bond us with place, and they nourish our individual self-esteem. They enhance joy in the construction of habitation. If played out in natural environments, they also bring us close to the earth and nature in ways that can engender a lifelong love of both. Such was my own experience as a boy of eleven to thirteen, when I sought little Edens in the forests of Alabama and Florida.

(Wilson 2003: 138–139)

However, if we accept that biophilia is an innate tendency in human nature, we must also accept the possibility, or even the likelihood, that 'biophobia' is just as natural. This is a subject that ecopsychologists are often conspicuously absent in addressing. The deep acceptance of the ambiguity of our relationship with nature found in Wilson is something Freud perhaps would have appreciated. As Wilson writes, throughout

most of human deep history there have been predators eager to snatch us for dinner; venomous snakes ready with a fatal, defensive strike to

the ankle; spiders and insects that bite, sting, and infect; and microbes
designed to reduce the human body to malodorous catabolic chemicals.

(2003: 141)

Thus, the 'reverse side of nature's green-and-gold is the black-and-scarlet of
disease and death' (ibid.).

In a similar way to biophilia, our biophobic tendencies can be encouraged and further developed, or reduced and alleviated, through critical
developmental experience.

> Like the responses of biophilia, those of biophobia are acquired by
> prepared learning. They vary in intensity among individuals according to
> heredity and experience. At one end of the scale are mild distaste and
> feelings of apprehension. At the other end are full-blown clinical phobias
> that fire the sympathetic nervous system and produce panic, nausea, and
> cold sweat. The innate biophobic intensities are most readily evoked by
> sources of peril that have existed in the natural world throughout
> humanity's evolutionary past. They include heights, close spaces,
> running water, snakes, wolves, rats and mice, bats, spiders, and blood.
>
> (ibid.)

This list looks almost like a description of the many terrors found in
Freud's case histories (see Chapter 9 for a discussion of the 'becoming-
animal' theme in horror). Wilson further points out that such prepared
learning is generally not found for contemporary threats which are objec-
tively far more dangerous, for example 'knives, frayed electric wires, auto-
mobiles, and guns' (ibid.). In ways compatible with psychoanalysis, the
expression of such fears can occur unconsciously. For example, when
psychologists flash images of spiders or snakes subliminally (15–30 milli-
seconds), subjects already conditioned negatively to these particular natural
'threats' react physically (for example by facial muscle changes) without
consciously registering the experience at all (Wilson 2003: 142).

As may already be apparent, biophilia and biophobia can be understood
as the ecopsychological equivalent of Freud's Eros and Thanatos. For more
research on the development of biophobia and biophilia, see for example
Wilson (2003, 1984); Kellert and Wilson (1993); and Orr (1994). In
Chapters 9 and 10 we shall explore biophobia from the point of view of an
ecopsychologically sensitive psychoanalytic and schizoanalytic approach to
the horror film, and its clinical manifestation in the form of animal phobias.

Liberating the ecological unconscious

> Those of us who feel trapped in an increasingly ecocidal urban, industrial
> society need all the help we can find in overcoming our alienation from the

more-than-human world on which we depend for every breath we breathe
. . . ecopsychology might be seen as a commitment by psychologists and
therapists to the hope that the biophilia hypothesis will prove true and so
become an integral part of what we take mental health to be.

(Roszak 1995: 5)

Ecopsychologists aim to move beyond anthropocentrism by drawing on
Deep Ecology's neoSpinozist affirmation of value *in* nature, beyond any
potential human practical or aesthetic benefit (Naess 1988; Tobais 1985).
Ecopsychology describes a historical process in psychology which moves
from a one-person focus on intrapsychic processes, to wider object relational, social or systemic – especially family systems (Koopmans 1998) –
perspectives. Beyond this 'ecopsychology proceeds from the assumption
that at its deepest level the psyche remains sympathetically bonded to the
Earth' and suggests the psychoanalytic idea that, at least in part, 'we can
read our transactions with the natural environment . . . as projections of
unconscious needs and desires' (Roszak 2002: 34).

Roszak (1995: 8) claims, in a way analogous to this book's emphasis on
the importance of ecology and complexity theory to psychoanalysis, that
psychology needs ecology to escape from the 'atomistic materialism of
19th-century physics' because ecology, perhaps the paradigm of the new
sciences, is the study of relationships. Mack (1995) relates the ecopsychological project to Freud's psychoanalysis:

Freud and his followers . . . invented psychoanalysis in response to the
fact that the extreme, deceitful ordering of men's and women's sexual
lives by a rigidified bourgeois society was becoming emotionally
intolerable and producing behavioral and physiological manifestations
that could not be understood or treated by the medicine or neuro-
psychiatry of the day. We confront now a new kind of problem . . . the
agonizing murder of the life systems of the Earth . . . What would a
psychology of the Earth be like? It would need to be comprehensive,
holistic, systemic . . . [and] dynamic . . . to explore profound, largely
ignored conscious and unconscious feelings, impulses, and desires in
relation to the physical world . . . to tell unpleasant or unwelcome truths
about ourselves . . . as we have learned to do from psychoanalysis.

(Mack 1995: 280–282)

Freud is still relevant here as his psychology is already at least implicitly
relational, exploring the interactions between intrapsychic agencies, individuals and groups. For Mack (1995: 282), however, a true 'relational
psychology of the Earth' would need to go further and include our relation
with other living beings and 'the Earth itself as a living entity.' Part of the
problem is that we are not used to thinking in this way. Indeed Mack

argues that Western culture views the Earth primarily as a 'thing', a dead object to be

> owned, mined, fenced, guarded, stripped, built upon, dammed, plowed, burned, blasted, bulldozed, and melted to serve the material needs and desires of the human species at the expense, if necessary, of all other species, which we feel at liberty to kill, paralyze, or domesticate for our own use.
>
> (ibid.)

For Metzner (1993: 66) this gets to the heart of our current crisis, as he argues that 'the entire culture of Western industrial society is dissociated from its ecological substratum', a 'dissociative split' also found in our religious and spiritual traditions where 'spirit' is envisaged as rising 'upward, into transcendent realms, whereas nature, which includes bodily sensations and feelings, draws us downward' toward the demonic. This split can also be observed in Freud's description of conflict 'between the human *ego* consciousness, which has to struggle against the unconscious, body-based, animal *id*, in order to attain consciousness and truly human culture' (Metzner 1993: 66–67).

We don't get much further with Jung, according to Roszak (1995: 11–12), who claims that 'Jung's collective unconscious . . . is filled, not with the tracks of beasts and . . . vegetative energies, but . . . ethereal archetypes' which is 'a conception . . . more to do with Plato than with Darwin' (although this critique of Jung within ecopsychology is unusual, as Jungian thought is strong in this tradition; see for example Rust [2004, 2008] or Carter [2010]). Ecopsychology sees itself as an attempt to heal such splits, and provide a psychology more sensitive to the Earth. Roszak (2009: 36) asks us to recall 'the courage with which Freud faced the radical madness of modern life in *Civilization and Its Discontents*' where he was prepared 'to psychoanalyze our entire culture.' Ecopsychologists 'now working to liberate the ecological unconscious are willing to do no less' (ibid.).

The ecological self

> The nonhuman environment is . . . considered entirely irrelevant to human personality development . . . as though human life were lived out in a vacuum . . . alone in the universe, pursuing individual and collective destinies in a homogeneous matrix of nothingness, a background devoid of form, colour and substance.
>
> (Searles 1960: 3)

The concept of the ecological self builds on the work of Searles (1960) and is defined by environmental philosopher Paul Shepard as a 'self with a permeable boundary. . . . Ecological thinking registers a kind of vision across boundaries' (cited in Roszak 1995: 13). Drawing on the new sciences of complexity and open systems, Joanna Macy (1995: 254) argues that what 'had appeared to be separate self-existent entities are now seen to be so interdependent that their boundaries can be drawn only arbitrarily . . . As open systems we weave our world, though each individual consciousness illumines but a small section of it, a short arc in vaster loops.' According to Shepard (1995: 36), from the beginning of life, the 'fetus is suspended in water, tuned to the mother's chemistry and the biological rhythms that are keyed to the day and seasonal cycles.'

The concept of the ecological self is crucial for creating a 'psychology as if the Earth mattered', with the claim that when 'the self is expanded to include the natural world . . . behavior leading to destruction of this world will be experienced as self-destruction' (Roszak 1995: 12). From a psychoanalytic point of view, Spitzform (2000: 265) argues that the ecological self needs to be incorporated into our developmental and relational models, because 'psychoanalytic developmental theory lacks a framework for understanding the role played by relatedness to the natural world for the emerging human self.' Furthermore, the very existence of this gap is difficult to see, 'like clean air, because we are so immersed in the natural world . . . there is a sense of self which emerges within an ecological context, and is maintained into adulthood by relationship with a wide range of non-human others' (ibid.).

Shapiro (1995: 235) writes that the ecological self's more flexible boundaries need to remain 'clear enough that we can hold our own as creative, responsible partners, yet pliable enough that we can bond and identify not only with our immediate family and ethnic heritage, but also with the whole spectrum of beings around us.' Others suggest that in attempting to foster an ecological self through reawakening the senses in natural surroundings 'people will experience periods of guilt and shame over their previously negligent or destructive environmental behavior, as well as a desire to make amends' (Gomes & Kanner 1995b: 91). This reparation is connected to a move to what could be called an ecological depressive position, entailing a sense of 'environmental remorse' arising 'as part of a healing process and in direct response to a strengthening bond with the land' (ibid.).

Gomes and Kanner claim that such experiences and the widening of vision they entail lead to 'more substantial and pervasive change than that induced by moral condemnation and other types of external coercion' (ibid.). E. O. Wilson makes a similar point, where he imagines humans surviving through the current crisis, but ending up lonely on a decimated Earth, with the sense of loss growing in us as we begin to realise what we have done, and what we are still doing at an alarming rate:

As habitats shrink, species decline wholesale in range and abundance. They slip down the Red List ratchet, and the vast majority depart without special notice. Being distracted and self-absorbed, as is our nature, we have not yet fully understood what we are doing. But future generations, with endless time to reflect, will understand it all in painful detail. As awareness grows, so will their sense of loss. There will be thousands of ivory-billed woodpeckers to think about in the centuries and millennia to come.

(Wilson 2003: 104)

As may be expected, ecopsychology often draws on the Gaia hypothesis (Lovelock 2000) which postulates that 'the biota, oceans, atmosphere, and soils are a self-regulating system that plays an active role in preserving the conditions that guarantee the survival of life on Earth' (Roszak 1995: 13). This can at times tend towards eco-mysticism, but it should not be too easily dismissed. The eco-therapist Sarah Conn claims that 'the world is sick; it needs healing; it is speaking through us; and it speaks the loudest through the most sensitive of us' (cited in Roszak 1995: 12–13).

Developmental ecopsychology and climate change

> The toddler who takes his first steps away from his mother makes active forays into the world . . . what the toddler is moving toward is as critical to him as what he is moving away from.
>
> (Barrows 1995: 108)

From a psychoanalytic perspective we should expect to find clues to the roots of our current crisis developmentally. Ecopsychology, however, asks us to fundamentally reconsider our ways of looking at human psychological development. Martin Jordan (2009: 27–28), a pioneer of ecotherapy, takes ecopsychology into the realm of attachment theory and developmental object relations, calling for us to 'explore how aspects of internal working models can be applied to relationships with nature' and in so doing find that perhaps 'the dominant attachment pattern that industrialized societies have to nature is one of avoidance and ambivalence' related to 'fundamental problems of dependency and vulnerability.'

In keeping with the ecopsychological tradition, for Jordan this understanding is crucial not only in terms of the current ecological crisis but also for human psychological well-being, and he explores developmental models leading towards a more healthy development of the ecological self, using a developmental framework that theorizes the importance of ecological relations as well as object relations. From the perspective of attachment theory, Jordan (2009: 28) suggests that 'nature can be seen as representing a secure base, an aspect of both our internal and external relational world that can provide great comfort.' In addition, drawing on research from environmental psychology, he claims that our relationship to the more-than-human world is an important aspect of our affect regulation (Fonagy *et al.* 2002).

Moving deeper into the psychological effects of an engagement with nature, Jungian ecotherapist Mary-Jane Rust (2008) draws from Deep Ecology founder Arne Naess (1988) to suggest that recovery from our current plight involves a kind of re-wilding of human nature, including inhabiting our bodies in a more real, sensual way. In a passage which partly echoes Winnicott's (1945) emphasis on the importance of 'unintegration' (as opposed to disintegration) and Marion Milner's writings on the creative process (Milner 2010; Glover 2009), Rust (2008: 17) writes that these experiences are 'profoundly healing':

> They are about dissolving and coming back together again, renewing ourselves in the process. We feel part of the larger living body of the universe . . . Perhaps our binges on food, drink or drugs are a misplaced attempt to experience that ecstatic state of oneness, our consuming of the earth a misplaced longing to re-unite with the earth.
>
> (ibid.)

According to Rust, by 'spending time in the wilds of nature, or just in our back gardens, we reconnect to the oneness of life.' She reminds us here of Jung's (1961: 225) words: 'At times I feel like I am spread out over the landscape and inside things, and am myself living in every tree, in the splashing of the waves, in the clouds and the animals that come and go, in the procession of the seasons.' Winnicott (1963) also described a related experience, when stating that the true self begins in 'the aliveness and vitality of body . . . not merely existing but . . . feeling real, authentic, and alive.'

Martin Jordan (2009: 30) claims that we defend against such experiences, largely due to a fear of dependency, a fear which he describes as 'a kind of madness, as the planet is so central to our survival . . . We fail to exhibit a mature dependency on nature and the planet and hold onto a psychotic idea that we are invulnerable.' As Jordan points out, such fears of dependency and vulnerability are very familiar to psychodynamic psychotherapists of all orientations. What, then, would a more healthy attachment to nature look like, if we were to extend Fairbairn's 'mature dependence' to include the non-human world and a recognition of the 'reciprocal interdependence' understood by the science of ecology? Drawing on the work of Searles (1960) and Spitzform (2000), Jordan argues that good mental health includes a self developing in secure attachment to non-human as well as human 'objects'.

As an important caveat to some tendencies within the ecopsychology movement, Jordan (2009: 30) warns against a 'naive positioning of nature in our object relational world', and to do so he draws on Klein (1987) in a way compatible with our earlier attempt to apply object relations theory to the ecological crisis, and perhaps with Wilson's (2003) inclusion of bio-phobia as the 'companion' to biophilia.

> Though some might disagree with Klein's bleak view of the 'depressive position,' where good and bad can coexist, I would argue aspects of this are central to a balanced view of nature's potential to both heal and destroy . . . The split with nature is at the heart of our environmental crisis. It cannot solely be laid at the heart of industrialization, for our emotional development has played a key role. For a mature dependency to develop, we have to acknowledge our ambivalence, perhaps not to get rid of it, but instead to live with it, and not acting out our defences in omnipotent or narcissistic ways.
>
> (Jordan 2009: 30)

This is where Jordan sees a potential place for a psychoanalytic eco-psychology, drawing us 'into relationship with nature in ways that celebrate the complexities of our emotional worlds, acknowledging not only the destructive tendencies of the human race, but also its capacity for love and reparation, and directing this capacity toward the natural world' (ibid.). Thus, as psychoanalysis opens itself up to a greater awareness of the web of life, the object-related self and the narcissistic self need to be viewed as developing alongside the ecological self.

How, then, should we envisage a new psychodynamic developmental psychology which takes such a relationship with nature seriously? According to Barrow (1995: 108) 'the toddler who takes his first steps away from his mother makes active forays into the world . . . what the toddler is moving toward is as critical to him as what he is moving away from', an idea which seems supported by research on the process of a child's developing relationship with their non-human environment (Wilson 2003; Sobel 2001). Whereas the child analyst Frances Tustin understands the 'awareness of bodily separateness' as the basic tragic fact of human life, Barrow argues the contrary, understanding this very sense of separateness as fundamentally an illusion. For Barrow (1995: 109), 'my skin is not separate from the air around it, my eyes are not separate from what they see.'

Barrow suggests that this illusion is unwittingly lent support by our conventional developmental theories as well as by our nature-disconnected society (Cohen 1997). Fundamentally, Barrow (1995: 109) claims that it is this which 'accounts for our loneliness, that isolates us and leads us to exploit and violate one another, the world we live in, and, ultimately, ourselves.' This is the heart of the ecopsychological critique. As Gomes and Kanner put it:

> From an ecopsychological perspective . . . It is clear that we depend on the Earth for our life . . . Yet we in urban-industrial civilization have

centered our identity as a species around the renunciation of this truth
. . . By dominating the biosphere and attempting to control natural
processes, we can maintain the illusion of being radically autonomous
. . . By acknowledging our dependence, we allow gratitude and reci-
procity to come forth freely and spontaneously . . . unacknowledged
dependence makes us act as parasites on the planet, killing off our
own host.

(Gomes & Kanner 1995a: 115)

A developmental perspective has also been usefully applied to understanding the complex psychosocial reaction, and inaction, to climate change.
Rosemary Randall's (2005) important paper 'A New Climate for Psychotherapy' combines ecopsychological and object relations perspectives to the
climate crisis, arguing that we need to think about the splitting, anxiety and
projection on an individual, social, and macro-economic level. She claims
that 'eco-anxiety' is often dealt with in our culture through addictive consumerism and our risk-averse society, as well as being privatized in therapy,
becoming one factor behind the reported increases in the severity of
problems therapists deal with (AUCC 1999, Royal College of Psychiatrists
2003, cited in Randall 2005).

Is it possible that the greater need for psychotherapy services stems . . .
from processes of social and collective denial which both use and
reinforce primitive defences in the population as a whole? . . . People
generally experience each other as less sane, less responsible and less
trustworthy than previous generations did . . . My suggestion is . . . we
are dealing with three interlocking social movements whose discon-
nectedness has come to seem wholly normal.

(Randall 2005: 171)

Randall draws on the long tradition of viewing the environment as
maternal but asks the important question: what kind of mother is she?
While some ecofeminists (e.g. Griffin 2000) have embraced the image of the
earth goddess as a positive image of 'deities of harvest, fertility and life',
Randall (2005: 171) views this as problematic to say the least, as it 'opens
the door to essentialist ideas of gender and sexuality which may valorise
women but still confine them.' Adopting instead a more 'depressive position' (Klein 1987) approach to the problem, she states that at various times
'mother earth' has been viewed as 'munificent, jealous, withholding, arbitrary or generous . . . as gloriously abundant or terrifyingly barren, fiercely
protective or desperately damaged' (Randall 2005: 171).

Within these attitudes we can tease out various aspects of our (often
infantile) relation to the 'environment mother' of the earth. Randall then
goes on to explore a series of common strategies deployed in the face of

climate change and relates them to specific developmental situations. First, *'I need'* (to drive because of work, to fly abroad to make sure I get sunshine on my holiday, etc.). In Lacanian terms a *demand* or *desire* is expressed as a *need* (mummy, I need another lolly). For Lacan (1977: 287), 'Desire is neither the appetite for satisfaction, nor the demand for love, but the difference that results from the subtraction of the first from the second.' To put it another way: 'Desire begins to take shape in the margin in which demand becomes separated from need' (Lacan 1977: 311).

However, beyond the insatiable demand of the child described by Lacan is a phantasy better explored within the Kleinian matrix, the phantasy of a mother who has an unlimited supply which involves the child in 'a refusal to respond to the reality principle' (Randall 2005: 172) and accept that this is not, and cannot, be the case. This developmental level, expressed by the phrase 'the world can take it' is of an infant who has 'not reached Winnicott's stage of concern', and therefore refuses 'to acknowledge that this munificent mother is the same person as the tired, depleted or unresponsive one' (ibid.). In Kleinian terms, this strategy is ultimately a defence against the pain, guilt, sadness, and regret, of the depressive position.

The second strategy is *'why should I? No one else is.'* Randall (2005: 172) describes this as 'the sibling's complaint' of being treated unfairly, and the primary-school protest: *'I don't want to. I don't like it. I can't be bothered. Do I have to?'* (ibid.). Here, mother has asked us to do something difficult and seems to favour a rival. Some destructive responses to climate change can be understood in this way, therefore, as a 'spoiling gesture, the willful or defiant protest that will upset mother's plans' (Randall 2005: 173). Here, mother is seen as 'mean, ungenerous and withholding' or alternatively as 'controlling, invasive and demanding' (ibid.) while the child is caught between wishing to return to being the privileged baby, and asserting a pseudo-maturity by attempting to trick mother or by rebelling against her plans.

A third strategy can be expressed in words such as: *'If it was really important, they'd have made us do something by now . . . They'll find a technological answer . . . these people like to frighten us'* (Randall 2005: 173). The phantasy is that this is a job for the adults and not a matter for the children. As Randall (2005: 174) stresses, what is so needed here, but so conspicuously lacking in reality, is an awareness of 'the generational shift as children become parents . . . and discover in their own maturity the pleasures of respect and care between the generations.'

Ecopsychology and health

> At a time of planet-wide environmental crisis, it seems . . . outrageous and irresponsible . . . [that] so few mental health clinicians connect the epidemics of mental distress in industrial societies with the devastating

impact of our suicidal destruction of our own habitat and ecocidal elimination of whole species . . . The environmental crisis . . . represents a crisis not only of uncontrolled pesticides or rampant sprawl, but of consciousness itself. Because the crisis ultimately springs from the unmanaged demons of the human psyche, hopes for an end to the long and self-destructive war between humankind and the Earth depend on repairing the damage inflicted on both.

(Buzzell & Chalquist 2009b: 19–21)

Heinberg (2009: 198) suggests that in our age of peak oil and climate change, we need also to consider the idea of *eco-grief*, the feelings of loss connected to ecological devastation and the threatened loss of a whole way of life, which, one way or another, is about to come to an end in what he calls *pre-traumatic stress disorder*, related in many ways to Freud's (1916) anticipatory mourning already discussed above. He suggests a psychological approach using the stages of grief described in the well-known Kübler-Ross (1973: 2005) model (denial, anger, bargaining, depression, acceptance) in order to understand where we are as a society and as individuals.

From this perspective, different types of interventions might be more or less 'effective for helping people accept our situation, depending on their current stage of adjustment' (Heinberg 2009: 198). He suggests, however, that the classic stages are not enough, because beyond acceptance there needs to be action, not only due to the ecological urgency, but because accepting 'the reality all too often leads to depression and despair.' In contrast, Heinberg argues that it is necessary to move beyond acceptance to become part of the collective effort to save the world, as this experience is 'empowering' and can generate the hope needed to combat despair. Heinberg also warns us all to prepare for the trauma to come:

In the decades ahead we will be going through hell . . . the only alternative to accepting the facts is to live in denial until the reality is inescapable and our room for maneuvering is even more restricted than it has already become . . . [A]s the full weight of resource depletion and climate change is felt, I think we can expect to see some of the worst excesses of human history . . . Part of the motivation must come from a positive vision of a future worth striving toward . . . The reality is that we are approaching a time of economic contraction. Consumptive appetites that have been stoked for decades by ubiquitous advertising . . . will now have to be reined in . . . *our central survival task . . . as individuals and as a species, must be to make a transition away from the use of fossil fuels – and to do this as peacefully, equitably, and intelligently as* possible . . . [Psychologists] should perhaps be gearing up to treat not only individuals but whole communities.

(Heinberg 2009: 200–204)

However, ecopsychology is not only interested in dealing with the negative impacts on health as a consequence of the degradation of the natural world, but also the positive consequences that can accompany reestablishing a more healthy relationship with nature and the other-than-human (or more-than-human as many ecopsychologists prefer). Although Sabastiano Santostefano (2004) cautions us against a naive version of ecopsychology that assumes nature automatically generates a sense of well-being and improvements in physical and mental health, there does seem to be an increasing amount of empirical evidence to support the contention that nature heals (e.g. Chalquist 2009; Mind 2007).

Researchers from the VU University Medical Centre in Amsterdam recently published results from a large study of 350,000 people showing that living near green spaces had substantial physical and mental health benefits (BBC 2009). The greatest benefits were for those living less than a kilometre away and the largest positive impacts were on anxiety disorders and depression. Living near green areas reduced depression rates by 21 per cent for children under 12. Physical disorders, such as heart disease, diabetes, stomach and respiratory infections, and neck, shoulder, back, wrist and hand complaints, also showed substantial improvements. In addition, research by Ulrich (1984) has shown that the view from a hospital window (whether natural or concrete) has a significant and measurable effect on the speed and completeness of a patients recovery (Ulrich 1984; Verderber & Reuman 1987).

Further evidence supports the therapeutic effect of nature and thus further confirms Wilson's (2003) biophilia hypothesis. Wilson summarises some of these findings:

120 volunteers were shown a stressful movie, followed by videotapes of either natural or urban settings . . . they recovered from the feeling of stress more quickly while experiencing the natural settings . . . supported by four standard physiological measures of stress: heartbeat, systolic blood pressure, facial muscle tension, and electrical skin conductance . . . The same result was obtained . . . [for] volunteers stressed by a difficult mathematical examination . . . Studies of response prior to surgery and dental work have consistently revealed a significant reduction of stress in the presence of plants and aquaria . . . Post-surgical patients recover more quickly, suffer fewer minor complications, and need smaller dosages of painkillers if given a window view of open terrain or waterscape. In one Swedish study covering fifteen years . . . clinically anxious psychiatric patients responded positively to wall pictures of natural environments, but negatively . . . to most other decorations (especially those containing abstract art). Comparable studies in prisons revealed that inmates provided window views of

nearby farmlands and forests, as opposed to prison yards, reported fewer stress-related symptoms such as headaches and indigestion.

(Wilson 2003: 139–140)

Together, these provide a remarkably powerful set of results. Pets can also have a major positive impact on our health, as independent research in Australia, England and the United States has shown. Wilson (2003: 140) writes that in 'one Australian study, which factored out variation in exercise levels, diet, and social class, pet ownership accounted for a statistically significant reduction of cholesterol, triglycerides, and systolic blood pressure' while in a similar US study 'survivors of heart attacks . . . who owned dogs had a survival rate six times higher than those who did not' (ibid.). Unfortunately, cat ownership did not provide the same positive effects.

For more information on the health effects of pets and natural environments, see Ulrich (1991, 1999, 2000); Ulrich, Lunden & Eltinge (1993); Ulrich *et al.* (1991); Kellert & Wilson (1993); Frumkin (2001); and Frumkin & Louv (2007). Following a review of this increasingly impressive body of evidence, the mental health charity Mind (2007) strongly supported the benefits of 'ecotherapy' and called for the 'greening' of mental health provision.

Ecotherapy

[Outdoor therapy] raises the important issue of the role of nature in the therapeutic process, how the client is forming a relationship with the natural environment as much as with the therapist, and the role of the therapist in this sense is as an expert at facilitating therapeutic conversations, not the professional with the answers and advice. It also highlights the idea of just how much unconscious power is contained in the traditional therapeutic frame, and how this power is perceived to be in the hands of the therapist. When moving into outdoor space a greater element of democracy can begin to enter into the process simply because the space is not owned or controlled by either therapist or client.

(Jordan & Marshall 2010: 349–350)

As we have seen, an increasing number of psychotherapists are seeing the connection between their work and the ecological crisis. Some have tried to create a special form of 'ecotherapy', taking therapy out of the confines of its urban indoor origins and moving into more natural spaces. While some embrace without reservation the idea that nature heals, there is a heated and important discussion occurring among others about problematic issues around boundaries, transference–countertransference dynamics, and the therapeutic frame which the idea and practice of ecotherapy raises, and this seems likely to go on for some time to come (e.g. Walker 2009; Jordan & Marshall 2010).

The first barrier to a 'greening of psychotherapy' is the fact, as we have seen, that so few psychotherapeutic approaches have conceptualized a proper role for the other-than-human world. Roszak (2009: 31) relates an anecdote from the opening scene of the film *Sex, Lies, and Videotape* (Soderbergh 1989) which is emblematic of this clinical blindspot. The woman begins by telling her therapist how anxious she is about all the rubbish and pollution piling up in the world and wishes she could do something. The therapist responds: 'Tell me more about your marriage.'

Joanna Macy (1995: 244) relates a similar experience: 'Once, when I told a psychotherapist of my outrage over the destruction of old-growth forests, she informed me that the bulldozers represented my libido and that my distress sprang from fear of my own sexuality.' Such responses limit the ability of psychoanalysts to discuss these issues openly. Characteristically, Searles (1972) already got to the heart of this issue all those years ago, and we are only just now beginning to catch up:

> My hypothesis is that man is hampered in his meeting of this environmental crisis by a severe and pervasive apathy which is based largely upon feelings and attitudes of which he is unconscious. The lack of analytic literature about this subject suggests to me that we analysts are in the grip of this common apathy . . . we fear that an active concern . . . will evoke, from our colleagues, nothing more than a diagnostic interest as to whether we are suffering from psychotic depression or paranoid schizophrenia.
>
> (Searles 1972: 361)

Psychotherapists have also felt restricted by an understandable fear of propagandizing. During the 1980s the Kleinian analyst Hannah Segal (1988) was very involved with the nuclear issue and described a similar problem with the seeming contradiction between engagement with these issues and traditional psychoanalytic 'neutrality':

> [W]hen patients . . . refer to nuclear issues, psychoanalysts remain faced with an ethical and technical dilemma . . . we must not collude with the patient's denial of any external situation . . . On the other hand, we must also be very wary of imposing on the patient our own preoccupations . . . If we do our job properly in dealing with the patient's basic defences, the relevant material will appear, because, in fact, below the surface, patients are anxious, even terrified.
>
> (Segal 1988: 56)

The idea of neutrality, so prized by psychoanalysts and for very good clinical and ethical reasons, was also dealt with by Riccardo Steiner (1989) with reference to Nazism, where he writes that 'the attitude of neutrality which psychoanalysts as clinicians must adopt cannot be sustained when the political situation threatens the values on which the psychoanalytic tradition is based. Silence and neutrality in such situations are tantamount to collusion and neutralization' (Steiner 1989, cited in Goggin & Goggin 2002: 38). Perhaps we might consider whether or not it is legitimate to add to Steiner's 'political situation' ecological matters as well, which similarly endanger 'the values on which the psychoanalytic tradition is based', as an analysis based on the consequences of accepting Guattari's (2000) model of the three ecologies would suggest.

How then does ecotherapy suggest we move forward? In his book *Wild Therapy: Undomesticating Inner and Outer Worlds*, Nick Totton (2011: 4) suggests that contemporary psychotherapy and counselling takes place largely in an 'imaginary world', a kind of 'bubble of unreality' where the grave ecological threats we are facing are simply not happening, 'where flying to Australia is a splendid adventure rather than an insult to the earth's atmosphere, where animals and plants and rivers and mountains exist not for themselves but to hold *our* projections and serve *our* material and psychological needs' (the page numbers here refer to the draft version Nick Totton kindly sent me while I was completing my book, although unfortunately without enough time to fully explore the potential of wild therapy that he describes).

His explanation for this 'bubble' is similar to my own. Psychotherapists, as human as their patients, are terrified to 'face the reality of the collapsing biosphere'. In addition to this anxiety they are threatened with 'grief and anger and despair', so much so that 'we don't know whether we could function in the everyday world if we fully admitted it' (ibid.). Aligning wild therapy with ecopsychology and ecotherapy, Totton claims there is a battle occurring within psychotherapy and counselling 'between our wish for status and social normality' and the field's historical relationship 'with the margins, the unconscious, the path less travelled' (ibid.).

Within this dynamic, those who draw attention to the realities of the ecological crisis are treated defensively as freaks who are outside the social consensus. We are then faced with the choice of attributing this marginality to our clients, helping them to adjust to an unsustainable social system, or 'we can recognise that *we too are clients*, and look for ways to support our own marginal perceptions and understandings' (ibid.). Totton suggests that the idea of wild therapy may be 'un-settling, for both therapist and client', because 'it moves us out of settlement, makes us leave our comfortable home and wander, following love . . . in all its many forms' (Totton 2011: 136).

For Totton (2011), wild therapy is drawn from three related areas. First, it emphasizes the need to heal the severed sense of connection with the 'other than human and more than human, to all beings with whom we share this universe' (ibid.: 132), drawing on the idea of the world not as external machine but as extended body (Robinson 1997). Second, it refers to the history of humanity, and the neolithic revolution which led to agriculture, cities, and the start of the domestication process, of ourselves as well as our livestock. Finally, Totton's (2011: 5) project relates to the regulation of psychotherapy debate, and important questions concerning 'what therapy is and should be, what values inform it and who should control its practice.'

Each of these themes relates to the issue of control and its impossibility, in a way which parallels my own complexity/chaos-based approach in this book. Totton (2011: 5) argues that by 'trying to control the world we have made it *other*, and therefore dangerous and frightening', and thus the 'more we seek control, the closer we seem to get to it, the further our goal recedes.' However, while his project of undomesticating humanity may appear to suggest a primitivist return to a pre-civilized Eden, Totton clearly states he does not mean to suggest something so literal. His call for a connection with 'wild mind' is, on the contrary, a way in part to avoid the very ecological collapse that may lead us to such a state:

> A reduction of humanity to Paleolithic population levels . . . will only happen through catastrophe . . . I want to explore the possibility of developing a wildness which is less literal, but perhaps none the less real and important: a reconnection with what I will describe as Wild Mind . . . a reconnection with the world and with the other beings which inhabit it . . . [involving] living, as well as thinking and feeling, in very different ways. Wild Mind refers to a state of awareness in which humans will not *want*, or be prepared, to damage the world for our own short-term comfort and convenience . . . A shift of consciousness and practice like this is perhaps only slightly less hard to imagine than return to hunter-gatherer lifestyle. However, it is necessary. Without it, a literal return to hunter-gatherer life (and population levels) may be the *best* we can hope for. I believe that psychotherapy and counselling . . . have a potentially important role to play in promoting and facilitating Wild Mind, or ecological consciousness.
>
> (Totton 2011: 5–6)

One form of ecotherapy seeks to use the power of the human–animal bond as a therapeutic tool (e.g. DeMayo 2009; Bradshaw 2009). Recent theories in evolutionary anthropology suggest that this could be grounded scientifically in our evolutionary history, arguing that the human–animal bond was crucial in human evolution, decisively influencing the origin of both art and language (Shipman 2010).

A further way to take the challenge of ecotherapy seriously is to attempt to take psychotherapy and counselling outside the traditional indoor consulting room into the outdoors (Buzzell & Chalquist 2009), in terms of both 'nearby nature' (Kaplan & Kaplan 1989) such as woods and parks, and 'wilderness' areas more remote from civilization (Macfarlane 2007). In their paper 'Taking counselling and psychotherapy outside: Destruction or enrichment of the therapeutic frame?', Martin Jordan and Hayley Marshall (2010) explore the various complex clinical factors involved in such a shift, in particular focusing on its impact on boundaries and the therapeutic frame.

In their research, they emphasize that a sense of frame is 'synonymous with particular spaces' and explore 'how these spaces may be both emotional and geographical (Bondi & Fewell 2003)' (Jordan & Marshall 2010: 345). The effects of opening out the closed, cut-off world of the emotional geography of the traditional consulting room is an interesting aspect of the process which Jordan and Marshall are exploring. Further developing such ideas concerning the spatiality of affect is an area where the philosophy of Deleuze|Guattari may have a lot to offer an ecologically informed psychoanalysis and ecotherapy.

Drawing on Langs' (1979, 1982) school of communicative psychotherapy and 'frame therapy', Jordan and Marshall (2010: 346) describe how the frame can be a 'safe containing stable space', a holding environment, but also result in a 'deep existential sense of the limiting and restricting nature of the therapeutic environment, which mimics the finiteness and vulnerability of life itself' and is therefore 'immensely anxiety provoking.' Jordan and Marshall (2010: 347) suggest that taking therapy outdoors challenges the notion of frame as being held in an indoor space, and may be 'seen by other psychotherapists and professionals as a "transgression" of the traditional boundaries of therapy.' However, they claim that this move also helps to further develop existing trends in psychoanalysis and psychotherapy, particularly those from the relational school (Aron 1996; Mitchell 1988), with its interest in intersubjectivity, co-construction, democratizing therapeutic power dynamics, and the 'fluidity' of boundaries in the analytic space.

Clinically, the work they describe involves two types of practice. The first involves 'conducting therapy with individuals in natural spaces over the time span of the traditional therapy hour. This work was very similar to one-to-one work carried out in a room with a client, and was typically carried out in "nearby nature" such as parks and woodland.' The second involves groups taken to more 'wild' areas such as mountains and 'typically extends over a weekend or longer and may involve camping out overnight in wilderness terrain' (Jordan & Marshall 2010: 347–348). They argue that the relational perspective is particularly suited to this kind of outdoor therapy (Santostefano 2004), and that outdoor therapy is a particularly suitable arena for conducting relational therapy, claiming that the 'relational encounter within the dynamic nature of the natural world can provide rich opportunities for a new experiencing with immediacy for both therapist and client, all of which can be fed in to the therapeutic process' (Jordan & Marshall 2010: 349).

Moving outdoors may also enhance mutuality (not identical with equality), given that the space within which therapy occurs is not owned by the therapist, and the process of choosing different terrain can become a more co-created ongoing experience within the therapeutic relationship. The outdoor environment also requires more flexibility with contracting, which needs to be both clear and explicit at the outset, to provide a container in the more unpredictable outdoor world, but also requires something along the lines of 'process contracting' (Lee 1997, cited in Jordan & Marshall 2010: 352). The result is that 'a truly fluid contracting process is called for as therapist and client face the outdoor terrain, and all the resultant challenges, together' (ibid.).

Of course, the largest single shift that this approach represents is in the issue of the role of nature itself in the therapeutic process:

> Relational psychotherapy has highlighted the mutuality of the thera- peutic process, but the physical environment has largely been ignored . . . and seen as a rather static backdrop. Placing therapy outdoors within a relational paradigm can mean that this backdrop now becomes a living presence . . . [where] therapist and client are constantly aware of (both consciously and unconsciously), and responding to, the presence of this vibrant living third in the dynamic. This moves therapy beyond the two person psychological world of relational psychotherapy in to a two and half person psychology (Tudor 2009) . . . a 'multi-directional' relating style and a methodological emphasis on what Tudor (2009) refers to as 'interspection: a process of reflecting on what is in between – and beyond – therapist and client'.
>
> (Jordan & Marshall 2010: 353–354)

However, clearly this can be a very challenging experience for therapists, involving problems around boundaries, frame issues, 'intrusions from the natural world, such as erratic, difficult weather conditions', and issues of the 'physical safety of clients on more dangerous terrain such as mountains and remote places far from urban life' (Jordan & Marshall 2010: 329). One of the authors described the experience of 'feeling exposed, as though aspects of my professional identity were stripped from me, and the common protections I used in the setting of the room were somehow taken away when moving outside' (Jordan & Marshall 2010: 356). This brought clearly to the foreground just how much of the therapist's identity 'is invested in the physical container of the room' (ibid.).

As well as recognizing these potential difficulties and anxieties, Jordan and Marshall adopt a cautious approach which acknowledges the potential for enactments on the therapist's part involved with the move outside for particular patients. Jordan and Marshall (ibid.) therefore strongly argue for the need for supervision and discussion with peers 'to explore fully the reasons both conscious and unconscious that might be involved in taking the therapy outside' for any particular patient.

They conclude with an idea they call the 'living frame', 'a movable and more dynamic encounter which includes relationality with the living world around us in the form of nature, the wind, rain, sunshine, the myriad of plant and animal life as well as the potentiality of encountering other humans' (Jordan & Marshall 2010: 357). Here, the frame is seen as a way of 'understanding the relationships and spaces that become therapeutic' and as such it 'can be reconstructed in a more fluid and dynamic way in the outdoors' (ibid.). While respecting the risks involved with outdoor therapy, and stating that it in no way supersedes or is necessarily 'better' than indoor therapy, they suggest that it can have the potential to provide an 'increased sense of immediacy and potential therapeutic vitality available for the client's benefit' (ibid.).

Idealizing the indigenous and the 'non-Western'

Ecopsychologists, and environmentalists in general, sometimes give the impression of holding to a simplistic division between 'good' indigenous peoples who lived in harmony with nature and knew its rhythms to which they related with spiritual awe and love, and the 'bad' technological-industrial Western society which breaks this intimate bond leading to ecocide. It is certainly true that the level and scale of ecological damage in our own time is something unprecedented. This is nowhere more true than for the tropical rainforests, which, while covering only 6 per cent of the planet's land surface, contain more than half of all known species (Wilson 2003: 59). Unfortunately, rainforests 'are also the leading abattoir of extinction, shattered into fragments that are being severely adulterated or erased one by one' (ibid.). The sheer pace of destruction has massively increased with modern technology, to the extent, Wilson (2003: 58) claims, that the 'loss of forest during the past half-century is one of the most profound and rapid environmental changes in the history of the planet.'

However, we should be wary of idealizing and romanticizing the indigenous and the native, whether the *Na'vi* inhabitants of *Avatar* (Cameron 2009) or the 'aboriginal' inhabitants of a land prior to the emergence of Western greed and destruction. Did these peoples really have such a harmonious connection with the rest of nature? Or is the real story more complex? Both Jared Diamond (2006) and E. O. Wilson (2003) point towards a history of waves of extinctions following the spread of humans to ecosystems which evolved without them and therefore were not pre-adapted to human co-habitation, with the largest and slowest moving animals falling first. As humans originated in probably 'a single area in Sub-Saharan Africa' (Manica *et al.* 2007), this applies to most of the world, and is possibly one reason why Africa still retains large megafauna that are extinct from many other regions.

For some specific examples, we can begin with the 'indigenous' Aborigines of Australia (who are not indigenous from the planet's point of view, as they arrived in Australia 46,000 years ago, millions of years after life began evolving there). Shortly after arriving, they quickly exterminated much of the megafauna of the regions they entered, including most of Australia's former giant marsupials (Diamond 2006: 9). Native American tribes, often looked to as a paragon example of societies living in harmony with nature, were also perhaps not always the exceptions to this trend that we would like them to be (Broughton & Siegel 2006). 'Traditional' non-Western medicine is also not necessarily more environmentally sensitive than Western medicine, despite its fashion in New Age circles. The last of the absolutely unique hairy Sumatran rhinoceros will probably disappear very soon, killed for its horn which is used in traditional Chinese medicine (Wilson 2003: 79–82, 94).

Islands are especially vulnerable to human impact. Indigenous Hawaiians and Maoris, for example, initiated major extinctions and extirpation (local extinction) events of native bird species soon after first arriving in Hawaii and New Zealand (Diamond 2006: 9–10; Wilson 2003: 43–50). The Moa, which included 11 species of flightless birds endemic to New Zealand and reaching up to 3.7 metres in height, were wiped out within decades of the Maori arrival, along with what had been the world's largest eagle (weighing up to 15 kilograms), previously the Moa's only predator (Holdaway & Jacomb 2000). Similarly, the arrival of the Polynesians on the Hawaiian islands initiated a large-scale extinction event for local bird species, with the large, flightless, ground-nesting birds going first. A second later extinction event begins with the first arrival of Europeans (Boyer 2008).

However, all this shouldn't lead us to conclude that humanity can never exist in a sustainable relation to the natural world, or that all societies are equally destructive. Genuine exceptions to the overall pattern do exist, and many of the societies mentioned above later learned to live in a less destructive relation to their environment. One particularly successful example is the Tikopia islanders, who have managed to regulate their population size and environmental behaviour so well that they are still living and thriving after 3,000 years of human occupation. This is despite their society being especially vulnerable to collapse due to being cut off from all outside support during almost their entire history, and living on an island just 1.8 square miles in size (Diamond 2006: 286–293).

The highlanders of New Guinea are another remarkable success story of humans living in an ecologically sensitive sustainable society, with sophisticated agricultural practices and silviculture (planned tree-planting and management for a variety of purposes). Diamond (2006: 285) writes that this allowed them to 'operate sustainably for tens of thousands of years before the origins of agriculture, and then for another 7,000 years after . . . despite climate changes and human environmental impacts constantly creating altered conditions.' Laddakh is a further fascinating case, which while being one of the highest and driest inhabited places on Earth, has for centuries supported a self-sustaining culture in the Himalayas based on Tibetan Buddhism. However, the road and airport connecting with the capital, Leh, has plunged this fragile ecology into the global economy, and is threatening to push this previously precariously balanced environment over the edge (Norberg-Hodge 2009).

Therefore, there are successes, but these are much rarer than we would like, and it is certainly not as simple as 'Western bad, indigenous good'. As Diamond (2006) argues, we need to learn from all the mistakes and the successes of the present and the past, from all regions of the planet, including the peoples described above. In fact, we are in a unique position here in that we *can* do this. No other previous civilization has had this opportunity to learn from all the failures and successes of their predecessors. We need to use all our knowledge, science, and the best traditions from humanity's history and relations with nature to build a more sustainable world. If it is the case that there are far fewer examples of good eco-practice in past or present 'indigenous' societies than we would like, this does not mean that we cannot, should not, or need not attempt to build such a world in the present and for the future.

It may be necessary, therefore, to look for, and help to create, a new bioethic of the future, rather than assuming that past human groups lived in an Edenic natural harmony with nature. The 'biophilic' ideas of the ecopsychologists are therefore still important here, even if the indigenous societies they sometimes idealize do not embody these ideas as much as our romantic projections would wish. In that sense ecopsychology is also about the creation of a new form of ethics along with a new understanding of mental health 'as if the whole world mattered', rather than necessarily a reprise of what has already gone before. But biophilia is not enough, it needs to be combined with sophisticated knowledge, science, and understanding of local and planetary ecologies and the varied consequences of human–environment interaction. Love, even the love of nature, is not *all* we need.

Working through environmental despair

> Until the late twentieth century, every generation throughout history lived with the tacit certainty that there would be generations to follow . . . children would walk the same Earth . . . That certainty is now lost to us, whatever our politics. That loss, unmeasured and immeasurable, is the pivotal psychological reality of our time.
>
> (Macy 1995: 241)

Joanna Macy suggests that *environmental despair* includes feelings such as terror, rage, guilt and sorrow, as 'confronting so vast and final a loss as this brings sadness beyond the telling', a pain we understandably tend to repress 'because it hurts, because it is frightening, and most of all because we do not understand it and consider it to be a dysfunction, an aberration, a sign of personal weakness' (Macy 1995: 241). She suggests that as a society we are caught between 'a sense of impending apocalypse and the fear of acknowledging it' and that these feelings 'cannot be equated with dread of our own individual demise' but rather express 'our pain for the world' (ibid.), for the larger (open) systems of which we are a part. She has thus developed what she calls 'despair and empowerment workshops' to try to help people to face these feelings, and through this open up to a wider vision of our interdependency and, as she puts it, 'remember our collective body' (Macy 1995: 255).

> The living system learns, adapts, and evolves by reorganizing itself. This usually occurs when its previous ways of responding to the environment are no longer functional . . . Bereft of self-confidence and hopefulness, we can feel as though we and our world are 'falling apart' . . . To experience pain as we register what is happening to our world is a measure of our evolution as open systems . . . our pain for the world is rooted in our interconnectedness.
>
> (ibid.)

The idea that our pain is not just personal but expresses a 'pain for the world', and Macy's systemic approach to the problem in general, is an interesting one with clear affinities to the work of Bateson (2000, 2002) which we shall turn to in Chapter 13, the penultimate chapter of the book. However, this kind of perspective is difficult, especially 'for a culture untutored in the perception of relationships' where 'it is precisely these systemic interactions that are hard to see' (Macy 1995: 243). Here lies perhaps the crucial task of our times.

> [W]e tend to live our lives as if nothing has changed, while knowing that everything has changed . . . Awesome and unprecedented in the history of humanity, the awareness lurks there, with an anguish beyond naming. Until we find ways of acknowledging and integrating that level of anguished awareness, we repress it; and with that repression we are drained of the energy we need for action and clear thinking . . . Uncovering the deep roots of repression is part of what psychology can offer environmentalists.
>
> (ibid.)

Macy goes on to explore the particular types of fears which prevent us from engaging or acknowledging our feelings. These include: *fear of pain;*

fear of guilt (of acknowledging our status as 'accomplices to catastrophe'); *fear of appearing morbid* in a society with optimism virtually required; *fear of appearing stupid* in a culture demanding instant solutions; *fear of appearing emotional* in a civilization with a 'dichotomy between reason and emotion'; and *fear of feeling powerless*, which Macy suggests 'springs less from actual powerlessness . . . than . . . fear of *experiencing* powerlessness' (Macy 1995: 248). The price we pay for maintaining our defences is ecological devastation, and what Lifton (1968) called, in the context of the holocaust, 'psychic numbing'.

Ultimately Macy retains hope in the face of environmental despair, a hope in what she calls 'the great turning', a dramatic and almost unprecedented shift in society and psychology on a global scale which she feels is now beginning, the level she believes is required if we are to be able to deal with the ecological crisis.

> Whatever happens, this can be a moment of unparalleled awakening. We have a sense of what it means for an individual to wake up. For the collective to awaken, we cannot even imagine what it will be like. The evolutionary pressure is on us now, which can feel so ghastly, pushes us toward this awakening . . . I don't think we've been given any absolute guarantee that conscious life on Earth will continue . . . In either case, this is a most extraordinary and beautiful moment. Because in this moment we can make a choice for loving life and taking care of each other.
>
> (Macy 2005, cited in Rust 2008: 11)

Ultimately, like Joanna Macy, Mary-Jane Rust shares this vision of nurturing hope in the face of despair:

> We are in the midst of an extraordinary process of transformation; stuckness, defeat . . . the addictive numbing of despair coexist with a myriad of awakenings . . . of new visions and energies and creative possibilities arising all around the planet. I have been trying to describe the journey towards sustainable living as a therapeutic journey . . . As the crisis quickens, the shadow of the myth of progress becomes ever more obvious . . . We may be living in the last hours of ancient sunlight. What are we going to do with our time? Busy ourselves shopping? Or spend time with those we love, in the places we love, and use the time to sort out our unfinished business with the earth?
>
> (Rust 2008: 20–21)

Chapter 8

Ecology without nature
Postmodern ecopsychoanalysis

> Strange as it may sound, the idea of nature is getting in the way of properly ecological forms of culture, philosophy, politics, and art . . . for it is in art that the fantasies we have about nature take shape – and dissolve.
>
> (Morton 2007: 1)

> Nature provides . . . signifiers, and these signifiers organize human relations in a creative way, providing them with structures and shaping them . . . the symbolic manifests itself first of all as the murder of the thing.
>
> (Lacan 1998: 20)

Ecology: The new opium of the masses?

> The image of nature as a balanced circuit is nothing but a retroactive projection of man. Herein lies the lesson of recent theories of chaos: 'nature' is already, in itself, turbulent, imbalanced.
>
> (Žižek 1991: 38)

The rhetoric of ecopsychology is very appealing, and powerful. However, without wishing to denigrate this tradition, it is important to consider dissenting voices, and it is to these we now turn, in particular to those from the Lacanian and postmodern traditions (Bertens 1995; Lyotard 1997). Timothy Morton's (2007) call for an 'ecology without nature', which has highly influenced Slavoj Žižek's (2007) own position, is important to deconstruct reified concepts of 'Nature', including those held within parts of the ecology and ecopsychology movements. In addition it helps to illustrate the way 'Nature' itself has long been an important object of phantasy. However, the danger of this approach is that it can lose sight of the fact that the ecological crisis ultimately reaches beyond any linguistic constructions, and is not itself a 'text' which can be 'deconstructed', but is a 'Real' beyond language, traumatically rupturing the 'symbolic' and the linguistic arrogance of certain trends within postmodern psychoanalysis.

However, we would do well to consider what the Lacanian approach has to offer, particularly Slavoj Žižek's work on ideology. Can we, in fact, analyze environmentalism as functioning as a new religion or ideology as the Czech President Vaclav Klaus suggests, but without denying the seriousness of the ecological crisis we are facing? Environmentalism has in fact provided a new direction for leftists disillusioned with the communist or socialist project, a new 'morally pure' domain for collective action unsullied by the stench of Stalinism, seemingly beyond the selfish aims to which even the class struggle basically came down to. In addition, Žižek (2007) suggests that it may in the long run actually prove to be a more potent opponent of capitalism, which so far has proved so good at recuperating all opposition.

This recuperation has already begun with ecology, where we have 'green' industries, green-wash, carbon credits, and new ecological reasons for old oppressions. Žižek (2007) suggests we can expect this to develop further in the future. However, catastrophic climate change may well represent a true 'limit-crisis' of capitalism as all these pseudo-attempts to deal with the problem fail to realize that this is not a purely social or psychological or even economic crisis but involves the real physical and ecological systems within which capitalism itself, as economic system and as social relation, is embedded.

We have already seen the echo of religion's strange attraction to apocalyptic 'eschatological' thinking in ecological imaginings of a 'world without us' (Weisman 2007). The religious dimension is most apparent in the 'New Age' wing of the movement with its 'mother earth' eco-spirituality. But even for many 'hard-nosed' scientists and large numbers of non-religious people ecology seems to provide a new basis for moral action, redemption and renewal in a secular and 'post-ideological' society (Žižek ridicules the idea that today we are somehow beyond ideology, claiming on the contrary that this very idea shows how we are more in the grip of it than ever). According to Žižek (2007):

> [W]ith the depoliticized, socially objective, expert administration and coordination of interests as the zero-level of politics, the only way to . . . actively mobilize people, is through fear, a basic constituent of today's subjectivity . . . No wonder, then, that the by far predominant version of ecology is the ecology of fear . . . [which] has all the chances of developing into the predominant form of ideology of global capitalism, a new opium for the masses . . . it takes over . . . religion's fundamental function, that of putting on an unquestionable authority which can impose limits . . . [F]or both, there is something of a transgression, of entering a prohibited domain.

Environmentalist and ecopsychological writings often emphasize the problem of our alienation from the 'life-world' of nature and how this leads to and results from the hubris of 'techno-scientific rationality', and the idea that we are not deeply embedded in nature but somehow beyond it or above it, which ecology shows us is false. Therefore, the ecopychological project is seen by many as an opportunity for psychological, social and spiritual renewal leading to a connection with natural, connected, 'life-worlds'. Žižek (2007) interrogates this claim, and argues the very opposite (as Žižek often does, whatever the initial proposition), that it is on the contrary our very embeddedness in our life-world that prevents us from seeing the problem.

When we flush the toilet, subjectively the waste simply disappears from our reality, into a non-existent non-space, or perhaps into that fecal space Meltzer (1992) calls the 'claustrum' which is explored with so much fascination and terror in horror films, and in the writings of Franz Kafka. Our sense of immediate living in our life-world cannot allow us to see the effects of our waste or the complex but very real abstractions into which it flows. We may intellectually know of the mass extinctions and the destruction of the rainforests but we cannot directly feel it. Therefore Žižek (2007) claims we actually need more alienation, and require even further distance from our immediate 'life-world' in order to better grasp the complex abstractions that we are involved in, rather than 'reconnecting' to immediate experience.

> Our attitude here is that of the fetishist split: I know very well (that global warming is a threat to the entire humanity), but nonetheless . . . (I cannot really believe it). It is enough to look at my environs . . . the green grass and trees, the whistle of the wind, the rising of the sun . . . can one really imagine that all this will be disturbed? You talk about the ozone hole but no matter how much I look into the sky, I don't see it . . . therein resides the horror of the Chernobyl accident: when one visits the site, with the exception of the sarcophagus, things look exactly the same as before . . . nonetheless we are aware that something is terribly wrong. The change is not at the level of the visible reality itself, it is a more fundamental one, it affects the very texture of reality. No wonder there are some lone farmers around the Chernobyl site who continued to lead their lives as before – they simply ignore all the incomprehensible talk about radiations.
>
> (Žižek 2007)

Thus, for Žižek the 'life-world' is no antidote for our 'techno-scientific' alienation, rather, the 'difficult ethical task is to "un-learn" the most basic coordinates of our immersion into our life-world: what usually served as the recourse to Wisdom (the basic trust in the background-coordinates of our world) is now THE source of danger.'

Ecology without Nature

In addition, Žižek argues that our very idea of 'Nature' may be the problem, hence his call, following Morton (2007), for an 'ecology without Nature'. For example, he takes issue with the idea that nature is a homeostatic, harmonious Gaia where all parts fit and interact perfectly with the whole, which humans then disrupt and destroy through techno-industrial hubris. In his essay 'Censorship Today: Violence or Ecology as a New Opium of the Masses', Žižek (2007) maintains that

> the main consequence of the scientific breakthroughs in biogenetics is the end of nature. Once we know the rules of its construction, natural organisms are transformed into objects amenable to manipulation. Nature, human and inhuman, is thus 'desubstantialized', deprived of its impenetrable density, of what Heidegger called 'earth' . . . nature is no longer 'natural', the reliable 'dense' background of our lives; it now appears as a fragile mechanism which, at any point, can explode in a catastrophic direction.

However, nature as a harmonious stable ground never existed to begin with, as more recent studies of evolution and complexity and catastrophe theory confirm (catastrophe theory studies sudden changes in events, involving combinations of attractors and bifurcations operating in self-organizing systems [see Kauffman 1993; Gould & Eldredge 1993]). Žižek (2007) calls on us therefore to 'accept the utter groundlessness of our existence: there is no firm foundation, a place of retreat, on which one can safely count', only violent cataclysms. This does not mean that humans have not caused immense damage, but that the idea of a holistically pure 'world without us' is false. Rephrasing Lacan's (1974: 68) famous aphorism about Woman, Žižek (2007) writes

> Nature doesn't exist . . . there is no big Other (self-contained symbolic order as the ultimate guarantee of Meaning); there is also no Nature *qua* balanced order of self-reproduction whose homeostasis is disturbed, thrown off the rails, by the imbalanced human interventions . . . what we need is ecology without nature: the ultimate obstacle to protecting nature is the very notion of nature we rely on.

One final important area of Žižek's commentaries on ecology (or 'žižecology' as Canavan [2008] calls it) concerns the wider sense of imminent destruction in our own times, whether from ecological collapse, terrorism or war, in a world where we can no longer 'rely on the safeguarding role of the limited scope of our acts: it no longer holds that, whatever we do, history will go on', in fact, for 'the first time in human history, the act of a single socio-political agent effectively can alter and even interrupt the global historical process' (Žižek 2007).

> The constellation is properly frustrating: although we . . . know that it all depends on us, we cannot ever predict the consequences of our acts – we are not impotent, but, quite on the contrary, omnipotent, without being able to determine the scope of our powers . . . [T]here is no 'big Other' to guarantee the . . . outcome . . . will be satisfactory. . . . [T]he lesson of ecology is that we should go to the end here and accept the non-existence of the ultimate big Other, nature itself with its pattern of regular rhythms, the ultimate reference of order and stability.
>
> (Žižek 2007)

Ecocritique: Deconstructing the ecological imaginary

Timothy Morton (2007: 1) agrees, exploring in his *Ecology Without Nature: Rethinking Environmental Aesthetics* how nature is represented in art and literature, especially from the Romantic era which 'still influences the ways in which the ecological imaginary works' today. Morton makes clear that his use of deconstructivist techniques does not mean adhering to a view that there is no such thing as nature, that coral reefs are not being destroyed, nor that the crisis we face is not desperate. However, this is a declaration of the author which doesn't necessarily fit well with the theoretical frame applied in that book. This may be changing, however, as in his more recent work he has developed an increasingly sophisticated philosophical engage-ment with materialism and the new sciences which moves some way beyond the framework of the earlier text.

Morton's crucial point is that our idea of nature is extraordinarily naive given the degree of theoretical criticism applied to other areas of thought. Morton's *ecocritique* aims at deconstructing the ecological imaginary, including not only negative but also positive idealizing projections, arguing effectively that 'putting something called Nature on a pedestal and admir-ing it from afar does for the environment what patriarchy does for the figure of Woman' (Morton 2007: 5). He therefore calls for an ecocriticism which 'does not think that it is paradoxical to say, in the name of ecology itself: "down with nature!"' (Morton 2007: 13).

Morton's ecology without nature refers above all to our idea of nature. This includes that reified and Romantic conception of 'Nature' which so much environmental (and anti-environmental) rhetoric, phantasy and behaviour relates to. In other words we can understand this project, in part, as the process of withdrawing our projections, which get in the way of more effectively dealing with the issues. To see the way Nature can become a vast arena for depositing our projections we have only to read Freud's patriarchal view of nature as a woman to be raped or subdued, forced into providing for us, but who ultimately may be more castrating than nourishing (Gomes & Kanner 1995a; Randall 2005).

Another example from my own experience is the moment in *Lord of the Rings: The Two Towers* (Jackson 2002) where trees rise up and fight back against their destruction by an evil Orcish industrialism. This evoked in me not hope but a feeling of mourning, not just for the lost nature (as actual physical world) but from a lost Nature (as idea or ideal). By bringing our Romantic idealistic projections onto Nature too much into the foreground, we are forced to mourn the lost ideal, as well as the lost 'real'. The trees are just not going to rise up to save the planet no matter how much environmentalists might want them to.

To bring the concept of the 'end of nature' down to earth (a possibly unfortunate expression in the circumstances), Morton (2010b) relates a common situation, and reflects on the fate of that traditional part of social relations and small talk, the 'weather' question, in the light of global warming:

> You are waiting at a bus stop. Somebody else rambles up. 'Nice weather isn't it?', she asks. You pause . . . You wonder whether she's only saying that to distract you from the latest news about global warming. You decide she isn't. 'Yes,' you say. But your reply holds something back. The awareness for you that it is not a particularly nice day, because you're concerned that the heat and the moisture have to do with global warming. This holding back may or may not be reflected in your tone. 'Mind you,' she says . . . 'Funny weather wasn't it last week? I blame global warming.'

Such conversations are now commonplace to the point of banality, but they reflect a deeper and more disturbing trend. As Morton (2010b) writes:

> In an age of global warming, the weather, that nice, neutral backdrop that you can talk about with a stranger . . . has taken on a menacing air . . . This failure of the normal rhetorical routine, these remnants of shattered conversations lying around, like broken hammers . . . is a symptom of a much larger and ontological shift in human awareness which is in turn a symptom of a profound upgrade of our ontological tools . . . [N]ature no longer exists in any meaningful sense except as nostalgia, or in the temporarily useful local language of pleas and petitions . . . We have a general feeling of . . . malaise and create nostalgic visions of Hobbit-like worlds to inhabit.

Of course simple disillusionment is not the answer (Winnicott 1987), and there is a real danger that the process of ecocritique can remove one of the main motivations binding the environmental movement together. Another danger is that all the talk of 'nature no longer existing' may feed into ideas or defences that argue that because 'nature' is already so altered by human activity everywhere that 'wilderness' in a pure sense does not exist, there is no reason to struggle to protect a nature which has no substance, or of which so little remains.

However, despite these dangers, ecocriticism is crucial in helping us to become more aware of how we use nature, not only physically through resource extraction, but psychologically and emotionally as a powerfully charged object, and aims to reach a situation where our projections and phantasies don't get in the way of more genuine environmental concern. A psychoanalytic deconstruction is also essential for the environmental organizations themselves. As Marshall (2001) writes: 'Environmental campaign organizations are living relics of Enlightenment faith in the power of knowledge', the idea that 'if only people knew, they would act.'

Dark ecology

The shift in perspective that climate change has forced us into is dizzying. Now that the seemingly stable neutral background we call 'environment' has dissolved into an all too contingent accident, the foreground itself disappears, in Morton's (2010b) view, as foreground cannot exist without background.

> Global warming . . . has performed a radical shift in the status of the weather . . . Because the world as such, not just a certain idea of world, but world, in its entirety, has evaporated. Or rather, we are realizing that we never had it in the first place . . . Global warming is a prime example of what I now call a hyper-object, an object that is massively distributed in space-time which radically transforms our ideas of what an object is . . . It's like suddenly discovering that you've been conducting your business in the expanding sphere of a slow-motion nuclear bomb. You have a few seconds for amazement as the fantasy that you inhabited, a neat seamless little world, melts away.
>
> (Morton 2010b)

The solution, according to Morton, is to abandon the comforting fantasy of our Hobbit-like Heideggerian 'life-worlds' and embrace what he calls a *dark ecology*, based on a 'melancholic ethics' (Morton 2007: 186), with interesting potential connections with a Kleinian ecopsychoanalysis shorn of certain of its ontological pretensions (Robbins & Goicoechea 1996), becoming what Steven Brown and Paul Stenner (2009) call a 'psychology without foundations'. Morton himself, in his latest book, *The Ecological Thought* (Morton 2010a), has emphasized the non-identitarian, nonsubstantialist and non-teleological interconnectedness that modern science, and especially ecology, leads us towards, in ways which we can relate to the discussion of Manuel DeLanda's (2005: 93) concept of 'meshworks' and to the perspective of this book in general. For Morton (2010a: 28), 'the ecological thought stirs because the mesh appears in our social, psychic, and scientific domains.'

Morton's (2010a: 83) call for a 'true materialism' which would consider 'matter as self-assembling sets of interrelationships in which information is directly inscribed' has resonances with my own views. This book argues that the call can best be answered by drawing on the philosophy of Deleuze and Guattari, and the sciences of complexity and chaos. The working through of these ideas in relation to psychoanalysis and the ecological crisis is the major theoretical task of the remaining chapters of this book.

Deleuze|Guattari: Towards a geophilosophy of nature

> There is nothing outside of the text . . . there has never been anything but writing . . . that what opens meaning and language is writing as the disappearance of natural presence.
>
> (Derrida, cited in Herzogenrath 2009: 2)

> We are so befuddled by language that we cannot think straight, and it is convenient, sometimes, to remember that we are really mammals.
>
> (Bateson 2000: 275)

The main problem with ecocriticism lies in the difficulty of deconstructive or postmodernist approaches in giving ontological space to nature and the material as anything other than an effect of language, or its negation as the 'Real'. A good example is Zita (1998: 89) who writes that: 'Nature . . . [is] a product of discourse or intersecting textualities, as the world becomes a ceaseless play of interlocking and conflicting texts, spoken from different locations and negotiated across different perspectives.'

With their mixed semiotics, Deleuze and Guattari (2000: 1) can offer a way out, with their view that: 'There is no such thing as either man or nature now, only a process that produces the one within the other and couples the machines together.' Herzogenrath (2009: 3) calls for a Deleuzo-Guattarian ecology, for 'a new perspective that allows for the incorporation of the workings of the "repressed" of representation (namely of the "real", of "nature", of "matter").' Similarly, Bonta and Protevi (2004) argue that:

> [J]ust as complexity theory's insistence on the natural creativity of open systems enables Deleuze and Guattari to outflank hermeneutic humanism at the same time as its thematization of signs as triggers of material

processes enables them to escape from the anti-humanist linguistic structuralism of postmodernism, their thematizing of the subject as an emergent functional structure embedded in a series of structures enables them to escape from methodological individualism. Complexity theory . . . focuses our attention on the subject as a functional structure emerging from a multiplicity . . . Despite Derrida's insistent revelation of the effects within written texts of an unnamable 'outside' or 'force' . . . Deleuze and Guattari's framework is more productive because of their historical situating of the signifying regime as one among several semiotic systems ('regimes of signs').

(Bonta & Protevi 2004: 5–7)

In a sense, the sciences of complexity have achieved Žižek's dissolution of 'nature' as a stable, homogenous ground and replaced it with chaos, flows, and nonlinearities. Perhaps the most basic distinction of all, that between order and chaos, has itself collapsed into something far more interesting. Bonta and Protevi (2004: 4) claim that with geophilosophy 'Deleuze and Guattari break not only with Levi-Strauss, but also with all forms of "postmodernism"' which 'by dint of an exclusive analysis of signifying texts wherever signs are deployed, has trapped too many philosophers and geographers in debates over problems of reference and the surplus production of meaning in signifying chains.'

Applying a similar reading to this book, Bonta and Protevi argue that a crucial element in the alternative offered by Deleuze and Guattari is their 'historically and politically informed engagement with complexity theory' which 'helps us break free of the postmodernist trap by rethinking sense and reference, and in so doing shatter the postmodernist equations of signs with signifiers' (ibid.). Complexity theory allows us a vision of sign systems beyond the linguistic register where 'at critical thresholds some physical and biological systems can be said to "sense" the differences in their environment that trigger self-organizing processes' (ibid.).

In this way, signs – thresholds sensed by systems – are not only conceptualized as occurring beyond the register of the human and even the organic, but also are understood as triggers of material processes. The problematic of the external reference of the signifier, which so troubles post-Saussurean doctrines, is thus bypassed. Signs are no longer limited to linguistic entities that must somehow make contact with the natural world, and sense or meaning need no longer be seen as the reference of signifiers to each other. Rather, the 'meaning' of a sign is a measure of the probability of triggering a particular material process.

(ibid.)

Deleuze and Guattari provide us not with a flight into mysticism, or a naive positivist reductionism, or even a postmodernist deconstructionist play of signifiers, but an 'intelligent materialism', or what they call 'geophilosophy'. However, despite Guattari's intense engagement in ecological issues especially, in particular in his final book, *The Three Ecologies* (Guattari 2000), and his joint publications with Deleuze which draw heavily on the flora, fauna and geostrata of the Earth, their ideas have rarely been taken up in ecological discourse. This seems to be just starting to change, with two recent important collections of essays (Herzogenrath 2008, 2009) exploring the way Deleuze and Guattari can help us with 'thinking environment[s]' from a number of points of view. For Herzogenrath (2008: 2), Deleuze and Guattari's concept of ecology, or *ecosophy*, offers a fresh take on environments as complex systems, and avoids 'dualisms such as "nature" versus "culture", "technology" versus "biology", or "natural" versus "artificial".' It seems therefore that the time for such an engagement is ripe.

Psychoanalysis with schizoanalysis

At this point in the development of the book, there is one important issue which must be dealt with before proceeding any further. Connecting the ideas of Deleuze and Guattari with psychoanalysis may seem unusual and even heretical, to both Deleuzo-Guattarians and to psychoanalysts, given Deleuze and Guattari's powerful attack on traditional Freudian and especially Lacanian approaches (Deleuze & Guattari 2000). What, then, does this book hope to achieve through articulating them together? While there are important exceptions (e.g. Genosko 1993, 2002; Schwab 2008), it could be argued that the followers of Deleuze and Guattari make their opposition with psychoanalysis much more absolute and less nuanced than the pair's original intention. Part of the aim of this book is to show how breaking down some of the strict borders between these fields may well be beneficial for both.

One possible symptom of this slide from the extended engagement (even if highly critical) with psychoanalysis to the relative lack of knowledge many 'Deleuzians' have of psychoanalysis today (certainly at least as far as concerns non-Lacanian or Freudian approaches) is the way the psychoanalyst Guattari (however unorthodox his clinical approach was) is often airbrushed out. He is replaced with the cipher of the philosopher 'Deleuze' to cover many concepts and ideas which have a much more heterogenous and interesting origin than the traditional, and very un-'Deleuzian', single 'philosopher-genius model' allows for.

Guattari was analyzed and trained by the psychoanalyst Jacques Lacan, and worked in the experimental psychiatric clinic of La Borde, under the Lacanian psychiatrist and psychoanalyst Jean Oury, until his death. Guattari's radical experimental clinical work, which Guattari termed 'schizoanalysis' (Deleuze & Guattari 2000: 322), is an area ripe for development, as students of Deleuze and Guattari have by and large not come from clinical backgrounds. Thus, there is a whole wealth of Deleuzian, or perhaps we should say Deleuzo-Guattarian, theory and clinical technique which awaits further development, which itself argues for the case for a renewed dialogue between Deleuze and Guattari and twenty-first-century psychoanalysis and group analysis.

Unfortunately, the reaction of many contemporary 'Deleuzians' to psychoanalysis is often not one of nuanced reflective thought or close critical reading but of reaching for the garlic and crucifix for fear of a psychoanalytic 'contamination'. This is especially ironic given that 'contagion', 'contamination', and 'viral infection' are processes celebrated by Deleuze and Guattari. The compulsive need to distance Deleuzian writings from anything even slightly resembling psychoanalysis has an overly defensive flavour, and it could be argued that psychoanalysis constitutes the 'unconscious' of schizoanalysis, just as Deleuze and Guattari's writing might be viewed as exposing the unconscious of an overly hierarchical and authoritarian psychoanalysis. To paraphrase the ecopsychological formula referred to above, this might lead us to the strange position of claiming that 'psychoanalysis needs schizoanalysis, and schizoanalysis needs psychoanalysis'.

Mark Solms once claimed that psychoanalysis is not important, rather it is *about* something important – the human mind. For Solms that meant that psychoanalysis should be open to dialogue with other approaches to the mind-brain such as neuroscience, as demonstrated by his own pioneering work in the field of neuropsychoanalysis (e.g. Solms & Turnbull 2003; Kaplan-Solms & Solms 2000). In addition, it means that psychoanalysts should be less involved with navel gazing arguments about arcane theoretical niceties of virtually no interest to anyone even slightly outside the psychoanalytic shutters. In particular he criticizes Talmudic exegeses about 'what Freud really meant', or didn't mean, about a given topic.

However, despite this, Solms argues that psychoanalysis, from its unique epistemological perspective, has crucial insights into certain aspects of the mind, human experience and subjectivity, in particular all that comes under that rather over-broad term 'the unconscious'. Similarly, Deleuze and Guattari are clearly onto something important in their own work, but despite their call for an experimental and 'rhizomatic' approach to reality and theory which would seem to militate against it, the creativity of 'Deleuzianism' has in many ways followed some of the same 'striating' and 'arborescent' dynamics that they warn so strongly against. This is a phenomenon psychoanalysts are all too familiar with from the history of their own discipline.

Historically, it can be argued that the critiques by those in fields adjacent to psychoanalysis, whether they be gender theory (e.g. Butler 2006; Chodorow 1991; Clover 1993; Irigaray 1985), history (e.g. Friedländer, 1978;

Felman & Laub 1991; Trezise 2008; Heinemann 2000), aesthetics (Elkins 1994; Glover 2009), philosophy (Derrida 1998; Ricoeur 1970; Marcuse 1998), or social theory (Foucault 1988; Adorno & Horkeimer 2002), to name just a few, have been especially productive for psychoanalysis. Such engagements have helped it to overcome serious blind spots which operate in the 'core' clinical as well as 'peripheral' applied fields (engagement with critiques from gender theory has been particularly important in this regard). Psychoanalysis has undoubtedly been enriched by these connections. In addition, psychoanalytic theory has been forced to develop increasing sophistication in response to the almost constant barrage of criticism it has enjoyed since its inception, a phenomenon which cannot only be attributed to 'resistance'.

This understanding of the ultimately productive nature of many of the attacks on psychoanalysis can be compared to Foucault's (1988) description of the productive, rather than purely 'repressive', nature of power. Deleuze and Guattari's powerful attack on psychoanalysis can be seen to follow in this tradition. Their writings on psychoanalysis do not constitute a cheap dismissal, which could be achieved in a few throwaway paragraphs, but instead emphasize schizoanalysis which involves an extended and detailed critical engagement with psychoanalytic thought which is at times subtle and nuanced even if at other times it can be rather overblown. In this sense it is not something to be disparaged by psychoanalysts, but rather, however cautiously, to be welcomed.

We could thus understand psychoanalysis itself as at least at times functioning as what Deleuze and Guattari (2003a: 21) call a *rhizome*, with countless connections to diverse fields from neuroscience to economics, politics to gender theory, film studies to aesthetics, and the study of organizations and groups. One side of psychoanalytic approaches here follows the model of the 'conquistador' (Freud 1900b: 398), an imperialist project to occupy and take over all fields of the human sciences. This colonizing dimension of psychoanalysis is certainly present in Freud's at times highly reductionistic claims.

In the *New Introductory Lectures On Psycho-Analysis*, for example, Freud (1933: 179) wrote, in a seeming attempt to annex all of the social sciences to psychoanalysis but referring in this example particularly to Marxism, that 'strictly speaking there are only two sciences: psychology, pure and applied, and natural science.' In this context, of course, 'psychology' is to be read as meaning psychoanalysis. Although, as always, there are other Freuds, some more subtle and open, some less so. However, where psychoanalysts, including Freud, tread more carefully, and genuinely attempt to listen and learn rather than impose pre-given grids of meaning, tremendous opportunities to develop are potentially available to both parties.

In some ways this shift follows a related shift in clinical psychoanalysis, from a view (partially a caricature) of the analyst as a fully analyzed master of 'his' domain, the 'subject-supposed-to-know' (Lacan 1998), to one based more on transference–countertransference interactions and co-construction of the field, whether conceptualized under the rubric of Kleinian theory, independent object relations, intersubjective, interpersonal or relational psychoanalysis (Mitchell 2007), or Jungian psychology, which tended from the start to be more open to the personality of the analyst being affected and changed (like two alchemical substances) by the ongoing process of therapy.

With this in mind, it is time to begin exploring what a nonlinear eco-psychoanalysis, one drawing on the philosophy of Deleuze and Guattari and the sciences of complexity might look like. We begin in the next two chapters with the contributions Deleuze and Guattari can make to traditional psychoanalytic approaches to the 'animal', whether they are found in dreams or reality, in phobias or symptoms, in literature or film, on the couch or in the forest. This will open up new opportunities for critical ecopsychoanalytic research into our ambivalent relationship with the world of nature, and the animal.

Chapter 9

Becoming-animal and horror

Through its depiction of the male monster as creature, the horror film addresses the issue of the animal in a more direct way than possibly any other film genre. It collapses the boundary between human and animal and in doing so raises the possibility of the end of civilization. Like woman, the animal is defined as 'other' in relation to the symbolic order of law and language and as such signifies the ruin of representation.

(Creed 2005: 201–202)

Horror and the primal uncanny of nature

This unheimlich [uncanny] place, however, is the entrance to the former Heim [home] of all human beings, to the place where each one of us lived once upon a time and in the beginning . . . the unheimlich is what was once heimisch, familiar; the prefix 'un' is the token of repression.

(Freud 1919: 245)

The word ecology comes from the Greek word oikos, meaning 'home' or 'a place to live' . . . German zoologist Ernst Haeckel coined the term oikologie, defined as the relationship of an animal to both its organic and its inorganic environment, particularly those plants and animals with which it comes in contact.

(Waffle 2003)

As we have seen regarding science fiction, cinema can be a crucial medium through which we can explore the ecological imagination and our civilization's complex and often highly ambivalent relationship with the other-than-human world. According to Steven King (1981: 131), 'horror films serve as a barometer of those things which trouble the night thoughts of a whole society', and from what we have learned about eco-anxiety from the psychological study of climate change, we might expect our night thoughts to be troubled by our relationship with the other-than-human world. This might be one place to study and explore that 'other side' of Wilson's (2003) biophilia, i.e. biophobia.

The horror genre is also an area where traditional psychoanalytic film theory has long been a dominant force (e.g. Clover 1993; Creed 1993, 2005, 2009; Day 1985; Schneider 2009; Twitchell 1988) and so there are potentially fruitful symbioses to be formed for an ecopsychoanalytic investigation into our relationship with nature, in particular through a study of the animal metamorphosis theme in horror. Drawing on psychoanalytic approaches along with Deleuze and Guattari's (2003a) theory of 'becoming-animal', we shall attempt to generate an ecopsychoanalytic perspective exploring how such film motifs relate to our civilization's ambivalent relationship to the other-than-human world, the 'primal uncanny' of nature. In Chapter 10, we shall see how this is related to the psychoanalytic clinic in the form of animal phobias, and attempt to open out a more ecological vision for psychoanalysis itself.

Horror can be understood as an exploration of many of our deepest anxieties such as persecutory anxiety – annihilation, fragmentation, destruction, dismemberment, engulfment, retaliation, biting/clawing, poisoning; depressive anxiety – guilt, destroyed inner world, death (see Klein 1987); sexual anxieties of different psychosexual stages – e.g. castrating father, engulfing mother; and the fear of madness itself (Fuery 2003). On the latter Winnicott (1974: 104) wrote that the 'fear of breakdown is *the fear of a breakdown that has already been experienced*', which Searles would connect to desires and fears of a psychotic merger with nature. Like Winnicott (1999), Deleuze and Guattari (2003b: 201–227) see much of what passes as sanity as a partly defensive structure:

> We require just a little order to protect us from chaos . . . That is why we want to hang on to fixed opinions so much . . . preventing our 'fantasy' (delirium, madness) from crossing the universe in an instant, producing winged horses and dragons breathing fire . . . *in flight from flight* . . . we reterritorialize on anything available.

There is a large existing psychoanalytic literature on horror going back to the first generation of analysts, from Freud's (1919) 'The Uncanny' and Marie Bonaparte's (1971) work on Poe, to Otto Rank's (1989) *The Double* and Ernest Jones' (2008) *On The Nightmare*, which as well as nightmares provides an early analysis of witches, vampires, werewolves and the Devil, the last of which was also dealt with by Freud (1991) himself. The obvious connection between horror themes and psychoanalytic ones leads Andrew Tudor (1997: 55) to claim that '*the genre itself invokes psychoanalytic considerations, at times borrowing its imagery from the symbolic apparatus of dream interpretation.*' But it works both ways. Not only does horror seem to have learned lessons from psychoanalysis, psychoanalytic accounts themselves often have the feel of horror films:

> Castration, sexual abuse, perversity, excrement, bestiality, animal phobias – Freud's case histories read like horror movies. They are alive with fears – fear of being bitten by a horse, fear of wolves, fear of having one's bowels gnawed by a rat . . . *Interpretation of Dreams* is permeated with anxieties and phobias of a similarly horrific nature – nightmares of falling, suffocation, ghosts, dead children, burning skin, urine and feces, people with bird's heads, snakes, men with hatchets, decapitations. In Freud's view, nightmares were the result of wish fulfillment from the unconscious, deadly dreamscapes of sexual origin in which he included murder and cannibalism.
>
> (Creed 2009: 188)

For William Day (1985: 177), the 'striking parallels between Freud's thought and the Gothic fantasy' are more than just coincidence in that they have 'a common, or at least related, origin.' Day suggests that both can be understood as 'responses to the problems of selfhood and identity, sexuality and pleasure, fear and anxiety as they manifest themselves in the 19th and early 20th centuries' (ibid.). From this understanding we could suggest that Klein fits better with today's more fragmented, schizoid world, with its more primitive and destructive horror films (zombie, gore, etc.) than the 'Gothic' neurotic forms which stalk Freud's *oeuvre*.

From an ecopsychological perspective, it is interesting that horror very often uses the theme of blurring the lines between human and animal (a line which in any case is already an artificial one, as Darwin taught us, and molecular biology has confirmed) or alien, and the anxieties and fascination connected with this. This theme is explored in numerous films such as *The Wolfman* (Johnson 2010), *The Fly* (Cronenberg 1986), *The Metamorphosis of Mr. Samsa* (Leaf 1977), *An American Werewolf in London* (Landon 1981) and *Alien* (Scott 1979) as well as of course in mythology and fairy tales. It is also striking how many of the 'horror' themes Creed found in Freud in the above quote involved animals, whether concerning merger (bestiality, people with bird's heads) or persecutory fear (biting horses, gnawing rats, devouring wolves, snakes). Barbara Creed's feminist psychoanalytic approach is particularly relevant here, and in particular her book on male monsters, *Phallic Panic: Film, Horror and the Primal Uncanny* (2005).

For Freud (1919), the uncanny is related to what is frightening, to what arouses dread and horror, to what should have remained hidden but has come to light, to the return of the repressed. In her discussion of Creed's book on male monsters, Anneke Smelik (2007) writes: 'The true horror of the male monster lies in its alignment with that which is most strange to it and that should be expelled from phallic masculinity: woman, animal and death' which signify 'the ruin of the male symbolic order.' Creed's 'primal uncanny' is that which blurs the boundaries between man/woman, living/ dead, and human/animal. Woman, animal and death, the 'other side' of phallic masculinity, are all associated in our culture with nature.

An ecopsychoanalytic perspective could therefore use such analyses to explore deep aspects of our subjectivity as it is structured by (and structures) our culture, to see what this reveals about the unconscious emotions affecting our relationship to the 'otherness' of nature. For Creed (2005: 16), the primal uncanny 'lives inside and alongside all forms of human subjectivity and signification. In the horror film it gives voice to its hidden and troubling presence through the body and being of the male monster, who is essentially a creature of the primal uncanny.'

Drawing on Kristeva's (1982) concept of abjection, Creed (2005: 17) argues that 'the male monster is made monstrous when he enters the domain of woman, animal and nature' via transformation into 'a menstrual or blood monster (vampire), a womb monster (mad doctor), a cannibalistic animal (werewolf), a blood beast (slasher) or a woman (transgendered monster).' Man also becomes monstrous when 'he seeks to destroy woman and her reproductive identity (the ripper) or deny woman as the origin of life and one who reminds him of his debt to the feminine and animal worlds (the mad doctor)' (ibid.).

One aspect related to the uncanny which Freud (1919: 44) describes and many theorists refer to is connected to the theme of castration:

> Dismembered limbs, a severed head, a hand cut off at the wrist, as in a fairy tale of Hauff's, feet which dance by themselves . . . all these have something peculiarly uncanny about them, especially when, as in the last instance, they prove capable of independent activity in addition. As we already know, this kind of uncanniness springs from its proximity to the castration complex.

Rather than the Freudian castration complex, Deleuze and Guattari (2003a: 149) might point, here to their idea of the 'body without organs' (see Chapter 13), or we could draw on Žižek's (2003) Lacanian commentary on their work in terms of 'organs without bodies', where he follows Lacan's appropriation of Kleinian 'part-objects' as 'partial objects', parts not necessarily connected to any whole.

Creed suggests that Freud greatly overestimated the importance of castration in his analysis, arguing instead that the ultimate referent to that strange combination of desire and dread which makes up the uncanny seems to be the idea of a return to mother's body, often appearing in substitute forms as dreams of a house or a familiar place or space or country, but especially as that fear which so haunted Edgar Allan Poe (1998) – being buried alive. 'To some people the idea of being buried alive by mistake is the most uncanny thing of all,' writes Freud (1919: 244). 'And yet psycho-analysis has taught us that this terrifying phantasy is only a transformation of another phantasy which had originally nothing terrifying about it at all, but was qualified by a certain lasciviousness – the phantasy, I mean, of intra-uterine existence.'

This uncanny theme of the grave-womb, studied by Creed (1993) as part of the monstrous-feminine, was also explored by Bakhtin (1984: 21) in his study of carnival, where he discusses the more productive, positive side of the grave-womb and its relation to the 'lower bodily stratum'. Freud (1919: 244–245) also suggested that this phantasy lay behind why 'neurotic men declare that they feel there is something uncanny about the female genital organs'.

> This *unheimlich* place . . . is the entrance to the former *Heim* . . . of all human beings . . . the place where each one of us lived once upon a time and in the beginning . . . there is a joking saying that 'Love is home-sickness' . . . whenever a man dreams of a place or a country and says to himself 'this place is familiar to me . . .' we may interpret the place as being his mother's genitals or her body. In this case too . . . the *unheim-lich* is what was once *heimisch*, familiar; the prefix '*un*' is the token of repression.
>
> (ibid.)

However, what for Freud are merely symbolic stand-ins for the mother's body may themselves point in a quite direct way to something even more 'primal': the idea of a return to the Earth itself, the home from which we come. Ecology, the study of this home ('*oikos*') concerns not so much the place itself but rather the web of relationships it constitutes. In horror at times these connections are more explicit. In *The Fly*, Jeff Goldblum transforms into a giant insect after a machinic rebirth in a metallic womb. In Dracula films, after each blood-feast the monster returns to his coffin containing ancient earth.

Bakhtin, the grave-womb, and the grotesque body of comedy

According to Creed (2005: 21), Freud saw woman and death as related. For Freud: 'Death is not something that exists apart from life, inhabiting a separate space of its own; death is an integral part of life.' In his dream of 'The Three Fates' Freud (1900a: 204–205) described his difficulty in accepting that 'we were all made on earth and must therefore return to earth.' He described how it was his mother's demonstration of the 'blackish scales of epidermis' produced by rubbing her hands together that led him in 'astonishment' to acquiesce to the belief that 'Thou owest Nature a death' (ibid.). The connection between woman, death and nature in the theme of the grave-womb is more explicit in Freud's (1913b: 301) 'The Theme of the Three Caskets', where he refers to the three aspects of the mother for man: 'the mother herself, the beloved one who is chosen after the pattern, and lastly Mother Earth who received him once more.'

These relations become more clear when we turn to Bakhtin's work on the grave-womb in his study of degradation and carnival reversals:

> 'Downward' is earth . . . an element that devours, swallows up (the grave, the womb) and . . . an element of birth . . . (the maternal breasts) . . . while in their purely bodily aspect, which is not clearly differentiated from the cosmic, the upper part is the face or the head and the lower part is the genital organs, the belly, and the buttocks . . . To degrade is to bury, to sow, and to kill simultaneously, in order to bring forth something more and better.
>
> (1984: 21)

This symbolism is ancient, with faeces/shit playing an important, productive and joyful role in Rabelais' carnivalesque prose (Rabelais 1965: 597), which Bakhtin takes as his starting point for his own exploration. The importance of shit in this universe of meaning is of being *intermediate between earth and body*, as something relating the one to the other' (Bakhtin 1984: 175). Shit here thus acts as a kind of transitional object (Winnicott 1999), occupying the *intermezzo* (Deleuze & Guattari 2003a). 'It is also an intermediate', Bakhtin (1984: 174) continues, 'between the living body and disintegrating matter.'

For Bakhtin, these themes are related to his distinction between the grotesque body and the classical body, the former being 'ambivalent and contradictory . . . ugly, monstrous, hideous from the point of view of "classical" aesthetics, that is, the aesthetics of the ready-made and completed' (Bakhtin 1984: 25). In contrast to the bourgeois classical body which is 'isolated, alone, fenced off from other bodies' (Bakhtin 1984: 29), the grotesque body is not cut off from the world.

> [I]t is unfinished, outgrows itself, transgresses its own limits. The stress is laid on those parts of the body that are open to the outside world, that is, the parts through which the world enters the body or emerges from it, or though which the body itself goes out to meet the world . . . the open mouth, the genital organs, the breasts, the phallus, the pot-belly, the nose.
>
> (Bakhtin 1984: 26)

This important work of Bakhtin, which has clear affinities to the work of Deleuze and Guattari, is crucial in that it is precisely in the grotesque, the horrific, the images of the grave-womb, that Freud's uncanny lies. But it can also entail a more joyful vision of the world, one that celebrates the carnival of life and death, without separating the two poles of becoming. In Creed's analysis of the primal uncanny in horror, this is also the place where animal, woman and nature meet:

> Nature and her prime signifier, the animal, constitutes another border that produces the uncanny, the line between civilized and uncivilized, the self and the non-self. In patriarchal cultures woman is aligned with the animal. Like the animal, woman also has a blood cycle, becomes pregnant, gives birth, sheds afterbirth, lactates, and suckles her young. Many societies erect taboos and cultural prohibitions in relation to the maternal procreative body. Unlike the idealized male body, the female body is not taut, discrete and classical; the female body is unstable. Because of her close alignment with nature and the animal, woman as monster threatens the male symbolic order of law, civilization and language. In the founding myth of Christianity, woman is depicted as aligned to the animal world.
>
> (Creed 2005: 22)

The distinction between classical and grotesque bodies, which Bakhtin puts in a historical and cultural perspective, also relates to the distinction between the isolated ego-self struggling to reach an impossible island-like autonomy, and the ecological self embodying the interdependent values and realities described by ecology and ecopsychology. It is important to note that Freud's uncanny involves a paradox. Due to the fact that it concerns something which is at once frighteningly alien and strangely familiar, it relates to some deep part of ourselves that has undergone repression.

Crucially, the feeling of familiarity is as important as the feeling of strangeness. The 'other' is thus not truly other but a core aspect of the self, it is *extimate*, in the words of Lacan (1992: 139), and it is uncanny *because* there is this feeling of recognition. This again returns us of Bakhtin's (1984: 150) thesis where he writes that once these grotesque images lost their roots with the popular life of carnival, 'the positive and negative poles of becoming (death-birth) are torn apart and opposed to each other in various diffuse images, they lose their direct relation to the whole and are deprived of their ambivalence. They then retain only their negative aspect.'

Comedy and tragedy, which Bakhtin claims were celebrated together up until the time of Shakespeare, were split apart and former grotesque images became either purely obscene or uncanny and terrifying. It is precisely the grotesque images within the category of the frightening that contain the 'special core of feeling' (Freud 1919: 219) recognized as part of the uncanny. Drawing on Bakhtin's (1984) 'history of laughter' it is possible to suggest that the uncanny is something that emerges when carnival, and all that it stands for, becomes repressed. The communal comic origins of carnival became in the Romantic period a kind of 'individual carnival, marked by a vivid sense of isolation' (Bakhtin 1984: 37), a world which would give birth to Hoffmann's gothic horror which in turn forms the basis of Freud's theory of the uncanny.

This connection of the uncanny with something close to the comic gains further support through a comparison between Freud's theory of the uncanny and his study of the comic, described most fully in his *Jokes and Their Relation to the Unconscious* (Freud 1905). For example, Freud's key thesis on the uncanny is that it represents 'that class of the frightening which leads back to what is known of old and long familiar' (Freud 1919: 220). In his joke book, Freud (1905: 340) quotes Melinand's (1895) theory of laughter which also related to the surprising discovery of the familiar: 'What makes one laugh is what is on the one hand absurd, and on the other hand familiar.'

If we turn to other categories of the uncanny we find similar correspondences. For example, Freud (1919: 226) offers Jentsch's view that the uncanny is caused by 'doubts whether an apparently animate being is really alive; or conversely, whether a lifeless object might not really be animate' as seen in the case of 'wax-work figures, ingeniously constructed dolls and automata . . . epileptic fits . . . insanity' all of which evoked 'the impression of automatic, mechanical process at work behind the ordinary appearance of mental activity.' Turning to his work on the comic, we strangely (uncannily) find almost this identical theme given as a key source of the comic, with Freud (1905: 65) explaining that 'the uncovering of psychical automatism is one of the techniques of the comic, just as is any kind of revelation or self betrayal.'

In *The Uncanny* (Freud 1919: 233) we get a hint at how this connection between the comic and the uncanny might work: 'Dolls are of course rather closely connected with childhood life. We remember that in their early games children do not distinguish at all sharply between living and inanimate objects, and that they are especially fond of treating their dolls like living people.' Thus, here we have again something from an earlier period which was *not* originally frightening, becoming uncanny only after it had been repressed. He describes the same sequence in his book on jokes, where he cites Bergson, a crucial influence on Deleuze and Guattari, who 'proceeds by a plausible train of thought from automatism to automata, and tries to trace back a number of comic effects to the faded recollection of a children's toy' (Freud 1905: 222).

The doll is of course the classic example of Winnicott's (1999) transitional object. If culturally we have repressed such 'borderline' phenomena, then their return will be traumatic. If in addition we don't have a place in us to put such things, if our potential space is either too small or crushed under the bombardment of a mass-media culture, then liminal experiences such as these may begin to be felt as uncanny, perhaps in the extreme even annihilating. It seems on a deep level that the comic is related to the uncanny; it is it's other side. When we are in the comic mood, it is still possible to connect ourselves to those things that our alienated state has generally caused us to find uncanny.

It is interesting here to bring in Bakhtin's own comments on masks and dolls/puppets. For Bakhtin, the carnival mask is a kind of transitional object, 'related to transition, metamorphosis, the violation of natural boundaries . . . It contains the playful element of life.' But, in Romanticism 'the mask is torn away from the oneness of the folk carnival concept . . . now the mask hides something, keeps a secret, deceives . . . loses almost entirely its regenerating . . . element and acquires a somber hue. A terrible vacuum, a nothingness lurks behind it' (Bakhtin 1984: 40). With the repression of carnival, the 'comic monster' doll loses its ability to defeat the cosmic terror through laughter, and instead becomes itself a source of terror. In Romanticism, 'the accent is placed on the puppet as the victim of an alien inhuman force, which rules over men by turning them into marionettes' (ibid.). Thus the familiar is turned into terror, the comic into tragedy, and laughter into uncanny horror.

A similar analysis can be applied to other themes of Freud's uncanny, including eyes (Bakhtin 1984: 316; Hyde 1998: 316; Freud 1905: 231), uncertainty (Freud 1919: 233), doubles (Freud 1919: 235–236) and repetition (Freud 1905: 128–129; 1919: 237). In fact, even within the text of *The Uncanny* itself, the harder Freud tries to pin down its meaning the more often comic stories recur, including two different comic ghost stories crammed into the second last paragraph (Freud 1919: 252).

The becoming-animal of the werewolf

> [T]he becoming-animal of the human being is real, even if the animal the human being becomes is not . . . The self is only a threshold, a door, a becoming between two multiplicities. Each multiplicity is defined by a borderline functioning as Anomalous, but there is a string of borderlines, a continuous line of borderlines (fiber) following which the multiplicity changes.
>
> (Deleuze & Guattari 2003a: 238–249)

In terms of the 'primal uncanny', our ambivalent feelings towards nature are connected with the fact that it is something so close to us, but this awareness has undergone a cultural repression. It is interesting for example that children can easily envisage in their books, stories and games becoming wolves, pigs, goats or grasshoppers without the anxiety adults feel when it appears in their art, most typically horror. We only need to think of Max in his wolf-suit in *Where the Wild Things Are* (Sendak 1988) to feel the pleasures in the becoming-animal of childhood. What child has never wanted to be a 'big bad wolf' and huff and puff against all civilized attempts to put up barriers against the wilds of nature?

Horror films' use of animal metamorphoses could then be understood as a kind of social nightmare, the return of the repressed from the ecological unconscious. However, if it remains trapped in this form such representations also serve to reinforce the repression, and embody one of the means by which it is achieved. Creed describes the uncanny effect of the becoming-animal in horror, a theme she relates to the borders we set up and attempt to police between the human and non-human world of nature:

> When man becomes animal, as in werewolf and apeman films, the primal uncanny is invoked. By aligning himself with the side of the feminine and the animal, man sheds his *heimlich* countenance and rapidly becomes *unheimlich* . . . This aspect of the uncanny – of becoming animal, of being unable to distinguish the human self from the animal self – is explored in narratives of metamorphosis and cannibalism, particularly the werewolf film. The monstrous human/animal beast is inherently uncanny . . . because the animal has always functioned as a signifier of the non-human.
>
> (Creed 2005: 24)

The opposition between nature and civilization is often embodied spatially in horror. For example, the contrast between the city and the forest is blurred by the figure of the wolfman, while 'the vampire erodes borders that run between whatever lies above ground and what lies beneath' (Creed 2005: 79). The male vampire, for Creed (2005: 84), 'signifies the primal uncanny through his relationship to the maternal body, to Mother Earth, to death, to woman's blood, and to the mythic association with menstrual rites' as well as representing 'the animal world through his power to metamorphose into a werewolf, bat, rat and other creatures of the night.' There is also an uncanniness in the very repetitiveness of his behaviour, in the need to draw blood, and the need to retreat to the safety of Mother Earth.

From the point of view of our civilization, which Freud simultaneously both represents and challenges, nature is that 'primal uncanny', the other that is actually part of the self. If our current ecological crisis can be understood as a symptom of the repression of Roszak's (1995) ecological unconscious, a project connected as we have seen to the paradoxical 'dialectic of Enlightenment' of Adorno and Horkheimer (2002), then the becoming-animal of horror films can be understood as its nightmare, the return of the repressed of the ecological unconscious.

However, these films point to more than this, in that they show us our desires as well as our fears. Creed (2005: 123) argues that werewolf films 'are subversive in that they point to the fragile boundary between nature and civilization, animal and human.' In doing so they also reflect the 'lure of the uncanny; the desire of the human to return to its primitive origins, which finds its strongest expression in folklore, popular culture, dreams and nightmares.' Animal metamorphosis as expressed in myth, film, literature, art, dreams and phantasy is a key motif for exploring these issues, and according to Creed (2005: 137) signifies 'a deep-seated anxiety over the definition of what it means to be male and human.' Ecopsychoanalysis is interested precisely in how these anxieties, and what it means to be human, are given a particular intensity and form by the ecological crisis.

> The definition of human is, more than ever, intimately bound up with the destruction of the natural and animal world . . . the horror and fantasy film represents the wolf-man as a sympathetic monster precisely because he represents potent characteristics of the natural world that modern man is in danger of losing in his pursuit of progress . . . the wolf-man signifies the ascendancy of nature and the ruin of classic patriarchal masculinity – a configuration that excludes woman, animal and nature. Hence the wolf-man is both terrifying yet immensely appealing.
>
> (ibid.)

Deleuze and horror

> Film, like literature, painting and philosophy itself, is a distinctively embodied thought process.
>
> (Powell 2006: 2)

Anna Powell (2006), in her book *Deleuze and Horror Film*, attempts to challenge psychoanalytic horror film studies with a schizoanalytic approach to the cinema of terror. She suggests that film *is* philosophy precisely through its affective physical impact (Powell 2006: 202), such that 'when the film appears to be over, it continues to run', as our own mind-bodies have become enmeshed with the filmic event, and continue to take the film forward.

Powell's approach to horror is not meant to replace psychoanalytic, gender, Marxist or postmodern approaches with a new Deleuzian ortho-doxy, but is rather designed to be 'complementary rather than oppositional' (Powell 2006: 3). However, while acknowledging the apparent 'fit' between horror film motifs and psychoanalytic 'primal schemata', exploited by Creed and others, she suggests that the 'interrogation of the dominance of psychoanalysis in horror theory is timely' (ibid.). This is timely for psycho-analysis itself, as without a continuous outside challenging its key insights, psychoanalytic orthodoxy always threatens to fall into stagnation. The suggestion that psychoanalytic approaches to nature can be reinvigorated by the Deleuzo-Guattarian critique is a key aspect of my own argument in this book. Such challenges are essential for keeping psychoanalysis vital.

Primarily, according to Powell, a Deleuzo-Guattarian approach to horror involves exploring 'the sensory affect of horror film *as* experience rather than allegory' (ibid.). Through Deleuze and Guattari, 'Psychoanalytic subjectivity is reconfigured . . . as a physical process in perpetual motion . . . aesthetics are viral in nature, being known "not through representation, but through *affective* contamination"' (Powell 2006: 4). By emphasizing that cinematic experience is a corporeal event involving machinic assemblages of image, sound, eye, brain and viscera, Deleuzian film studies problematizes traditional (especially Lacanian) understandings of spectators as a 'disembodied set of eyes'. As Powell writes: 'Our eyes are embedded, and embodied in flesh as only one part of the complex perceptual apparatus stimulated by film' (ibid.). In fact, eyes are an 'extension of our brain; part of the imagination's operations; part of the camera's machinery and part of the "machinic assemblage" of cinema' (ibid.).

In many ways this perspective correlates well with recent attempts to form a neuropsychoanalytic aesthetics of art and film (Holland 2003, 2007; Oppenheim 2005) including also specifically the horror film (Dodds 2011a), as well as more affectively attuned neo-Kleinian psychoanalytic writings. In 'The Monstrous Brain: A neuropsychoanalytic aesthetics of horror?' (Dodds 2011a), I suggested that despite all the talk in psychoanalytic film theory of the 'body' and the 'spectator', virtually no empirical studies have been carried out by psychoanalytically informed researchers on the way actual bodies and actual spectators respond to film, including the gendered spectators so beloved of film theory. The new tools of neuroscience, particularly affective neuroscience and social neuroscience, combined with the rapidly developing theoretical and experimental project of neuropsychoanalysis, can open up new opportunities for experimental research into psychoanalytic film theory. Horror is an obvious place to start as it is above all others a 'body genre', with intense affective engagement being such an integral part of the viewing experience.

Deleuze's approach seems useful here, with the suggestion that the 'spectator does not exist as a separate entity, but is subsumed in the film event *as part of it* . . . The assemblage of viewer and text co-operates a dynamic experiential process of becoming' (Powell 2006: 4). By overcoming divisions between mind and body in the cinematic experience, both neuropsychoanalytic and Deleuzian approaches to film offer a way to overcome some of the binary distinctions between the human and the 'other-than-human'. As Powell (2006: 5) writes, in such an approach we understand that 'we meld and become part of the material technology of cinema in its movement, force and intensity.'

This idea fits well with the theme of ecopsychoanalysis with its emphasis on overcoming destructive dichotomies. However, in its attempt to distance itself from psychoanalytic approaches, Deleuzian writing on cinema like Powell's at times goes too far in the disclaiming of meaning, metaphor and signification. What is left when these areas are abandoned to (traditional) psychoanalytic approaches is a cinematics of style, surfaces, textures, and techniques, without reference to character or narrative. Ideally, from the perspective of this book, both can be usefully employed. How does this approach specifically relate to horror cinema? For Powell

> Horror's frequent undermining of normative perspective by fragmented images and blurred focus operates in tandem with the erosion of the subjective coherance and ego-boundaries of its characters. It also affects the spectator's sense of cognitive control over the subject matter as our optic nerves and auditory membranes struggle to process confusing data. Our projected coherence is undermined as we slide into a molecular assemblage with the body of the film. Formal properties, like the camera shake and blurred images strikingly expemplified by *The Blair Witch Project* [Myrick & Sanchez 1999], intensify this melding. The viewer's sensory participation intensifies by viral infection as the film literally gets inside and sets up home there.
>
> (Powell 2006: 5)

While Powell (2006: 15) at times seems highly ambivalent about psychoanalysis, she finally suggests that a 'borderline lies between psychoanalysis and the deterritorialisation of the "intensive voyage" of schizoanalysis.' It is on this productive line of flight that ecopsychoanalysis makes its *unheimlich* home, between the 'primal archeology' of psychoanalysis and the 'cartography' of schizoanalytic intensity (Powell 2006: 20). In seeking to move beyond representation, schizoanalytic approaches to horror have what Powell (2006: 23) calls 'a micropolitical function to free us from the habitual schemata of representational templates and to start us thinking in new ways', leading to 'new becomings.' New readings of *Psycho* (Hitchcock 1960), for example, explore the 'becoming-bird' of Norman, as well as the more traditional psychoanalytic focus on his 'becoming-mother' (Powell 2006: 24–25).

By excising traditional psychoanalytic approaches to representation and narrative, Powell attempts to 'highlight the contrast between the critical methodologies of schizoanalysis and psychoanalysis' (ibid.). However, the actual experience of film, as she acknowledges, involves 'a fluctuating assemblage of molar and molecular responses that operate an ensemble rather than being divided off artificially' (ibid.). Thus, this divide is partly a temporary tactic, to allow new ways of understanding and becoming to fully emerge, and is not intended to set up a binary division between psychoanalytic and schizoanalytic modes of criticism. In fact, Powell (2006: 25) seeks 'to open up a dynamic interchange by tracing a plane on which they may fruitfully intersect as *"particles* entering into each other's proximity".'

Powell's book is important because it opens up Deleuzain film studies beyond what she calls Deleuze's own 'bourgois' cinematic preferences of the Parisian *cineaste* which she criticizes when discussing the way Deleuze 'disparages the "pitiful twitches and grimaces" and "haphazard cuts" of music videos and refers scathingly to the "bad cinema" of explicit violence or sex . . . [which] "travels through lower-brain circuits"' (Powell 2006: 6). In her book Powell (2006: 9) describes how she 'perversely' applies Deleuzian and Bergsonian approaches to film against the grain of the film narrative, writing that: 'These perversely applied terms include molecularity (genetic engineering); schizoanalysis (dangerous madness); the body without organs (enforced prosthesis); and duration (haunting).'

Turning to our own current topic of interest, the becoming-animal and becoming-monster of horror, Powell (2006: 10) suggests that such trans- formations involve a 'radical re-working of the subject/object binary', a project which 'is central to Deleuzian aesthetics.' Here intense experiences of affect and sensation 'subsume the subject and connect it to the external world in a molecular meld' (ibid.). In particular, in horror film, such becomings involve 'desubjectified affects', the analysis of which can help to explore 'fantasies of transmutation such as the shape-shifting of the feline woman in *Cat People* [Schrader 1982]' (ibid.).

In order to explore the process of becoming in horror, Powell locates this process in Deleuze and Guattari's concept of the 'body-without-organs', in order to provide a new way of looking at 'body horror', and also the theme of the movement-image and the time-image. In terms of the latter, Powell (2006: 11) argues that the 'temporal movements of the horror film are fractured and nonlinear', where the 'past impregnates the present in a haunting which seeks to block the flow of present into future' in such neo-Gothic films as *The Haunting* (Wise 1963) or *The Others* (Amenabar 2001). We shall return to the subject of nonlinear temporalities in Chapter 13.

At moments in her text, Powell comes close to the particular focus of my own book, describing how such intense becomings allow us to re-imagine our relationship with the non-human world. For Powell (2006: 53), 'as well as being the subject matter of myth and modern fiction, becoming-animal has broader philosophical and political implications.' In particular, it has the 'potential to extend human becomings, and can re-think human rela- tions with the natural world' such that our 'fictional engagement in the becomings-animal of fantasy potentialises new connections' (ibid.).

One example she provides of becoming-animal in horror is in the film *Natural Born Killers* (Stone 1994), where 'Mickey has the dangerous force of wild horses and the deadly poison of reptiles.' His body is 'tattooed with snakes and a scorpion', which 'displays and intensifies his own sense of becoming-animal.' Relating to her focus on becoming as offering the potential to extend what it means to be human, and open up new, vital connections, the Navajo shaman figure in the film, in fact, seems to act as a key mediator between the human and 'natural' realms. According to Powell (2006: 54), he thus transforms the protagonists 'protective totem into a vengeful force against them' and refutes 'white culture's split of the human and animal kingdoms.'

As with Creed, for Powell becoming-animal is closely linked to becoming-death. However, the model of death as an 'experience' is very different in her eyes to Freudian Thanatos, and closer to Nietzsche's eternal return. Death here is 'the deterritorialised circuit of all the cycles of desire' (Deleuze & Guattari 2003a: x) and the work of horror, according to Powell (2006: 52), involves a process of 'schizophrenizing death'.

> By the experience of death here, [Deleuze] intends the 'death of the subject' as it becomes-schizo in intensive states. In the unconscious, the experience of death is common, and occurs 'in life and for life, in every passage of becoming'. Intensive emotions tap into and control the unconscious experience of death. Death is enveloped by every intense feeling and is '*what never ceases and never finishes happening in every becoming*'. As every intensity if finite, and finally extinguished, so 'every becoming itself becomes a becoming-death!' (Deleuze & Guattari 2000: 330).
>
> (Powell 2006: 52)

What is the function of becoming-animal, becoming-anomalous in horror, according to Powell? She writes that:

> Women and men who become with other life-forms are among the anomalies of horror cinema. Inhuman entities possess human bodies. Bodies without souls have non-human life of their own, and spirits without their former bodies become-ethereal. These entities refuse to remain the objects of our aesthetic contemplation and seek to incorporate us into the dynamic hybrid of their virtual assemblage. We also become with the monsters as mutant spectators. Despite formulaic attempts to restore order at the end of many films, we continue to become long after the film has ended . . . Anomalies subvert fixed notions of subjective wholeness and undermine cultural attempts to maintain self-consistent typological and species norms.
>
> (Powell 2006: 64)

Powell (2006: 66), drawing on Deleuze and Guattari's use of Bergson's 'vitalism', views 'becoming as the continual process of movement and flux', or as Deleuze and Guattari (2003b, cited in Powell 2006: 66) put it: 'We are not in the world, but we become with the world . . . We become universes. Becoming plant, animal, molecular, becoming zero.' In this process, according to Powell (ibid.), 'subject/object boundaries meld in molecular fusion to form new entities' and 'we experience other, more dynamic, ways of being in the world.' Furthermore, becomings are always molecular, because 'the animal, flower or stone one becomes are molecular collectivities, haecceities, not molar subjects, objects or forms that we know from the outside and recognise from experience, through science or by habit' (Deleuze & Guattari 2003a: 275, cited in Powell 2006: 67).

Becoming-animal, whether in folk tales or horror films, suggests 'that the boundaries of humans and other life-forms are not fixed, but that molecular flows conjoin singularities' (ibid.). As Deleuze and Guattari (2000: 107) write: 'Man does not become wolf, or vampire, as if he changed molar species; the vampire and the werewolf are becomings of man . . . proximities between molecules in composition, relations of movement and rest, speed and slowness between emitted particles.' Thus for Powell (2006: 67), 'vampires, werewolves and other hybrids of horror fantasy are inspirational images of human affinity with beasts, plants and minerals.'

One of the great examples of this in horror is Ripley's transformation in *Alien Resurrection* (Jeunet 1997). After being brought back to life through her DNA and genetically fused with the alien, her status as neither fully human nor alien undermines species difference, even more than her character was seen in critical discussions of the earlier films as undermining gender differences. 'Our clear-cut identification with Ripley as hero in the previous films is undermined' as we 'are no longer sure of her nature, her powers or her agenda' (Powell 2006: 75). In addition, the film 'conveys a strong mutual desire for reconnection between the artificially spliced blocs, alien and Ripley, drawing them irrevocably together' (ibid.). This is most clearly demonstrated when Ripley is taken to witness the alien queen (her 'child') giving birth to her 'grandchild'.

> Ripley is both more than and other than human. [She] . . . wallows with luxuriant abandon in a sea of tentacles. These resemble writhing rats' tails of dark brown glistening wetness, with an abject, excremental aspect. She is briefly engulfed as the mass pulses in and out, then emerges to spread her limbs with easy confidence. Without fear, she sinks back into it by folding up her arms with a rhythm and speed corresponding to those of the pulsing mass itself.
>
> (ibid.)

While acknowledging the obvious psychoanalytic themes within such a scenario, Powell instead gives it a more 'Deleuzian' angle, which foregrounds *mise-en-scène* and affective becoming:

The embrace in which the alien carries Ripley to the queen is both repellent and beautiful. Its special quality is enhanced by strobe-lighting and stirring incidental music, with drum rolls and horns in a lyrical melody. These effects combine with slow editing rhythms to enhance a sense of timelessness as the two beings embrace . . . Her facial expression is blissful and serene. The alien, however, has a blunt, eyeless head, with a protuberance resembling an insect's proboscis . . . After witnessing the birth, Ripley lies down wet, slimy and relaxed. She appears to have undergone a new form of birthing herself, which acknowledges her own amorphous nature. In a parallel process, the alien baby is becoming-human . . . [with a] familiarly humanoid skull, torso, teeth and deep blue eyes. It is this human coding that will further complicate our feeling when Ripley destroys the infant for the sake of human survival in the 'happy ending' imposed by the generic template.

(Powell 2006: 76)

Staking her position in opposition to Creed's use of abjection theory, Powell (2006: 77) argues that a schizoanalytic reading 'opens up a more radical possibility' compared with what she calls, perhaps a little unfairly, 'Creed's negative Kristevan reading', and suggests that the 'intimacy between anomalous life-forms need not constrain the viewer to horrified repulsion, but initiates more congruent becomings.' I am not so certain that such a radical disjunction exists between these two important theoretical approaches, a fact which Powell also at times appears to acknowledge.

Furthermore, according to Powell, this scene in *Alien Resurrection* is especially 'Deleuzian', first due to its emphasis on the 'speeds and slow-nesses' of different life-forms, with Ripley as coordinating between human and alien rhythms. Second, the wordless nature of the scene opens up a 'non-verbal communication and intensive rapport' (Powell 2006: 77). Kleinian and object relations psychoanalysis has much to say about this level of affective communication, especially compared with the Lacanian discourse Powell criticizes, although this is not the place to explore this in detail. Finally, this sequence, which is quite separate stylistically from the rest of the film, is full of what Deleuze (1989: 6, cited in Powell 2006: 77) calls '"opsigns" and "sonsigns" . . . "pure optical and/or sound situations" that break from the narrative drive of the movement/action image to pro-duce a "moment of pure contemplation" for the spectator . . . [which] suspends the narrative flow and enables speculative thought.'

With such concepts, Deleuzian approaches open up new ways to think about not only film, but also the complex and often non-symbolic systems of communication involved in the psychoanalytic process itself (see Chapter 12). Along with 'opsigns' and 'sonsigns', another non-representational sign system in film is the 'tactisign'. In the film *Suspiria* (Argento 1977), for example, Powell (2006: 142) writes that 'Argento incorporates as many senses as possible to frighten and arouse the spectator in their experience of the film event' so that 'tactility is evoked with a particularly repellent force.' Tactisigns bring us closer to non-linguistic semiotics such as stigmergic communication, which we shall turn to later in the context of complexity theory approaches to ecology (see Chapter 11).

> Tactisigns reveal 'a touching which is specific to the gaze' . . . Horror films appeal to the sensorium as comprehensively as possible by including haptics in their range of affects. The tactisign is pivotal in scenes of sensory horror and enhances the potency of their virtual presence. As well as terrfying sights and sounds, we perceive affective textures of a repellent nature, such as the wet stickiness of human blood, or the slimy trail of the monster.
>
> (Powell 2006: 142)

Powell seems ambivalent about the relation between schizoanalysis and psychoanalysis. At times she appears to suggest that we would do better to abandon psychoanalysis for the new worlds that Deleuzian film theory opens up, but at other times she appears to find the two approaches potentially complementary. Powell (2006: 208) ends her book on a more conciliatory note, stating that: 'I advocate an interstitial, transverse connection across existing approaches, whilst continuing to push the frontiers of the field further. I feel it is definitely time to re-draw the map of existing horror Film Studies, but not to kick it away just yet.' Such an 'intersititial, transverse connection across existing approaches' is precisely what the ecopsychoanalytic project requires, and it is increasingly necessary in our ecologically precarious world.

The strange ecology of the rhizome

As a counterpoint to animal metamorphosis in horror, it is interesting to return to *Avatar's* theme of transformation into a non-human body. Should this be seen in a positive light for ecopsychology? Unlike its treatment in horror, this more positive transformational experience could be seen as blurring the anthopocentric divide between human and non-human, undoing the artificial barriers between ourselves and nature, a blurring not experienced as anxiety-provoking but joyful and liberating. Or should we read it as taking our alienation from our bodies even further? – the whole film was a computer-generated virtual world; and even within the film the hero's body is a virtual body, manipulated externally by remote control by plugging his human body into a machine and allowing it to starve, shrivel and lose contact with life.

The backdrop to the film suggests the whole story could be read as a phantasy of the hero to escape the limitations of his wheelchair-bound body.

Like the experience of computer game players who lose themselves in their 'avatars' which exist only in the digital realm, when this develops into an internet addiction the individual can end up spending more and more of their life online, with little time left over for their embodied 'offline' self. As viewers to the spectacle in the cinema we are also immersed in a virtual world in a similar way to the characters of the film who go inside their avatar. Žižek (2010) seems to suggest a similar 'virtual' approach to the film:

> [A]lthough *Avatar's* narrative is supposed to take place in one and the same 'real' reality, we are dealing – at the level of the underlying symbolic economy – with two realities: the ordinary world of imperialist colonialism on the one hand, and a fantasy world, populated by aborigines who live in an incestuous link with nature, on the other. (The latter should not be confused with the miserable reality of actual exploited peoples.) The end of the film should be read as the hero fully migrating from reality into the fantasy world – as if, in *The Matrix* [Wachowski & Wachowski 1999], Neo were to decide to immerse himself again fully in the matrix.

We feel awe at the beauty of a nature 'even better than the real thing', and perhaps our very pleasure frightens us. So is *Avatar* a liberation or a trap? It is not a question of either/or but of both/and. An ecopsychological approach would be to bring out the radical potential in such film motifs, using Deleuze and Guattari to help to escape the cultural binaries which Freud identified (or identified with). In their challenge to hierarchical tree-branch 'arborescent' thinking, Deleuze and Guattari use what they call a rhizomatic approach:

> [U]nlike trees or their roots, the rhizome connects any point to any other point . . . it brings into play very different regimes of signs, and even nonsign states. The rhizome is reducible neither to the One nor the multiple . . . It has neither beginning nor end, but always a middle (*milieu*) from which it grows and which it overspills . . . When a multiplicity of this kind changes dimension, it necessarily changes in nature as well, undergoes a metamorphosis . . . the rhizome is an acentered, nonhierarchical, nonsignifying system without a General and without an organizing memory or central automaton, defined solely by a circulation of states.
>
> (Deleuze & Guattari 2003a: 21)

It is no accident that in both cases ('arborescent' and 'rhizomatic') an ecological metaphor is used (we might also recall the complex systems of virtual roots, trees and rhizomes in *Avatar* itself), although Deleuze and Guattari would not use the word metaphor, but would suggest that a single very real 'abstract machine' operates simultaneously on various registers. But they are wary of replacing one arborescent binary with another binary (trees versus rhizomes):

> [T]here is no dualism . . . There are knots of arborescence in rhizomes, and rhizomatic offshoots in roots . . . there are despotic formations of immanence . . . just as there are anarchic deformations in the tran-scendent system of trees, aerial roots, and subterranean stems . . . We invoke one dualism only in order to challenge another . . . Each time, mental correctives are necessary to undo the dualisms we had no wish to construct but through which we pass.
>
> (Deleuze & Guattari 2003a: 20)

Deleuze and Guattari's approach of 'becoming-animal' distinguishes 'Oedipal' animals (pets, domesticated animals) from 'State' or mythic animals (British Lion, American Eagle) and from 'nomadic', wild or pack animals, a distinction they claimed Freud was blind to when he kept reducing the Wolf Man's wolf to the 'analyst's bow-wow' (Deleuze & Guattari 2003a: 29). Whatever else Freud found in the Wolf Man's elabor-ate dreams, phantasies and symptoms, he could not see the wolves but only a totemic substitute for the father, or displacements of the primal scene.

Deleuze and Guattari introduced the concept of 'becoming-animal' in the 'Becoming-Intense, Becoming-Animal, Becoming-Imperceptible . . .' chap-ter of their *A Thousand Plateaus* (2003a) with a discussion of the 1971 horror film *Willard* (Mann 1971). Willard is a social misfit with an intense relationship to 'his' (Oedipal) rat Ben and the many other rats he 'collects' and fails to kill at various moments in the film. He eventually rejects these rats in favour of a human relationship with a woman, at which point he plans to poison Ben and the other rats, which respond with an attack; the rat pack (swarm) devours Willard, the film ending with a close up of Ben's face.

The horror of such scenes represent a kind of reversal of the scapegoat process, where the animal to be abjected instead abjects the human subject. Representing the transversal, interstitial approach discussed by Powell, this concept of the scapegoat helps to relate Deleuze and Guattari's becoming-animal with Creed's (1993) use of Kristeva's (1982) abjection in relation the primal uncanny in horror films as revealed in animal metamorphosis.

> A first expiatory animal is sacrificed, but a second is driven away, sent out into the desert wilderness. In the signifying regime, the scapegoat represents a new form of increasing entropy in the system of signs: it is charged with everything that was 'bad' in a given period, that is, everything that resisted signifying signs . . . everything that was unable to recharge the signifier at its centre and carries off everything that

spills beyond the outermost circle. Finally . . . it incarnates that line of flight the signifying regime cannot tolerate . . . an absolute deterritorialization.

(Deleuze & Guattari 2003a: 116)

Deleuze and Guattari's 'becoming-animal' is not a matter of imitation, metaphor, analogy or even identification, but a new way of being-becoming where heterogeneous elements recombine into new assemblages ('becoming O . . . becoming a walker' being so different from 'learning about walking', [Bion, cited in Meltzer 1994: 467]). They consider in this context the becoming-wolf of Freud's Wolf Man, the becoming-horse of Little Hans, the becoming-orchid of the wasp, the becoming-wasp of the orchid and the resulting wasp-orchid 'assemblage' (see also Dodds 2011b).

While Deleuze and Guattari do not use this term we could understand their work, their 'geophilosophy' (Bonta & Protevi 2004), as moving from 'becoming-animal' to 'becoming-ecological', where the individual animals becomes less important than the heterogeneous relationships and becomings they embody in the trans-individual and sub-individual web of connectivities. Rather than anthropomorphism, Deleuze and Guattari (2003a: 318–319) call us into a 'geomorphism', 'the becoming-earth of the bird through song . . . in which the bird is in rhizomatic communication with the earth' creating 'melodic landscapes' through constant processes of deterritorialization-reterritorialization.

Just as Deleuze and Guattari emphasize the deterritorialization of organs, in this case the bird's mouth being deterritorialized from its original function of eating in order to free it to sing, Bateson (2000) has a similar argument, which in addition draws on the emphasis in chaos theory of recursive loops:

The distinction which is commonly drawn between perception and action, afferent and efferent, input and output, is for higher organisms in complex situations not valid . . . every item of action or output may create an item of input . . . percepts may in some cases partake of the nature of output. It is no accident that almost all sense organs are used for the emission of signals between organisms. Ants communicate by their antennae; dogs by the pricking of their ears.

(Bateson 2000: 292)

Here, the 'home' of ecology is no longer a fixed, stable place of habitation but becomes a strange ecology, an uncanny ecology deterritorialized into a web of animal-human-plant-mineral-climatic assemblages or 'haecceities' (Deleuze & Guattari 2003a: 263). Utilizing Deleuze & Guattari's work in terms of an ecopsychoanalytic approach to animal metamorphosis allows us to move beyond the anthropomorphized animal as projection of human traits to the pleasures (and anxieties) that such a transformation entails – making 'it impossible to say where the boundary between the human and animal lies' (Deleuze & Guattari 2003a: 273) – and to the potential of new creative connections with the ecological webs beyond.

Chapter 10

The zoological imagination

> That day, the Wolf-Man rose from the couch particularly tired. He knew that Freud had a genius for brushing up against the truth and passing it by . . . Freud knew nothing about wolves, or anuses for that matter. The only thing Freud understood was what a dog is, and a dog's tail . . . Who is ignorant of the fact that wolves travel in packs? Only Freud. Every child knows it . . .
>
> (Deleuze & Guattari 2003a: 26–28)

Psychoanalysis and the phobic animal object

Deleuze and Guattari's critique of psychoanalysis opens up a potential path towards an ecopsychoanalysis which may offer new ways of engaging with the other-than-human world, a task made more urgent by the current ecological crisis. If our ambivalent relationship to the animal can be explored in the horror genre, perhaps we can also gain some insights into the psychoanalysis of animal fears and phobias, which stand at the origin of clinical psychoanalysis.

Turning to the famous painting by Freud's notorious patient, the 'Wolf Man' (*Plate 1*), we can reflect on the importance of the *ecological imaginary*. Our minds, films, and artwork are populated with flora and fauna of all kinds, some related to 'real' existing lifeforms in the external world, some more the product of phantasy and ecologies of the inner world. For Deleuze and Guattari (2003b: 184) 'art is continually haunted by the animal.' As an expression of our inner space, these creatures stalk our dreams, our stories, our myths, our fairy tales, our films, and our nightmares. They also influence the way we deal with the nature around us.

Environmental philosopher Paul Shepard (1995: 36) notes that '[g]ames and stories involving animals serve as projections for the discovery of the plurality of the self.' There is an ecology of the inner world, an ecology of mind (Bateson 2000), just as there is an ecology of nature, and perhaps we can also speak here of a cinematic or aesthetic ecology. The ecopsychologist

Plate 1 Drawing by the 'Wolf-Man' (Sergei Konstantinovitch Pankejeff 1886–1979)

Source: Freud (1918: 30) © The Freud Museum, London

Stephen Aizenstat (1995: 96) goes as far as to argue that these inner creatures 'are real, have imaginal weight and body, and act in dreams on behalf of themselves . . . the elephant that appeared in my dream last night was fully engaged in his activity, not mine . . . the dream image is an independent presence in a broader psychic ecology, a dreamscape where there is room for many beings to 'walk around' and be regarded by one another.' This eco-Jungian approach to 'minding the animal psyche' is developed further in the spring 2010 issue of the journal *Spring* (Carter 2010).

What do we see when we look at the Wolf-Man's picture? What did Freud see? Well, we know what Freud saw, as he was only too happy to keep repeating to his patient: Daddy, penis, castration. He didn't see the wolves, the other-than-human world. According to Deleuze and Guattari (2003a: 29), Freud domesticates the wolves into an 'Oedipalized wolf or dog, the castrated-castrating daddy-wolf, the dog in the kennel, the analyst's bow-wow.' The wolves themselves were irrelevant, it was only what the wolves stood for that was important. The same goes for the tree, snow, plants, and earth depicted in the painting. This is central to Deleuze and Guattari's critique of psychoanalysis. Whatever the patient says, Freud says Oedipus. Whatever emerged from the Wolf-Man's ecological imagination, Freud replies: 'mummy, daddy, me.'

'Nature', 'the environment'. What are the status of these things? Are they merely a backdrop for our projections? A tapestry where we can weave our phantasies and dreams? Resources to be extracted? Psychoanalysis and group analysis have done fascinating and crucial work on otherness in race and gender (Dalal 2002; Clarke 2003; Seshadri-Crooks 2000; Chodorow 1991; Clover 1993), but we have hardly even begun to think about the other-than-human world. Much of our current 'thinking' in this area can therefore be said to take place in the medium of film, art, and literature.

What do we see when we look at this picture? Even the question is perhaps too anthropocentric. Perhaps we should instead ask: what do the wolves see when they look at us? Genosko (1993) points out that 'wolves often engage humans and non-humans in that way, in what has been called a ceremonial exchange, the conversation of death' and suggested that even within his own framework 'Freud might have made use of this theme . . . since the intense stare thrown by the wolves at the dreaming child fits in well with the threat of castration that Sergei feared.'

Wolves, rats and horses: Totemism and Oedipus

> Nothing . . . can be of greater value to a young person than a love of nature and understanding of natural science, particularly animals . . . In my case they were wolves.
>
> (The 'Wolf-Man', cited in Gardiner 1972: 315–316)

Genosko (1993) explores this area in some depth in 'Freud's Bestiary: How Does Psychoanalysis Treat Animals?' and uses Deleuze and Guattari's critique of Freud to open up a what he calls a 'zoological vision' for psychoanalysis. He notes that Freud's interpretation of the scene depicted in the painting involves a reversal so that it is the (human) child 'who takes the active position while other non-human animals assume the passive role of being looked at' (Genosko 1993: 614). We can see this move as representative of the repression of the ecological unconscious (Roszak 1995) in Western culture, as 'Freud initiates a unidirectional communication appropriate to the collector: animals are exhibited, mounted or unmounted, in display cases . . . a full-blown domestication of the scene' by which the 'gaze of the other is emptied . . . becoming an unseeing look like that of zoo animals, objects for our inspection' (ibid.). As we might expect, Deleuze and Guattari (2003a: 28) are highly critical:

> It was already decided from the very beginning that animals could serve only to represent coitus between parents, or, conversely, be represented by coitus between parents. Freud obviously knows nothing about the fascination exerted by wolves and the meaning of their silent call, the call to become-wolf. Wolves watch, intently watch, the dreaming child; it is so much more reassuring to tell oneself that the dream produced a reversal and that it is really the child who sees dogs or parents in the act of making love.

Animals stalk the pages of Freud's other case histories too. Erst Lehrs had his own 'becoming-animal' by being transformed through his case history into the 'Rat Man'. He was also given the nickname 'corpse-bird', and Freud in addition labelled him 'an osphresiolagniac, a snooping and sniffling dog-child' (Genosko 1993: 603). Freud himself is well known for his love of dogs. Even in the last year of his life, dying of cancer, when the Royal Society took the unprecedented step of going to Freud's house so he could become a Fellow, he still went regularly to visit his beloved dogs in quarantine. Even his famous love of science did not elevate the Royal Society, that most august of scientific bodies which includes Darwin and Newton, above his love for his dogs. Freud's dogs were also often an important 'third party' during his analytic sessions with patients – which is often not commented on – which inevitably affected the transference.

Creed (2005: 123) argues that in his description of the Wolf-Man, 'Freud focused too much on his own phantasy of the castrating paternal figure and not enough on his fearful folkloric counterpart, the wolf-man in sheep's clothing.' Deleuze and Guattari (2003a: 38) hold a similar position when they write: 'The trap was set from the start . . . Talk as he might about wolves, howl as he might like a wolf, Freud does not even listen; he glances at his dog and answers, "It's daddy."' This is true of Freud's work more generally, where both animal totems and animal phobias involve (at least for the boy) a substitute for the Oedipal father. In 'The Return of Totemism in Childhood' in *Totem and Taboo*, Freud (1913a: 187, cited in Genosko 1993: 608) claims that animal phobias are 'a very common, and perhaps the earliest, form of psychoneurotic illness occurring in childhood.'

For Freud, the 'ambivalent attitude (to obey and transgress) toward the two principal taboos of totemism' (Genosko 1993: 608) is identical to 'the primal wishes of children and the two crimes of Oedipus.' Thus 'both animal phobias and totemism are parallel "products" of phylo- and onto-genetic complexes' (ibid.). By displacing anxieties relating to the father onto an animal substitute, the animal turns into an object of both fear and fascination, such as Litte Arpád's chickens (Ferenczi 1952), and Little Hans' horse:

> Hans identified with his father by becoming a horse, trotting around the household, neighing, wearing a nosebag, and, finally, by biting his father and behaving in a fearless way toward him [Freud 1909a: 213–214] . . . Ferenczi's 'Little Chanticleer' expressed that he had become a chicken in numerous ways . . . cackling and crowing . . . singing songs with chicken themes, play[ing] with toy fowls by 'slaughtering' and 'caressing' them.
>
> (Genosko 1993: 608)

The horrific aspect of the horse was explored psychoanalytically in Ernest Jones' classic, *On the Nightmare* (Jones 2008), the cover of which depicts a horse image as part of Henry Fuselli's 1781 painting *The Nightmare*. It is also utilized well in film, for example in Yamamura's (2007) award-winning animation of *Franz Kafka's A Country Doctor*, where the uncanny movements of the horses, which move between catatonic freezes and extreme velocities, occur in the film in moments related to themes of death or sexuality. Such movements can be understood using Deleuze's (1986, 1989) concepts of the movement-image and the time-image in the workings of cinema. The rhythm of editing, flow, and freezing in cinematic technique is followed by the viewer's eyes and neuro-affective systems which form a coupled machine, following a similar flickering movement, thus turning 'virtual movement-images into actual intensive moments' (MMU 2005). Yamamura's horses gaze at the country doctor in key moment of the film with vacant, staring, lidless eyes, to powerful filmic effect.

According to Deleuze and Guattari, both art and consciousness itself operate on what they call a 'plane of immanence' whose 'perpetually shifting motion is replete with speed and slowness, floating affects', an immanent process which 'produces desire' and 'possesses density as well as surface, moved by the non-subjective powers of affect' (MMU 2005). The movement of Yamamura's horses can further be understood as switches between the intensive speed of paranoia and the frozen time of the catatonic (Deleuze & Guattari 2000). The becoming-animal of horror and of patients' phobias, as well as art and cinema, involves a plunge into the (potentially creative) chaos of the swarm (Bonabeau *et al.* 1999; Sole & Goodwin 2000; Camazine *et al.* 2001; Marks-Tarlow 2008), a plunge with its joys and its terrors.

Creed (2005: 130) connects the totemism described by Freud to the cannibalism theme of the werewolf myth: 'Through metamorphosis and cannibalism, the wolf-man points to the "instability of the paternal metaphor" and the failure of civilization.' For Creed, 'the cannibal meal of the wolf-man myth symbolizes a pact not with civilization but with nature and wilderness' (ibid.). The wolfman is an uncanny creature of the *inbetween*, being neither man nor beast, and belonging to neither city or forest while dwelling in both. Thus, cannibalism constitutes an attack on the meaning of civilization, but in a way which suggests that the Hobbesian state of nature 'is not a real epoch chronologically prior to the foundation of the City but a principle internal to the city' itself (Creed 2005: 132). Therefore, the werewolf, as myth, as film motif, and as clinical phantasy and phobia refers not simply to the return of repressed desires which the City has blunted and eroded, but rather:

> [T]he wolf-man signifies those indeterminate, uncanny animal spaces necessary to the creation and definition of their opposite: the familiar, civilized human city. The wolf-man does not leave the town or city to live in exile in the forest; he is compelled to live as an exile within the city . . . he engages in a modern reworking of murder and the totem meal which celebrates not the emergence of civilization but its end.
>
> (Creed 2005: 133)

The zoological imagination and the multiplicity of the pack

From an ecopsychological perspective one important aspect of Freud's descriptions of animal phobias is an implicit suggestion that psychological health involves overcoming such ambivalences, enabling a return to the previously 'excellent relations' with animals. Freud (1913a: 187) writes that sources for animal phobias are both 'textual', where animals are 'only known to the child from picture books and fairy tales', and 'contextual' through direct contact, depending on the geographical location of the child: 'horses, dogs, cats, less often birds, and with striking frequency very small creatures such as beetles and butterflies.'

> Freud . . . said little about prephobic relations except that children identify strongly with non-humans . . . seen as 'full equals' . . . he showed little interest in the positive relations that may again obtain

between children and animals after a successful analysis . . . it was not only that Hans 'ceased to be afraid of horses.' Rather, he recovered the pleasure that they gave him and the wonder they inspired . . . Psychoanalysis . . . [has] a certain unrealized potential in reconstituting the relations between children and animals.

(Genosko 1993: 610)

According to Genosko (1993: 606) Freud lacked a true 'zoological vision', and suggests that 'Deleuze and Guattari isolate a trend in Freud's thought, one that he would not allow to emerge even though he had stumbled upon it: the becoming-animal of analysands'. At the heart of Deleuze and Guattari's (2003a: 240) critique of Freud is their claim that 'the only kind of animals that psychoanalysis understands are individuated animals, family pets, sentimental, Oedipal animals each with its own petty history, "my" cat, "my" dog.'

For them, Freud could not allow the Wolf-Man to become Wolf and join the pack but instead worked to 'Oedipalize' the Wolf-Man's animal becomings, rather than recognising that 'every animal is fundamentally a band, a pack' (Deleuze & Guattari 2003a: 239). We might use these terms to read the change in Willard's (Mann 1971) relationship with Ben from an Oedipalized pet into a member of the pack or swarm. According to Deleuze and Guattari (2003a: 6–7): 'Rats . . . are rhizomes. Burrows are too, in all their functions of shelter, supply, movement, evasion, and breakout when rats swarm over each other.'

In this context it is interesting to mention an anecdote Felix Deutsch relates concerning Freud's pet dog Liin: 'Have you ever heard of a dog with a false pregnancy? . . . this dog is a psychosomatic case, indeed! . . . I am almost inclined to say: That can only happen to the dog of an analyst!' (Jones 1957: 226–227). Ernest Jones (1957: 15) described Freud's love for his dogs as 'evidently a sublimation of his very great fondness for young children which could no longer be gratified', but this episode suggests something more than an anthropomorphic projection but rather what we might call an *anthropomorphic projective identification* in that the animal-recipient comes to actually embody what we place there. This kind of inter-species psychodynamic process remains virtually untheorized among psychoanalysts. And yet, as Genosko (1993: 615) writes, we can't 'escape the fact that canines are mediated semiotically for anthropomorphism as meaning-vehicles "designed" for human families.'

Genosko claims that there is also something missing in Deleuze and Guattari's own 'zoological vision', in particular their assumption that every animal is fundamentally a pack, providing the zoological example of the solitary pair, also found in some 'pack' animals. This may however be missing the point of the pack, or the swarm, which is that every individual is also fundamentally a pack, an emergent product of the self-organization of the swarm (Bonabeau *et al.* 1999; Camazine *et al.* 2001; Dodds 2008), forming 'assemblages' both below and above the level of the individual human subject. As Deleuze and Guattari (2003a: 29) write, 'Freud tried to approach crowd phenomena from the point of view of the unconscious . . . he did not see that the unconscious itself was fundamentally a crowd.'

> The wolves will have to be purged of their multiplicity . . . Seven wolves that are only kid-goats. Six wolves: the seventh goat (the Wolf-Man himself) is hiding in the clock. Five wolves: he may have seen his parents make love at five o'clock, and the roman numeral V is associated with the erotic spreading of a woman's legs. Three wolves: the parents may have made love three times. Two wolves: the first coupling the child may have seen was the two parents *more ferarum*, or perhaps even two dogs. One wolf: the wolf is the father, as we all knew from the start. Zero wolves: he lost his tail, he is not just a castrater but also castrated . . . The wolves never had a chance to get away and save their pack.
>
> (Deleuze & Guattari 2003a: 28)

Deleuze and Guattari (2003a) are '*Anti-Oedipus*' because they feel psychoanalysis uses Oedipus to constrain flows, to limit and cage the pack, as a process of stratification. For them, 'psychoanalysis . . . subjects the unconscious to arborescent structures, hierarchical graphs, recapitulatory memories, central organs, the phallus . . . not only in its theory but also in its practice . . . it bases its own dictatorial power upon a dictatorial conception of the unconscious' (Deleuze & Guattari 2003a: 17). Freud's 'Oedipalizing' method is thus an example of what Deleuze and Guattari call strata or stratification:

> Strata are Layers . . . They consist of giving form to matters, of imprisoning intensities or locking singularities into systems of reson-ance and redundancy, of producing upon the body of the earth molecules large and small and organizing them into molar aggregates. Strata are acts of capture . . . like 'black holes' or occlusions striving to seize whatever comes within their reach. They operate by coding and territorialization upon the earth . . . The strata are judgments of God . . . (but the earth, or the body without organs, constantly eludes that judgment, flees and becomes destratified, decoded, deterritorialized).
>
> (Deleuze & Guattari 2003a: 40)

The Wolf-Man's contextual pack included other wolves, other dogs, including Anna Freud's Alsatian 'Wulf', which also looked like a wolf (Freud 'paternally . . . entered into Anna's fondness for her dog' [Gay 1995: 540]). The Wolf-Man also described his father's estate as 'wolf country' with 'primeval forests, ponds, lakes . . . a remnant of nature still untouched by man. There were wolves in the forests . . . every summer a wolf-hunt was organized by the peasants of adjacent villages' which included 'Siberian wolfhounds, white borzoi, staghounds' and even a specially trained golden eagle (Gardiner 1972: 12).

Genosko (1993: 617) claims that these animals are harder to place in Deleuze and Guattari's domestic/wild dichotomy, or even their Oedipal/State/Nomad triad, and suggests instead the need for the concept of a 'mixed pack . . . a loose pack, an unpacked pack that reflects the diversity of pack phenomena, and includes wolves banished from their pack, dog-wolf hybrids, lone hunters that become pack-like only during the mating season, solitary pairs, and so on.' In many way's this fits better with Deleuze and Guattari's overall thrust, which is to move beyond the binaries they are forever reconstituting despite themselves. Genosko's aim is to 'open the associative chain to animals not so easily subsumed under the morals of castration and father surrogate' while avoiding romanticizing the schizo-swarm by 'treating the Wolf-Man as a psychotic whose body was trampled by wild packs and teeming swarms, a body . . . that never turned off, that never stabilized, and knew no decathexis' (ibid.).

One example Genosko gives of such a pack is from Freud's (1921: 130) *Group Psychology* which includes a reference to Schopenhauer's porcupines, which need to huddle together for warmth only to be driven away by their spines. For Genosko (1993: 627), these represent a mixed pack that is 'stable in its instability, inasmuch as it composes and decomposes itself in its very unfolding.' Here we could make a 'complexity' reading of the pack, the 'strange' pack as a dissipative structure, a fractal pattern with complex interminglings of order and disorder arising from far-from-equilibrium interactions at the 'edge of chaos' (Kelso 1995).

Complexity theory allows us to open up the ecological vision of psychoanalysis through the gap prised open by Deleuze and Guattari's critique. What is the primal animal in psychoanalysis' zoological imagination? Genosko (1993: 629) argues that it is not the wolf, the rat, or even Freud's bow-wow, but the Sphynx. That strange 'hybrid' animal is already a pack, already the becoming-human of the animal and the becoming-animal of the human.

Art and nature

Freud's (1930: 92) civilization derives from the taming of the wild, including the wild within, which 'enabled humankind to exterminate many wild animals and breed others as domesticates' but 'caused for Freud a fundamental disruption in the relations between the primal sons and their father surrogate, the totem animal (and other animals as well)' (Genosko 1993: 628). Freud (Freud & Einstein 1933) went beyond discussing the domestication of animals to claim that civilization is primarily about the 'domestication' of humans (see also Totton 2011). Taking Deleuze and Guattari's 'becoming-animal' seriously would mean that true psychological health requires a restoration of our ecological vision, the rediscovery of a joyful connection with the animal less burdened by the weight of Oedipal meaning, and an opening up of the becoming-wild, the becoming-ecological of Freud's domesticated, discontented civilization. There are always spaces of wildness, or what Deleuze and Guattari call 'lines of flight'.

Art and film, including the horror film's use of animal metamorphosis, are important places to explore this, to engage with the return of the repressed, the primal uncanny (Creed 2005) of the ecological unconscious. Marcuse (1998: 172) saw art and the 'aesthetic dimension' as one of the few remaining reservoirs of the pleasure-principle, where we can imagine other worlds, other reality principles. Similarly, for Genosko:

> Freud drew a parallel between the mental realm of fantasy . . . and nature reserves. The former is split off from the reality principle; the latter are established against the civilizational forces that seek to dominate nature . . . Freud suggests to us that fantasies that are informed by wildness and wilderness . . . produce a crack in the near-ubiquitous domestication of life, and thus provide for the child's and adult's enchantment of their relations with animals.
>
> (Genosko 1993: 629–630)

As Deleuze and Guattari (2003b: 186) write, 'if nature is like art, this is always because it combines these two living elements in every way: House and Universe, *Heimlich* and *Unheimlich*, territory and deterritorialization, finite melodic compounds and the great infinite plane of composition.'

Part IV

Nonlinear ecopsychoanalysis

Nobody likes it when you mention the unconscious, . . . because when you mention it, it becomes *conscious*. In the same way, when you mention the environment, you bring it into the foreground . . . it stops being the environment. It stops being That Thing Over There that surrounds and sustains us.

(Morton 2007: 1)

Climate, wind, season, hour are not of another nature than the things, animals, or people that populate them, follow them, sleep and awaken within them . . . animal-stalks-at-five-o'clock.

(Deleuze & Guattari 2003a: 263)

Chapter 11

Entering the nonlinear world

> The most important task today is . . . to learn to think in the new way.
> (Bateson 2000: 468)

> Chaos Physics and Complexity Theory . . . underlie much of Deleuze's thought, its autopoietic capacities reveal themselves at states 'far from equilibrium' . . . These capacities are hidden at a state of equilibrium, and yet it is exactly this state . . . that in 'traditional science' is regularly taken as *the* characteristic and essential feature of matter. Thus strategies of slowing down, stabilizing, and homogenization of matter result in an account of matter as passive, chaotic, and 'stupid' – a mere 'mass' or object to be 'informed' by an outside spirit, force, subject, or God.
> (Herzogenrath 2009: 6)

Fractals and phase space

> Clouds are not spheres, mountains are not cones, coastlines are not circles, and bark is not smooth, nor does lightning travel in a straight line . . . Nature exhibits not simply a higher degree but an altogether different level of complexity . . . The existence of these patterns challenges us to study forms that Euclid leaves aside as being formless, to investigate the morphology of the amorphous. Mathematicians have . . . chosen to flee from nature by devising theories unrelated to anything we can see or feel.
> (Mandelbrot 1983: xiii)

Throughout this book we have referred to the importance of complexity theory in helping to provide a new framework for thinking through our current crisis, along with the philosophy of Deleuze & Guattari. It is now time to begin to enter this nonlinear world, initially through the concepts of *fractals* and *phase space*. The latter represents all possible states of a system, which can be defined by its *attractors* (introduced in Chapters 2 and 3) and its *dimensions*, which 'represent the "degrees of freedom", or relevant ways of changing' the system (DeLanda 2006: 29).

In Deleuze and Guattari an *abstract machine*, or *virtual diagram*, is the phase space portrait which 'lays out what an assemblage can be made out of and what it can do, not just in its current state, but in future states as it enters into becomings or transformative relations with any of the other assemblages it can reach by virtue of inhabiting a "plane" allowing for mutual interaction' (Bonta & Protevi 2004: 48). The same 'diagram' can apply to a number of different registers (e.g. social, biological, psychological, ecological, geological) and is thus for them more than a metaphor. Deleuze and Guattari derive their concept from Gregory Bateson (2000: 76–77), that most 'transversal' of scientists, who wrote that when 'we compare a social problem with a problem of animal differentiation, we are at once provided with a visual diagram in terms of which we may be able to talk a little more precisely.'

This book suggests that the nonlinear swarm may well help to provide the diagram we need now. It is best visualized through *fractals* (Mandelbrot 1983), which are geometric structures in fractional dimensions. How long is the British coastline? This does not have a conventional answer as it all depends on scale. The line you see on a map is not correct because the closer you go the more irregularities you see, and thus the longer the line becomes. In fact, coastlines have a dimension of 1.42, being more than a line (one dimension) but not yet a surface (two dimensions). There are other fractals that are intermediate between two dimensions (surfaces) and three dimensions (volumes). One example, from Patrzalek (2010), is that for human chromosomes, 'the basic architecture . . . is tree-like; every chromosome consists of many "mini-chromosomes", and therefore can be treated as fractal', with dimensions (D) of 2.34. Fractals can in theory exist in up to n dimensions, although mostly here as 'mathematical objects'. Fractals provide a new way of thinking about nature, and can be found on all scales, from the structure of our lungs, to the branching of trees, the patterns of ant trails, interconnected river systems, or stock market fluctuations.

The *Mandelbrot set* is sometimes referred to as the 'thumb-print of god'. It is infinitely complex (you could continue zooming for ever), but is produced through a remarkably simple (one-line) mathematical equation, which has the property of *recursivity* where the product of the equation feeds back into itself in a never-ending series of iterations (Guastello 2004). The boundaries of the chaotic (or strange) attractor, discovered by Lorenz in 1963, are fractal in shape, and fractals have the property of being self-similar at all scales, with repetitions never precisely identical, where the whole set seems to reappear (almost) at various different levels of magnification, as we see from the successive zooms into the Mandelbrot set in *Plate 2* (up to 60,000,000,000 times magnification), which on an ordinary monitor represents a set with a diameter of 24 million kilometres. For an animated version of a similar zoom sequence see Zom-B (2010). More recently three-dimensional versions of the mandelbrot set, called mandelbulbs (Topia

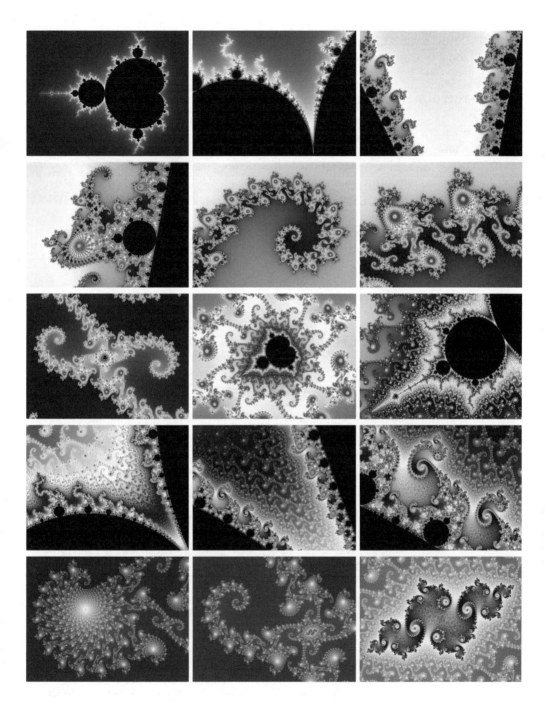

Plate 2 The Mandelbrot set. Successive zooms up to 60,000,000,000 times magnification

Source: Adapted from Beyer (2003)

2010), have been created, which looks set to capture our imagination for some time to come.

Introducing the swarm

> The emerging picture of a human agent as a swarm of competing interests shaped by evolutionary forces is hard to reconcile with our traditional sense of ourselves as conscious egos or souls or selves, willing our intentional actions by free decisions that must issue from our private sanctuaries in the mind.
>
> (Dennett 2003: 219)

> [I]nsect is closer, better able to make audible the truth that all becomings are molecular.
>
> (Deleuze & Guattari 2003a: 308)

Complexity theory is made up of a cluster of fascinating concepts with important relevance to ecology and ecopsychoanalysis. Here we will explore some of the conceptual planes (Deleuze & Guattari 2003b) these concepts occupy, and show their rhizomatic interconnectedness. Much of the material below comes from the study of social insects, the results of which have been applied to a variety of other complex systems, ranging from brains to societies to swarm robotics. *Swarm intelligence* points to a new form of thinking, which may help us in our current crisis – our becoming-insect. As Bonabeau *et al.* (1999: 122) write

> At a time when the world is becoming so complex that no single human being can really understand it, when information (and not the lack of it) is threatening our lives, when software systems become so intractable that they can no longer be controlled, perhaps the scientific . . . world will be more willing to consider another way of designing 'intelligent' systems, where autonomy, emergence and distributed functioning replace control, preprogramming and centralization.

Social insects 'are capable of generating amazingly complex functional patterns in space and time', despite the fact that 'they have limited individual abilities and their behavior exhibits some degree of randomness' (Bonabeau *et al.* 1999: 206). These structures were initially understood through an anthropomorphic model where 'individual insects were assumed to possess a representation of the global structure to be produced and to make decisions on the basis of that representation', however this proved to be false; rather '*Insect societies . . . are organized in a way that departs radically from anthropomorphic models*' (ibid., emphasis added). As Deleuze and Guattari (2003a, 2003b) point out, the 'anthropomorphic model' doesn't do justice to human subjects either.

Self organization (SO) and stigmergy

> Self-organization is a process in which pattern at the global level of a system emerges solely from numerous interactions among the lower-level components . . . the global pattern . . . is an emergent property of the system, rather than a property imposed on the system by an external ordering influence . . . [E]mergent properties are features of a system that arise unexpectedly from interactions among the system's components . . . In a school of fish . . . each individual bases its behavior on its perception of the position and velocity of its nearest neighbors, rather than knowledge of the global behavior of the whole school . . . an army ant . . . bases its activity on local concentrations of pheromone laid down by other ants rather than on a global overview of the pattern of the raid.
>
> (Camazine *et al.* 2001: 8)

Self-organization (SO) involves structures formed 'through interactions internal to the system, without intervention by external directing influences' (Camazine *et al.* 2001: 7) and thus provides a way of studying Deleuze and Guattari's 'assemblages', formed through intensive processes, incorporating material flows from a wide range of 'registers'. SO involves 'the possible existence of several stable states (multistability)' with structures emerging 'by amplification of random fluctuations' (Sole & Goodwin 2000: 151), with dramatic changes occurring at bifurcation points. SO allows us to 'arrive at a collective-level description of social insects in terms of nonlinear dynamics and emergent phenomena', where 'order out of individual chaos emerges through simple interactions between units' (ibid.). The *multiple interactions* essential to SO can also be achieved by a single individual ant where 'trail-following events can then interact with trail-laying actions' (Bonabeau *et al.* 1999: 11).

SO is a general pattern-forming process found in many seemingly disparate systems such as 'sand grains assembling into rippled dunes, chemical reactants forming swirling spirals, cells making up highly structured tissues . . . fish joining together in schools . . . a raiding column of army ants, the synchronous flashing of fireflies . . . the complex architecture of a termite mound . . . lichen growth, pigmentation patterns on shells, fish and mammals (Murray 1988; Meinhardt 1995), and the ocular dominance stripes in the visual cortex of the macaque monkey brain (Hubel & Wiesel 1977)' (Camazine *et al.* 2001: 7–8).

Here we come to one of the 'regimes of signs' Deleuze and Guattari (2003a: 140–142) refer to, allowing rhizomes to self-organize out of assemblages of living (e.g. rats, termites) and non-living matter, the latter including, for example, the 'bits of dirt and fecal cement that make up the termite mound' (Bonabeau *et al.* 1999: 18). The concept of *stigmergy* or *sematectonic communication* was developed by Pierre-Paul Grasse (1982–1986) to describe indirect communication through the environment in insect societies, where termite nest-building is coordinated, not by individual workers, but by the nest itself. Each action performed by a termite modifies the stimulating configuration of the nest, triggering further actions by other termites. Eric Bonabeau (cited in Small 2010) has described it as 'a profound concept, the consequences of which are yet to be explored'.

Grasse further distinguishes between *quantitative stigmergy* which occurs when 'a stimulus of a certain intensity is transformed into the same stimulus with a higher intensity' and *qualitative stigmergy*, where 'a stimulus is transformed into another, qualitatively different, stimulus as a result of the building activity of the insect which may in turn release a different response from other insects' (Camazine *et al.* 2001: 58). Sematectonic communication or stigmergy is relevant to Deleuze and Guattari's (2003a: 68) emphasis on a-signifying communication and signalling and Bateson's (2000) understanding of the environment as part of mind, which he sees as immanent to the feedback arcs which don't necessarily start and finish within our skin. In the case of a man cutting a tree with an axe we can see stigmergic processes at work that Bateson would call 'mental':

> Each stroke of the axe is modified or corrected, according to the shape of the cut face of the tree left by the previous stroke. This self-corrective (i.e. mental) process is brought about by a total system, tree-eyes-brain-muscles-axe-stroke-tree . . . [which] has the characteristics of immanent mind . . . What is transmitted around the circuit are transforms of differences . . . a difference which makes a difference is an *idea*. But this is *not* how the average Occidental sees the sequence of tree felling. He says, 'I cut down the tree' . . . invoking the personal pronoun . . . restricting mind within the man and reifying the tree. Finally the mind itself becomes reified by the notion that, since 'self' acted upon the axe which acted upon the tree, 'self' must also be a 'thing'.
>
> (Bateson 2000: 315)

Similarly, Bateson describes a walking stick as part of the mind-system of a blind man (while he is using it), forming in Deleuze and Guattari's (2003a) terminology a man-stick assemblage. From a systems perspective, 'the stick is a pathway along which differences are transmitted . . . so that to draw a delimiting line *across* this pathway is to cut off a part of the systemic circuit which determines the blind man's locomotion' (Bateson 2000: 318).

Stigmergy is a path towards complexity. As a termite colony grows, 'starting from a single unhelped foundress, more and more stimuli are likely to appear . . . forming a richer and richer stimulatory environment . . . thereby inducing new types of behavior (Bonabeau *et al.* 1999: 207). Construction is therefore a *'morphogenetic process*, during which past construction sets the stage for new building actions' (ibid.). Stigmergy can sometimes get started using *templates* 'in the form of environmental physical or chemical heterogeneities' (ibid.) and in some species the body of the queen herself (see also the weaver bird *Ploceus cucullatus*, in Camazine *et al.* 2001: 56). This process is highly suggestive from the point of view of psychoanalysis, where the internalized maternal object forms the nucleus or template around which the psyche begins to emerge and cohere into that complex nonlinear dynamic structure we call self, involving constant iterative internal and external feedback with mental, social and natural ecologies.

Like fractals, stigmergy is therefore a *recursive* process whereby 'stimuli provided by the emerging structure itself . . . guide further activity' (Camazine *et al.* 2001: 23).

> Stigmergy is effective for coordinating building activity over great spans of space and time. The structures built by social insects . . . are often thousands of times larger than the builders and require many lifetimes to complete. Stigmergy also eliminates the need for individuals to be equipped with an inherited image or mental blueprint of the nest.
>
> (Camazine *et al.* 2001: 58)

Decentralized control

> To these centered systems, the authors contrast acentered systems . . . in which communication runs from any neighbor to any other . . . and all individuals are interchangeable, defined only by their state at a given moment such that the local operations are coordinated and the final, global result synchronized without a central agency . . . The solution without a General is to be found in an acentered multiplicity possessing a finite number of states with signals to indicate corresponding speeds . . . this kind of machinic multiplicity, assemblage, or society rejects any centralizing or unifying automaton as an 'asocial intrusion'.
>
> (Deleuze & Guattari 2003a: 17)

SO is characterized by *decentralized control* and decision making, pointing to a radically different way of thinking about mind, systems, and societies, which is more ecological, anarchical, and rhizomatic. According to Bonabeau *et al.* (1999: 328) 'a social colony is a decentralized system composed of cooperative, autonomous units that are distributed in the environment.' SO involves two distinct information pathways. *Signals* are shaped by natural selection to convey information (for example ant trails formed from chemical pheromones), unlike *cues* (such as deer trails formed through repeated trampling) which are non-organic forms not acted on directly by evolution (Lloyd 1983; Seeley 1989b, cited in Camazine *et al.* 2001: 59–60). This enables non-living structures not shaped by natural selection to be incorporated into the feedback loops Bateson calls mind in a unique architecture of information flow.

> A school has no leader . . . in schools containing thousands of fish it is inconceivable either that one supervisory individual could monitor everybody's position and broadcast the moment-by-moment instructions needed to maintain the school's spatial structure, or that individual fish within the school could monitor the movements of the leader and follow accordingly. Coherence is achieved, instead, by each fish gathering information only about its nearest neighbors and responding accordingly . . . Fish do not have time to gather more than momentary impressions of the movement patterns of their nearest neighbors before they must act.
>
> (Camazine *et al.* 2001: 22–23)

Decentralized pathways include communication that is individual-individual (whether animals, cells or robots), group-individual (through signals and cues), or via the environment (stigmergy), which together 'provide the essential means of interaction among the components in a self-organizing system' (Camazine *et al.* 2001: 60). The ant colony can therefore be characterized as a *dense heterarchy* where 'higher levels affect the lower levels' and 'induced activity in the lower units feeds back to influence the higher levels' with any member 'likely to communicate with any other' (Wilson & Holldobler 1988: 65) in a highly interconnected structure.

> If a network is densely connected, this implies that the network is *not* set up in a hierarchical manner like the partitioned hierarchies of human armies and factories, in which instructions flow down parallel independent groups of members through two or more levels of command . . . *the highest level of the heterarchy is the whole membership . . . the queen is not at the head of the heterarchy.*
>
> (Wilson & Holldobler 1988: 67, emphasis added)

DeLanda (2005: 93) calls such rhizomatic organizations *meshworks*, which occur at all levels of the three ecologies (see Chapter 13). There are clear *cybernetic* problems with central authority because it requires 'an effective communication network among individuals' and places 'formidable, if not impossible, burdens of information acquisition, processing, and transmission on the leader, especially if the group is large and the pattern being built is far larger than any individual group member" (Camazine *et al.* 2001: 64).

> [In] a colony of *Macrotermes* termites . . . group size can exceed a half million individuals and the construction is some ten million times more massive than any of its builders. Even in smaller groups of animals such as beavers, extensive complex habitats may be modified over many generations . . . natural selection has favored a decentralized, self-organizing approach to pattern formation rather than relying on the 'direct intervention of some kind of "little architect" or "construction demon"'.
>
> (ibid.)

As Bateson writes (2000: 444): 'We do not live in the sort of universe in which simple lineal control is possible. Life is not like that.'

(Radical) emergence, complexity, and nonlinear dynamics

> [W]hat would thinking be if it did not constantly confront chaos? . . . chaos has three daughters . . . the Chaoids – art, science, and philosophy . . . [Each] cut[s] through the chaos in different ways. The brain is the junction – not the unity – of the three planes.
>
> (Deleuze & Guattari 2003b: 208)

Emergence is an essential component of swarm intelligence and SO. 'Squareness', for example, is impossible to find in any one line of the square, but is an emergent property of a particular *relationship* among the four component lines. With half a million termites, or the virtually infinite number of interactions possible between neurons in the human brain, the complexity (and unpredictability) of the system becomes immense. The relationship between the higher-level properties and lower-level components is nonlinear and complex.

As Sole and Goodwin (2000: 18) write: 'Self-organizing behavior emerges unpredictably in systems at different levels' with emergent properties which 'provide the recognition that nature can be creative while denying the occurrence of miracles.' In order to describe emergent properties beyond the quantum level, Silberstein (1998) uses the term *radical emergence*, in which he includes *consciousness* (the psychoanalyst would of course extend this to the *unconscious* mind and look at complex iterations between conscious and unconscious mental processes).

Radical emergence, as a property of complex systems, functions as an 'abstract machine' (Deleuze & Guattari 2003a) embodying a structural pattern of relationships occurring in many separate registers, including the psychological, ecological and social of Guattari's (2000) three ecologies. Supporting Deleuze and Guattari's contention that every individual is fundamentally a pack, the mind/brain itself is increasingly being studied through the 'virtual diagram' of the swarm. For example, we can use a single abstract machine to consider how 'memory' needs to be re-conceptualized as something that can occur not only in brains but in collectivities of all types (including social), and even non-living structures such as chemical gradients and the physical environment (involving stigmergy).

> [L]ike the brain, the colony is formed by many individuals in inter-action; individual units can switch from one type of activity to others; they can fail or be removed without any harm to the collective . . . the main differences arise from connectivity: direct contact between indivi-dual ants is a transient phenomenon, whereas synaptic connections among neurons usually have a long lifetime . . . This is partially com-pensated (particularly in large colonies) by the use of chemicals, which can create spatial structures that clearly involve long-term memory effects.
>
> (Sole & Goodwin 2000: 148–149)

In *What is Philosophy*, Deleuze and Guattari (2003b: 210) argue that 'it is the brain that thinks and not man – the latter being only a cerebral crystallization' and that philosophy, art, and science are not 'mental objects of an objectified brain but . . . three aspects under which the brain becomes subject, thought-brain . . . the rafts on which the brain plunges into and confronts the chaos.' To make sense of this we need to see how complexity, especially the complexity required to reach that level we call psychology, emerges from lower-level interactions of the brain.

If we look at a single neuron, it is not very interesting. Similarly: 'One ant alone is a disappointment; it is really not an ant at all' (Sole & Goodwin 2000: 148). However, because of emergent properties produced through self-organization, 'insect societies share basic dynamic properties with other complex systems, such as brains' (Sole & Goodwin 2000: 148). Deborah Gordon (1999) suggests that a similar 'diagram' can be found behind 'molecular interactions within a living cell, the unfolding pattern of cells and tissues in an embryo, and the activity of the neurons that produce the mind.' Any complex system can be viewed as a *morphogenetic cascade*, which can include flows from all registers.

> The nest develops as if it were an embryo, starting as an undiffer-entiated cell, the copularium, which transforms into the royal cell and becomes progressively more complex, with many different parts . . . Complexity unfolds progressively (Bonabeau *et al.* 1998b); increasingly

diverse stimuli . . . facilitate the construction of ever more complex structures. In termites, as the nest grows, air streams develop to become new sources of stimulation for the builders . . . African wildebeest self-organize into large-scale migration fronts comprised of thousands of individuals.

(Camazine *et al.* 2001: 492)

Thus we can see how the scientific apparatus of complexity theory, along with the philosophical perspective of Deleuze and Guattari, can help to provide a meta-perspective from which to connect the various levels of mind, brain, society, ecology and climate, which this book argues is necessary to allow joined-up thinking on the topic of climate change and the psychological dimensions of the ecological crisis.

Chaos

The obsessional appeal of science, based as this is upon the presence of a compulsive need for orderly arrangement and meticulous accuracy, has, of course, long been recognized; but the schizoid appeal is no less definite.

(Guntrip 1995: 249)

Opinion offers us a science that dreams of unity, of unifying its laws . . . Nevertheless, the dream of capturing a bit of chaos is more insistent, even if the most diverse forces stir restlessly within it. Science would relinquish all the rational unity to which it aspires for a little piece of chaos that it could explore.

(Deleuze & Guattari 2003b: 206)

Climate change is sometimes referred to as 'climate chaos' because of the increasingly unpredictable nature of natural systems. A nonlinear perspective is thus crucial for climate science, but it also provides ways of engaging with the crisis on the social and psychological levels. *Chaos theory* shows us, paradoxically, that chaos is far from the opposite of order and structure. This position is consistent with Deleuze and Guattari (2003b: 118) who see chaos as productive and 'defined not so much by its disorder as by the infinite speed with which every form taking shape in it vanishes . . . not a nothingness but *a virtual*, containing all possible particles and drawing out all possible forms.'

Chaos is a feature of all nonlinear systems, which show us that traditional linear approaches to scientific analysis only describe a special case situation within a larger nonlinear world. As Deleuze and Guattari (2003b: 119) write: 'Science is haunted not by its own unity but . . . by all the limits or borders through which it confronts chaos.' We can see this relation between chaos and nonlinearity in Camazine *et al.* (2001: 43):

> As r [randomness] is increased . . . the system not only fails to reach a stable value but also does not oscillate among a number of fixed values. Instead, no pattern occurs . . . The system is said to be chaotic . . . [involving a 'strange' or chaotic attractor] . . . Deterministic chaos is the unpredictable behavior of a nonlinear system within a certain parameter range . . . What is so unexpected, however, is that a deterministic equation can yield unpredictable results.

Chaos is essential for SO as the latter involves the amplification through positive feedback of fluctuations created by phenomena such as 'random walks, errors, random task-switching' (Bonabeau *et al.* 1999: 10). The fact that ants regularly get lost used to puzzle scientists who wondered why this 'inefficiency' wasn't eliminated by evolution; but lost foragers can sometimes find new food sources and therefore randomness enhances the creativity of a system or what Bateson (2000) calls its *ecological flexibility*. This is true in psychological, social, biological and even non-living systems. In the context of swarm robotics, Bonabeau *et al.* (1999: 19) write that: 'Randomness or fluctuations in individual behavior, far from being harmful, may in fact greatly enhance the system's ability to explore new behaviors and find new "solutions".'

Similarly, and counterintuitively, studies of EEGs (electroencephalograms), ECGs (electrocardiograms) and other biorhythmic measurements that show *healthy* rhythms have 'greater irregularity (turbulence, complexity)' whereas 'unhealthy systems gravitate toward periodic and simplistic output (Goldberger *et al.* 2002; Kauffman & Sabelli 1999)' (Guastello 2004). Chaos also plays a crucial role in brain dynamics, an area increasingly explored by *neuropsychoanalysis* (Grigaby & Stevens 2000).

We can also see examples from birds of what Deleuze and Guattari (2003a) call the territorializing effects of the familiar. Sole and Goodwin (2000: 138) explain how 'chaotic [brain] dynamics (as shown by the observed strange attractors) represented the normal state when the animal was attentive' but that 'these attractors underwent dramatic changes when some familiar odor was introduced' resulting in much more ordered neural fluctuation. The spatiotemporal pattern 'exhibited a well-defined stable structure . . . characteristic for the specific odor' (ibid.).

On the emotional level, Jaak Panksepp (2004), a pioneer of affective neuroscience and neuropsychoanalysis (Solms & Turnbull 2003; Stora 2007), argues that the basic emotion systems in the mammalian brain form *attractor landscapes* involving vast assemblages of neurons operating at far-from-equilibrium states. Similarly, Skarda and Freeman (1987: 161–195) see chaos 'as an emergent property of intrinsically unstable neural masses.' This chaos is also creative, in that it 'continually produce[s] novel activity patterns' (Sole & Goodwin 2000: 138) and thus provides a souce of flexibility in the system (Bateson 2000). Paradoxically the nonlinear processes of chaos give rise to stability by allowing the system to creatively adapt to environmental change, something increasingly urgent in our current crisis.

This same virtual diagram has been used to approach phenomena as far apart as organizational behaviour (Dooley 1997) and communication dynamics within families (Pincus 2001). As Guastello (2004: 6) writes: 'The general principle is that the organism is a complex adaptive system, and that the turbulence or complexity in its behavior allows for the broadest range of adaptive responses.' With chaos, biology is no longer the 'bedrock' on top of which separate psychological and social worlds form, because the brain is itself formed through nonlinear interactions with the world, culture and experience (Edelman 2006).

We can understand more fully the function of chaos through its border with more stable states, a region called the *edge of chaos*. Living systems attempt to balance themselves on the fractal border zone between stability and instability which provides maximum ecological flexibility, producing the *dissipative system* of life. Dissipative systems are open systems in constant reciprocal interaction with and adaptation to their environments and exist at far-from-equilibrium conditions where they can maintain themselves within a dynamically ordered structure. In ant colonies, for example, it has been noted that at a critical density 'random individual activations become able to propagate through the whole colony, but the density is low enough to prevent activity from remaining a long time in the system' (Sole & Goodwin 2000: 164). This is a fundamental challenge to long-held Western philosophical and scientific views on the relation between order and chaos as order arises from chaos in a specific scientific sense.

Keslo's (1995: 26) work suggests that the brain itself 'is a self-organizing, pattern-forming system that operates close to instability points, thereby allowing it to switch flexibly and spontaneously from one coherent state to another . . . By living near criticality, the brain is able to anticipate the future, not simply react to the present.' This can also be understood as a dynamic interplay between Deleuze and Guattari's (2003a) deterritorialization/territorialization systems in constant flux. A system poised at the edge of chaos is described by Deleuze and Guattari as a 'rhizome' or 'consistency', in contrast to 'stratas' which are linear homeostatic systems involving negative feedback loops which damp out fluctuations and return quickly to a stable point.

According to Bonta and Protevi (2004: 37) while 'stratified "organisms" force their organs to serve the system of which they are parts . . . consistencies have changing virtual realms: they amplify diversity by virtue of positive feedback loops.' They warn however that 'successful consistencies are always dampened by negative feedback loops to avoid a suicidal explosion – the fascist war machine lacks precisely this "instinct for self-preservation"' (ibid.). Returning to the language of complexity theory, Camazine *et al.* argue that:

> With such self-organization, environmental randomness can act as the 'imagination of the system', the raw material from which structures arise. Fluctuations can act as seeds from which patterns and structures are nucleated and grow. The precise patterns that emerge are often the result of negative feedback provided by these random features of environment and the physical constraints they impose, not by behaviors explicitly coded within the individual's genome.
>
> (Camazine *et al.* 2001: 26)

Swarm intelligence: Nomadic war machines

Army ants don't build stable territorialized nests, but instead form 'bivouacs', 'temporary clusters of half a million ant bodies packed together' (Schneirla, cited in Sole & Goodwin 2000: 165). These break up and start to swarm once the light reaches a critical threshold and 'the swarm behaves as a single entity, searching and expanding over space as though guided by some kind of intelligence' (Sole & Goodwin 2000: 150) – a *swarm intelligence*. In the swarm there are interactions between two main levels, the individual level of the ant responding to local information such as the local chemical gradient, and the global level of the whole chemical field. 'These levels are strongly connected, and in fact they cannot really be separated' (Sole & Goodwin 2000: 150), a phenomenon which Hermann Haken (1995) terms 'circular causality'.

Interestingly, studies have shown that the large variation found between swarm patterns in different species can be accounted for without assuming genetic differences; rather, it can be seen as a direct consequence of SO and crucial environmental variations in the distribution of prey (Camazine *et al.* 2001: 282–283).

> For an *Eciton burchelli* raid nearing the height of its development in swarming, picture a rectangular body of 15 meters or more in width and 1 to 2 meters in depth, made up of many tens of thousands of scurrying reddish-black individuals . . . [N]otwithstanding the chaos and confusion that seem to prevail within the advancing mass . . . organization exists, indicated not only by the maintenance of a general direction but also by the occurrence of flanking movements . . . [H]uge sorties of *burchelli* bring disaster to practically all animal life that lies in their path and fails to escape . . . Out of the initial cluster, a raiding

column emerges. The colony starts to walk through the rain forest looking like a giant amoeba magically exploring the forest floor . . . in a purposeful way, up to 1000 square meters a day. Its foraging trails . . . often form complex dendritic structures resembling fractal trees.

(Schneirla, cited in Sole & Goodwin 2000: 165)

Pathologies of the swarm: The collapse of civilizations

We will end this chapter with a hint at some of the dangers this research points us towards. First, from a clinical point of view, it is interesting to note that there can be pathological, aberrant patterns in swarms (Camazine *et al.* 2001: 282). What this research shows is that in a highly complex and interconnected system, relatively small changes of one parameter can sometimes have disastrous (and unpredictable) effects on the whole. This has important implications for the effect of climate change on the social, psychological, climate and ecological systems in Guattari's (2000) three ecologies. We shall see in the next chapter how this is also relevant for the clinical domain at the core of psychoanalysis.

Our study of swarm intelligence and SO has thus far focused on interactions between large numbers of (relatively) simple agents producing highly complex emerging structures and processes. A new level of complexity is reached when we take the self-organizing human mind as the individual agent interacting with large numbers of other minds in human societies and with the non-human environment, which leads to 'many more degrees of freedom in what self-organization can accomplish' (Camazine *et al.* 2001: 493). Thus we reach the level of (human) psychosocial phenomena crucial to understanding our collective response to a changing climate. Here, we need to take the plunge into chaos, emotionally and intellectually, in order to free up the creativity needed at this moment of crisis, but this path has no guarantees of success.

This can bring a complexity-based approach to Jared Diamond's (2006) research on the collapse of civilizations, and the important roles he uncovered for systemic social interconnectivity, environmental damage, and climate change. Crucially, many of these societies entered the period of collapse shortly after reaching their apogee of power and wealth. One example we could look at is the Anasazi Chaco society in North America, which built by far the tallest buildings in that continent prior to Chicago's skyscrapers of the 1880s. Following centuries of development, their advanced society collapsed rapidly in one decade after reaching its peak, between the years 1110 and 1120.

According to Diamond (2006: 155), this should make us 'hesitate to be too confident yet about the sustainability of our First World economy, especially when we reflect on how quickly Chaco society collapsed after its peak . . . and how implausible the risk of collapse would have seemed to

Chacoans of that decade.' According to Diamond's research, the leading causes for this particular collapse were deforestation and arroyo cutting, climate change in rainfall and temperature, and an increasingly interdependent, complex society (arroyos are water-carved creeks or channels and can be increased in unpredictable ways by irrigation systems and deforestation, both of which occurred in Chaco). The gradually increasing complexity and interdependency of the Anasazi Chaco society enabled an advanced and rich society to function well while it lasted, but in the long run put the whole society at risk of collapsing.

The pattern is uncomfortably close to that of our own society. In the course of six centuries, Chaco's population grew, along with its demands on the environment, leading to environmental resource depletion and degradation. In Diamond's words, it became a society 'living increasingly close to the margin of what the environment could support' (2006: 156). The droughts which finally pushed the society over the edge were merely the proximal cause, as the same society with a lower population density and more remaining environmental resources would have been able to survive the changing climate. When the Anasazi society in Chaco did collapse, 'its inhabitants could no longer reconstruct their society' as 'the initial conditions of abundant nearby trees, high groundwater levels, and a smooth floodplain without arroyos had disappeared' (ibid.).

For Diamond, the conclusion is sobering and instructive for our own civilization. Like the Anasazi, we 'can get away with a lot of waste when the economy is good', but we forget that 'we may not be able to anticipate when conditions will change', by which point 'we may already have become attached to an expensive lifestyle' from which we cannot extricate ourselves in time (ibid.). Climate change appears to have played an important part in the rise and fall of previous civilizations, including ones as mighty as Rome, as recent scientific research has found (Büntgen *et al.* 2011). We do not yet know whether our own civilization will share the fate of many that have gone before, but we would do well to grasp the complex, nonlinear effects involved. As Sole and Goodwin (2000: 302) put it, 'complex societies spontaneously evolve toward a hyper-coherent state where failure in one part of the system affects all the other parts in a domino theory of disaster.'

> We still do not know why civilizations collapse. We need some new explorers able to penetrate the jungles of complexity and find the theories that will help us locate ourselves in our complex world . . . a fascinating but counterintuitive universe, a nonlinear and unpredictable world operating by rules still to be discovered. These laws will show us how our ecosystems are organized as they are and how fragile they can be. They will tell us more than we can imagine about our brains and societies . . . Let us remember, when walking through the ruins of those

great ancient cities . . . that they all had something in common: a long time ago, their citizens believed that those cities and those civilizations would last forever.

(ibid.)

Chapter 12

Psychoanalysis, ecology and complexity

> To react with apathy to our present pollution-ridden 'real, outer' world is, I think, equivalent to defending oneself unconsciously against the experience of becoming an individual human self, a self which, in the very nature of human living, must contain a whirlpool of emotional conflicts, at times so chaotic as to threaten the dismemberment of one's very self.
>
> (Searles 1972: 372)

> In spite of all the muddled thinking that Freud started, psychoanalysis remains as *the* outstanding contribution . . . to our understanding of the family – a monument to the importance and value of loose thinking.
>
> (Bateson 2000: 84)

The emergent ego

> In many ways, psychoanalysis can produce the most reliable data available anywhere for the study of complex processes . . . Integrating disconnected contents into the ego is the business of psychoanalysis . . . The reorganized ego emerges from the integration and coordination of its component parts through a process of self-organization. These components are themselves organizations at a high level of complexity . . . Psychoanalysis is a coevolutionary ecosystem in which the patient's self-knowledge is reorganized through his adaptation to the analyst's increasing knowledge of him.
>
> (Palombo 1999: xviii)

Now we come to the difficult task of attempting to integrate complexity theory and ecology into psychoanalytic thought. Complexity and chaos theory have strong implications for psychology (Abraham 1995; Piers, Muller & Brent 2007) and psychoanalysis, and have been usefully applied to studying phenomena ranging from schizophrenia and bipolar disorder (Guastello 2001; Hornero *et al.* 2006) to family system dynamics (Gottman *et al.* 2003; Pincus 2001). According to Guastello (2004: 4): 'At the broadest level of analysis . . . [it] appears to have changed the basic concept of the human mind itself.' Iwakabe (1994: 1) has written that what he calls the 'nonlinear revolution' in psychotherapy is 'providing a new worldview of ecology, human beings, and nature.' Furthermore, Moran (1991: 224) argues that psychoanalysis itself is inherently nonlinear:

> The interaction of various mental features is taken for granted in most psychoanalytic models . . . the psychoanalyst takes this view of the mind (as interacting with itself, or intra-acting) into account when he considers, for example, the interdependence of the patient's affect, verbal associations, and sensations of physical posture on the couch . . . [T]hese . . . variables . . . must be considered not only additively, but as to *how they relate to each other*, in order to understand the nature of the psychoanalytic process at any moment.

In his book *The Emergent Ego*, Palombo (1999: 28) suggests that psychoanalysis needs complexity theory to replace 'the limitations of nineteenth-century ideas in physics and biology' embedded in psychoanalytic thought. He suggests that psychoanalysis 'seems to many people outside the field to have been treading water scientifically', a fact contributing to the gradual 'decline in the prestige of psychoanalysis' (Palombo 1999: 29), the loss of which however may provide the crucial incentive it needs to change.

For Palombo (1999: 341), while some of the 'anachronisms in traditional psychoanalytic theory . . . have been ameliorated by object relations theory' they still 'must be embedded in a larger theory that takes account of the body and the brain as well as the manner in which people internalize their relations to one another.' From the point of view of the three ecologies, this would entail integrating object relations, social relations (Clarke & Hoggett 2008) and ecological relations. More recently, Palombo (2007: 1) has reiterated his claim that complexity theory should be regarded as the 'parent science of psychoanalysis'.

> The theory of emerging properties in complex self-organizing systems offers an opportunity for a systematic reconceptualization of psychoanalytic theory . . . [which] neutralizes the threat of reductionism . . . The theories of coevolution and self-organized systems provide a new framework for investigations into the nature of the process . . . Complexity theory offers a comprehensive basis for understanding the adaptive ego as an emergent product of evolution rather than a relic of frustrated biological urges.
>
> (Palombo 1999: 339)

Iwakabe (1994: 1) suggests that nonlinear models more closely match the nature of the psychoanalytic process. In linear approaches, 'the interaction . . . is modeled by creating two independent linear models: one for the client's effect on therapist behavior, and the other for the therapist's effect on client behavior' but this cannot account for 'interaction effects.' In contrast, nonlinear interdependence models study 'mutual influential effects without breaking them down to two independent linear systems' and 'without simplifying the nature of complex, mutually affecting variables' (Iwakabe 1994: 4). It thereby avoids the reductionistic trap into which many attempts to apply scientific methods and theories to psychoanalysis are in danger of falling.

Goldstein (1995: 240) also argues that Freud's equilibrium model is 'limiting because it assumes that all important dynamics are internal to the system' and therefore that 'the connection to the environment is disregarded.' The result is that it consequently 'underestimates the importance . . . of unexpected crises, fortuitous events, and accidents' (Goldstein 1995: 250) particularly if we stick rigidly to Freud's stance of psychic determinism. On the other hand a 'nonlinear and nonequilibrium model that adequately accounts for evolutionary transitions across development stages' (ibid.) can open out psychoanalytic metapsychology in its full complexity.

Donald Meltzer (1994: 143) implies just such a shift when he writes that 'the problems of relationships between objects of whatever sort are more comprehensively understood in terms of communication than in terms of energy, and more accurately measured in terms of a gradient from chaos to order than in terms of closed systems of dynamic equilibria.' But just as Einsteinian physics does not reject the physics of Newton but merely makes it a special (limiting) case within a broader system, Goldstein (1995: 240) argues that: 'Within this nonequilibrium perspective, equilibrium has a crucial role to play in identifying the attractor characterizing the initial stuck condition of patients in psychotherapy.'

Self-organized criticality

> The sandpile had self-organized to an unstable critical state. When another grain was added, and the critical threshold surpassed, the organization of the pile broke down. The sizes of the avalanches were neither random nor uniform . . . [T]he magnitudes . . . were inversely proportional to the frequencies of occurrence for each size, following a power law.
>
> (Palombo 1999: 96)

For Palombo (1999: 24) SO is 'the most significant missing ingredient in psychoanalytic theory', which shows how 'small bits of insight assembled themselves into larger and larger structures . . . from the bottom up.' Additionally, since complexity theory deals with how systems change and evolve, 'the process of change in analytic treatment shares its basic features with all other kinds of progressive change in nature' (Palombo 1999: 82).

Describing the sandpile situation above, Bak (1994: 481) notes that once the pile reaches the state of *self-organized criticality* 'any analysis based on individual grains of sand ceases to be useful'; instead 'the pile of sand must be viewed as a whole because even grains considerable distances apart are linked through an elaborate network.' When plotted, the resulting *power law* forms a self-similar fractal graph, a virtual diagram applying equally to earthquakes, ecosystem extinctions (Kauffman 1993), volcanic eruptions, cloud formation, solar flare activity, and financial instability (Scheinkman & Woodford 1994).

Further illustrating its effectiveness for linking diverse levels of analysis, Michio Kaku (1995: 84) applied SO and phase transitions to both psycho-developmental stages and social processes such as the French Revolution. Bak and Chen (1991: 53) claim that: 'Throughout history, wars and peaceful interactions might have left the world in a critical state in which conflicts and social unrest spread like avalanches.' The historian Michael Shermer (1995), for example, found that dramatic social movements such as the European witch trials share certain similar social conditions such as feelings of loss of control and responsibility, and that these movements often rapidly spread through society until a critical peak when the smallest event can cause a rapid collapse, as the new event reverberates and resonates through the entire system.

On the psychological level, Miller (1999: 364) understands psychoanalytic change as following a similar power law, with most change confined to the local level and absorbed by the wider psychic defences. However, as the system reaches self-organized criticality, the tiniest local shift 'can cause related schemas to destabilize and consequently loosen their ties with one another' and eventually 'precipitate a cascade of disorganization throughout an entire system' leading to 'qualitative changes in a patient's affective states and in his or her beliefs about himself or herself and the world' (ibid.). Following Deleuze and Guattari, these self-similar patterns between levels should not be understood in terms of metaphors (one being 'like' another) but as the result of the same pattern-forming process occurring in different registers. Such analyses are crucial for the dramatic psychological and social shifts required to combat the dangers of climate change.

Coevolution and the fitness landscape

> In an intimate two-person system . . . the fitness of one person depends
> to a great degree on the behavior of the other. Like the bee and the
> flower, or the fox and the rabbit, the two are interdependent. Adaptive

> interdependence tends to accelerate evolutionary change, as each adapting system adapts to changes in the other . . . The patient and the analyst are two interacting self-organized systems . . . made up in turn of many connected interacting components. The interacting systems adapt over time to changes in each other's behavior in their shared ecosystem. When . . . successful, each system in the ecosystem evolves to an optimal degree of internal connectedness as well as to a higher level of fitness.
>
> (Palombo 1999: 115)

For Miller (1999: 360), the 'mental activity of the patient cannot be understood apart from the context to which the patient is adapting, namely, the interaction with the analyst.' Evolutionary theory provides the model of a 'fitness landscape', its own equivalent of 'phase space', where each helpful mutation allows the species to move closer to a local adaptive peak ('There is no genetics without "genetic drift"' [Deleuze & Guattari 2003a: 53]).

However, Richard Dawkins' (1997) well-known metaphor of 'climbing Mount Improbable' for the gradual ramp of evolutionary change towards adaptive complexity, while providing a useful way of visualizing how complexity can arise without the intervention of an omnipotent designer, is ultimately misleading. The metaphor implies that evolution has a relatively fixed goal (the adaptive complexity of, for example, an eye), and a fixed ramp to get there with relatively little deviation from the true path. In fact, as Dawkins would be the first to acknowledge, the fitness landscape is in fact constantly shifting and morphing in new directions along with each change to the organisms it contains, the ecological relations between them, and the always unpredictable effects of shifting climatic and non-organic factors.

One interesting consequence of the fitness landscape is that when a species reaches a local optima it can get 'stuck', as change in any direction represents a loss of fitness, even though it might allow it to reach a higher and more adaptive peak in the long run (but evolution has no foresight, the watchmaker is blind [Dawkins 1996]). Palombo (1999: 114) applies this model to psychoanalytic treatment where 'temporary loss of fitness is a regression' and the patient 'suffers for the sake of further exploration and growth.'

However, the fitness landscape of psychoanalysis, like its evolutionary counterpart, is also not fixed, as the patient is part of a co-evolving system with the analyst. Therefore, the 'patient can escape more easily from a local optimum if the landscape changes, so that the descent from his current location is less abrupt' (ibid.). This occurs through shifts in the analyst's behaviour resulting from 'coevolutionary change in the analyst's view of the patient', keeping the analysis from 'stagnating on the patient's local optimum' through deforming 'the patient's fitness landscape to facilitate further movement' (ibid.).

Here we have a novel explanation for 'resistance' in psychotherapy, which can also be applied to deadlocks in the wider culture concerning climate change. Despite the increasingly obvious fact that we are on a dangerous and destructive path, individual and collective resistances suggest an inability to leave a local peak in order to find a more adaptive mountain. Applying this model to tackling the social defences around climate change would involve attempting to deform the fitness landscape to make descent less difficult. In addition, as with the random errors of ants, Kelly (1994: 470) suggests that 'honour your errors' is a useful rule here, where, 'by nurturing small failures, a system can make large failures less probable . . . small cracks can prevent larger fractures.' This is true whether we are looking at ants foraging, genetic mutations, psychological defences, or whole societies, ecosystems or civilizations.

The edge of chaos in the psychoanalytic process

> Traditional psychoanalytic theory does a very sketchy job of relating the texture of psychoanalytic work from hour to hour with the emergence of significant change in the patient's inner mental structures. What psycho-analysts need is a way to think about how small, even unobservable, changes in the moment to moment analytic interaction can lead to larger, stable, observable changes in the patient.
>
> (Palombo 1999: 125)

For Palombo (1999: 124), the emergence of repressed material, which is central to psychoanalysis, is a result of a phase transition occurring when 'connectedness of the system reaches a critical level that permits the patient a higher degree of self-observation.' While Palombo doesn't make this link, there are some striking similarities here with Bion's (1962a) theory of thinking, in particular his concept of the 'selected fact' which he derived from the mathematician Poincaré who used it to describe how a new element gives coherence to a group of previously scattered data. For Bion this involves an emotional experience 'by which the mind transforms a chaotic, persecutory experience into an experience that is integrated, representable, and thinkable' (Houzel 2005) corresponding to Klein's move from the paranoid-schizoid to the depressive position.

Miller (1999: 355) also focuses on the transformational process taking place 'within the creation and evolution of the complex adaptive system (CAS) of the analytic dyad.' In this framework, transference–countertransference and psychopathology can be studied through 'how complex adaptive systems self-organize, develop, and evolve', allowing new ways of approaching old analytic controversies such as mutative change. Thus for Miller a single framework is able to encompass 'principles . . .

concepts and techniques that have hitherto been described by a number of conflicting theories' (ibid.).

Therefore, on the conceptual level, complexity theory may prove useful as a 'selected-fact' which can bring coherence to the current fragmentation of psychoanalysis. For example, we can reconceptualize 'fixation' or 'regression' (including 'therapeutic regression' [Winnicott 1989]) as occurring in dynamic systems which 'continue to evolve, carrying forward into new iterations their pathological organizations' (Miller 1999: 372). Regressions here, however, should not be understood as a return 'to an earlier state of the organism, but to a less well-organized state of the current system . . . in which the ties that bind the elements . . . enter a more chaotic state' (ibid.). In a similar way, Perna (1997) has pointed out that such a regression towards a more chaotic state 'is the prelude to reorganization, even if that reorganization is to a more pathogenic state' (Miller 1999: 372).

More recently, from the perspective of self psychology, Christine Kieffer (2007) has suggested that the concept of the 'analytic third' can best be envisaged through complexity theory as an emergent phenomenon, truly embodying something more than either analyst or patient by themselves. From this perspective, analysis works at the edge of chaos, in the creative space for play and spontaneity, with therapeutic movement involving nonlinear oscillations between rupture and repair of the therapeutic alliance. Therefore, the edge of chaos concept can be viewed as an effective model for psychoanalytic change (Palombo 1999: 180).

The Boston Change Process Study Group (2008) has been taking this perspective further and continues to generate fresh insights. While flexibility is not necessarily the most adaptive for all situations (crocodiles and cockroaches are virtually unchanged after 100 million years), 'when change is advantageous, as it is when the ecosystem changes significantly, organisms evolve in a direction that promotes adaptation.' In our current crisis our ecosystems are changing dramatically, therefore the other two ecologies (psychological and social) must be ready for changes too, and not necessarily in orderly ways. Psychoanalysis is above all a method that allows for deep psychological change and restructuring, which, for Palombo (1999: 181), 'involves increasing the connectedness and complexity of the patient's mental contents.' However:

> Patients in psychoanalysis, especially in the early stages, may not appreciate the adaptive value of working toward the edge of chaos. They may find the hazards of life near the edge of chaos frightening, and may actively seek to avoid them. When this form of resistance is not dominating . . . co-evolution leads to longer and longer trains of associations (the songs of the psychoanalytic patient) . . . that leads to stabilization of an ecosystem near the edge of chaos.
>
> (ibid.)

From this perspective Palombo is able to reframe some of the most heated problems dividing different psychoanalytic schools, such as the difference between the working relationship (Greenson 1967), the therapeutic alliance (Zetzel 1965), and the holding environment (Winnicott 1965):

> Greenson and Zetzel both intended to describe a relationship between the neurotic patient and the analyst when poised near the edge of chaos . . . Winnicott's point was . . . that for many seriously ill patients, the first stage of treatment must be the establishment of a Nash equilibrium . . . Kohut gives the appearance of believing that the achievement of a Nash equilibrium is all that is necessary for any patient . . . Obsessive patients with a dependency phobia find the Nash equilibrium state itself to be threatening . . . Here, the analyst's action to move the patient toward the edge of chaos is not only optimizing but essential to the continuity of the analysis.
>
> (Palombo 1999: 248–249)

We might also consider in 'edge of chaos' terms Meltzer's (1994: 316) description of Klein/Bion's PS↔D as a dynamic system balanced 'between paranoid-schizoid and depressive value systems', teetering on 'the knife-edge of sparing-the-self vs. sparing-the-object.' Bion's update of Klein provides a model of health less to do with purely depressive position functioning, and more as a flexible dynamic balance on the cusp of these two attractor systems.

Finally, we cannot complete this section on the edge of chaos in psychoanalysis without considering dreams. Palombo (1999: 262) describes dreaming as 'a continuous phase transitional state . . . the biological equivalent of controlled nuclear fusion.' Similarly, Scalzone and Zontini (2001: 263) have discussed a related approach suggesting that dreams provide the 'chaotic link, or interface, between the unconscious wish, which constitutes an attractor, and the conscious thought' so that 'the structured linearity of conscious thought can emerge out of the nonlinear chaos of the drives.' Dreams, which have always been so central to the psychoanalytic project, perhaps provide the ultimate fractal graph of the psyche, a model of mind which (in health) is dynamically poised at the edge of chaos.

Attractors

> Pathological unconscious infantile attractors are more primitive . . . [less] structured . . . [than] the usual psychological attractors of everyday life . . . [e.g.] the fixed point attractor of an idée fixe and the closed curve attractor of an obsession . . . In a successful psychoanalysis one would surely find an increase in the strangeness of the patient's unconscious

attractors . . . [which provides] a good model for the flexibility required
by a healthy mind in a changing environment.

(Palombo 1999: 184)

Priel & Schreiber (cited in Iwakabe 1994: 213) also use attractors to understand psychopathology, particularly in terms of the repetition compulsion,
and like Palombo they see the psychoanalytic process as a 'destabilization'
in order to help develop and change 'limited (periodic) cycle attractors to
chaotic (strange) attractors' through allowing 'stretching and folding of the
whole system by providing information by interpretation, and by facilitating the patient's remembering and reconstruction of the past' (see also
Galater-Levy 1995; Lonie 1995). More recently, Busch (2007: 429) has
worked from a similar framework, viewing 'pathological attractor sites' as
'*black holes in psychological space*, sucking everything in that comes near its
orbit, remaining outside of awareness and thus unable to be modified by
other structures.' While complex attractors give stability to the system 'due
to their greater number of neural pathways', simple (pathological) attractors 'guide a system in a rigid manner, and are profoundly affected by
minor external factors' (ibid.).

Defence mechanisms keep the pathological attractors simple by keeping
them unconscious, thereby closing off developmental possibilities through
new interactions with the outside world. As we have seen from our study of
swarms, 'systems that restrict or inhibit information exchanges with their
environments tend to be unstable' (Miller 1999: 370). This also applies to
the system psychoanalysts call 'self' so that 'in severe states of system
closure . . . the rigid connections between the elements that constitute the
particular attractor state degrade, because there is no energy or information
to sustain them, causing fragmentation and disintegration of the sense of
self' (Miller 1999: 371). This analysis can be applied to each of Guattari's
three ecologies, as 'a maladaptive organization can exist on any level of a
system' (Miller 1999: 371).

> From a dynamic systems perspective, the aim of psychoanalytic
> treatment is to transform rigidly ordered, closed systems into more open
> and adaptive states . . . The analyst thus maintains two positions . . .
> the person who induces change and the one who provides a safe haven
> in which reorganization can take place . . . in the dynamic balance
> between order and chaos that is required to adapt to the context
> provided by the analytic relationship.
>
> (Miller 1999: 372–373)

In addition, Scharff (2000: 181) has integrated a complex system perspective with Fairbairn's object relations, with its emphasis on the personality

being in perpetual dynamic flux between various objects, and suggests that this allows us to re-think transference–countertransference interactions in terms of 'complex self-organizing systems as they tend towards higher levels of organization.' Similarly, in a related paper, Miller (1999: 364) argues that '*transference* is a periodic attractor state of the patient' embodying 'a complex and dynamic interplay of contextually specific memories and states, derived . . . from developmental and relationship histories.'

This allows us to view transference as a multidimensional experience in constant, complex interaction with the analyst's countertransference, involving synchronization (like the flashing of fireflies in the evening). Studies of the therapeutic process (Tschacher & Scheier 1997) and mother–infant interactions (Sander 1983) suggest that an 'ordered dyadic system emerges out of the synchronization of . . . physiological-cognitive-emotional patterns' (Miller 1999: 367). Similar dynamics were found in studies of psychotic states which 'self-organized from within the complex, linearly unpredictable mental systems of these patients' (Miller 1999: 372). Grostein (1990, cited in Iwakabe 1994: 10) also used the nonlinear approach to research psychotic states, which he described as 'seemingly random, yet . . . organized in a complex mechanism of nonlinearity.'

Nonlinear subjectivity and intersubjectivity

> Chaos theory offers a paradigm for psychoanalysis that improves our powers of understanding . . . it offers an explanation for the essential unpredictability of complex dynamic events, it relieves analysis of the burden of prediction, and at the same time enables it to offer enhanced understanding of complex and repetitive patterns of psychic organization and interpersonal interaction.
>
> (Scharff 2000: 181)

One further important researcher in this field who needs to be mentioned is Terry Marks-Tarlow. In her paper, 'The Self as a Dynamical System' (2004), she emphasized the fact that chaos and complexity show us new universals in nature, so it is not so much about 'applying' them to psychology, but rather about discovering that they are already there. In ways which echo the concept of the ecological self that we studied earlier, she conceptualizes the self', as 'an open, complex, dynamical system' where 'healthy selves self-organize and evolve to the edge of chaos, where they are capable of flexible reorganization in response to unpredictable social and environmental contingencies' (Marks-Tarlow 2004: 311).

Chaos theory also adds to our understanding of *intersubjectivity* as it suggests not only that the self is 'fractal' in nature but that the boundaries between self/world and self/other 'are dynamically fluid and ever changing, mediated by complex, recursive feedback loops existing simultaneously at physical, social, cultural, and historical levels' (Marks-Tarlow 2004: 311). Galatzer-Levy (1995) suggested that the mind itself can be understood as having a 'fractal' quality, arguing that psychoanalysts can take advantage of self-similarity as a means of data reduction as core concerns of the analysand are detectable from the smallest material, with dreams being the clearest example of this fractal nature.

Marks-Tarlow's latest book, *Psyche's Veil: Psychotherapy, Fractals and Complexity* (2008), remains one of the most fully worked out attempts to put these concepts to use clinically including, for example, the loss of complexity in disorders such as depression. However, while providing a new power and vision for analytic work, the complex systems perspective is also humbling, as the one thing it can never have is certainty.

> Psychoanalytic treatment is a messy business . . . There are no discrete moments to be analyzed or events to be processed, but . . . a continuous flow of experience . . . always under construction. In the creation of this experience, the worlds of the patient and the analyst intersect, join together, and disjoin . . . Chaos and complexity theories provide models within which analysts can comprehend the messy, ever changing nature of the therapeutic interaction and their influence on it.
>
> (Miller 1999: 377)

Understandably, there have been criticisms of this point of view. Mayes (2005), for example, writes that 'attractive as these metaphors are, there is still much work to be done to translate them into either empirical or operational terms that may then be more closely examined for their theoretical utility' (Mayes 2005). Iwakabe (1994: 17) also suggests that there are major practical difficulties in applying these ideas empirically as well as conceptually and this is certainly still a problem area (however, see Dodds 2008; Dietrich *et al.* 2008).

In addition, Iwakabe (1994: 16) argues that there is an 'ontological mismatch between concepts of chaos theory and those of psychoanalysis' and that the '[m]etaphoric use of chaos theory is problematic.' As we have seen, Deleuze & Guattari (2003a) and DeLanda (2006) go some way towards claiming these are not merely metaphors but refer to the same virtual diagram or abstract machine already in operation in these various different assemblages. To his credit, despite these criticisms Iwakabe (1994: 18) agrees that 'tolerance of even crude experimentation of ideas may be more rewarding than rejection of the new methodologies and ideas.'

Group dynamics at the edge of chaos

> From chaos, *Milieus* and *Rhythms* are born.
>
> (Deleuze & Guattari 2003a: 313)

We now move to the fractal border zone between the three ecologies, especially those areas between mental and social ecologies. Complexity approaches have much to offer group analysis, and Bion's (1961) basic assumptions can be studied as attractors towards which group life is pulled, with phase transitions between different basins of attraction. Similarly, Foulkes' (1990) theory of group transferences as forming continuously re-integrating networks seems to beg for such an approach. This process has already begun in the field of 'systems psychodynamics', which Fraha (2004: 65) defines as an interdisciplinary field combining influences from psycho-analysis, group relations, and open systems perspectives (see also Gould, Stapley & Stein 2006).

Eidelson (1997: 53) shows how complexity-based models are useful in studying phenomena of crucial relevance to climate change, such as the bystander effect and other 'tragedies of the commons' (Hardin 1968; Ostrom 1990; Vlek 1996), as discussed in Chapter 1. Eidelson's complexity-based models suggest that by creating subsystems inside a large group they can potentially produce 'pockets of collaboration' that can spread, moving the larger system to a new basin of attraction (Glance & Huberman 1994). Here Bion's description of the emotional oscillation of a basic assumption dependency (baD) group is useful:

> The group is compelled to recognize that the spontaneously chosen leader is seriously disordered . . . At the same time it is compelled to believe that he is the dependable leader . . . this can only be done by a series of oscillations . . . If I refuse to intervene . . . the oscillations become very rapid . . . The result is that the group can no longer contain the emotional situation, which thereupon spreads with explosive violence to other groups until enough groups have been drawn in.
>
> (Bion 1961: 124–125)

The aim here is 'to bring in so much inert material in the way of outsiders from the group, who do not share the emotional situation, that the new and much larger group ceases to vibrate' and 'the violent and disagreeable mass oscillation' ceases (Bion 1961: 125). However, the danger is that 'the oscillations spread to the hitherto inert' leaving a situation 'more disagree-able than ever' (ibid.: 125–126), with much depending on the speed and effectiveness with which other groups are brought in, and the pre-existing emotional states of the 'outside' groups.

In 'Complexity at the "Edge" of the Basic Assumption Group', Stacey (2006: 91–114) has attempted to develop further just such an articulation of Bion's group analysis with the Tavistock Institute's group relations approach and complexity theory, asking what would happen 'if we move from a membrane metaphor of an organization's boundary to a fractal metaphor in which it is problematic to say what is inside and what is outside.' (Stacey 2006: 95). This returns us to Freud's uncanny. In his book dedicated to exploring Freud's concept, Royle (2003: 2) writes that the uncanny 'disturbs any straightforward sense of what is inside and what is outside' and 'has to do with a strangeness of framing and borders, an experience of liminality.'

Stacey argues that self-organization theory provides an important shift in perspective for group relations consultants and group analysts, shifting the focus 'away from regulation at a boundary to the manner in which the system's transformation process transforms itself' (Stacey 2006: 94). By moving from a model of 'rational design and regulation' to one of 'spontaneous self-organizing processes', the complexity approach can help to reveal and understand the possibilities latent in the group for developing 'the creative potential of disorder' (Stacey 2006: 94–95). Thus the nonlinear geometry of the fractal precisely undermines any clear line between inside and outside, providing new ways to think about the individual and the group, moving from a membrane metaphor of the boundary to a multi-dimensional fractal border zone.

One example of this creative shift in perspective can be seen through a new way of approaching Bion's (1961) distinction between the work group and the basic assumption group. For Bion, *work group* functioning is the conscious purpose of the group, its 'official', reality-based ego-function. This is easily disturbed by more unconscious, primitive behaviour and thought, which Bion calls the *basic assumption group*. It is important to emphasize that these are not different groups, but different aspects of group *functioning*; all groups always contain a mixture of both. Pure work groups are impossible and would be emotionally sterile, while pure basic assumption groups would not have enough reality-based functioning to survive for long and are the group equivalent of severe psychosis.

These groups also unite individuals together in different ways: *cooperation* (work group) and *valency* (basic assumption group). The latter 'requires no training, experience, or mental development. It is instantaneous, inevitable, and instinctive' (Bion 1961: 153). Connected with basic assumption groups is what Bion called *group mentality*, the 'unanimous expression of the will of the group, contributed to by the individual in ways of which he is unaware, influencing him disagreeably whenever he thinks or behaves in a manner at variance with the basic assumptions' (Bion 1961: 65). Bion (1961: 160) identified three main basic assumption (ba) group constellations which 'give form and meaning to the complex and chaotic emotional state that the group unfolds to the investigating participant': fight-flight (baF), dependency (baD) and pairing (baP) (see *Figure 4*, p. 66). Further basic assumption groups have been suggested, such as Hopper's (2002) Incohesion: Aggregation/Massification (ba I: A/M), but this is not the place to explore them.

As with Klein's developmental positions, each basic assumption can be understood as a complex 'attractor' definable along the six dimensions in *Figure 4*, p. 66. Stacey (2006: 98–101) argues that Bion's (1961) work group ↔ basic assumption groups interact to create regions of stability and disintegration with potentially creative fractal regions of bounded instability at the edge of chaos between them. This movement towards an ecological and complexity-based group psychoanalysis is further aided by the ecological dimension already existing in Bion's work, where he describes the way different group relations (at all levels) constitute commensal, symbiotic, parasitic and paranoid connections (Meltzer 1994: 401).

As with Bion's basic assumption theory, Elliott Jaques' (1955) *social phantasy systems* can be understood from a complexity perspective as emerging through the self-organization of individual defence mechanisms, with global patterns feeding back to affect lower levels recursively. Thus social formations, 'individual' mind/brains, and communities can be studied as dissipative structures and swarms. In terms of climate change, Nicholsen (2003) has offered a group analytic hypothesis that at an unconscious level, American group cohesion is connected to a continuous sacrifice of nature. Thus, unless we can move the group phantasy to a new basin of attraction the group is likely to remain dangerously stuck in its abusive relation to the natural world.

Repression and guilt in the social phantasy ecosystem

> Repression, guilt and an over-developed super-ego seem to be the fate of those who become active. People in this position have to repress the desires for unbridled consumption which they share with the rest of the population . . . renunciation rarely leads to public support, let alone gratitude . . . an irritated car driver is more likely to knock you off your bicycle than to thank you for reducing the nation's carbon emissions. It can be a lonely position and one effect of repression can be an emphasis on the moral high ground.
>
> (Randall 2005: 10–11)

To see an example of a nonlinear social phantasy (eco)system in action we can turn to Randall's (2005: 175) analysis of the 'relationship between a majority population which avoids or denies guilt and a minority into whom this same guilt can be evacuated.' The non-active majority project their environmental concern onto activists which has the effect that activists function as containers for the split-off collective environmental superego (supereco). Then, by mocking those labelled as 'bearded killjoys', the external threat as well as the 'presence of guilt are both neutralized' so that there is: 'Nothing to worry about. Business as usual' (Randall 2005: 175).

Using a nonlinear social systems perspective allows us to more fully identify the feedback loops which don't end in the first projection, but get carried around the circuit with complex social and psychological effects, reverberating back and forth in new iterations as the system moves forward in time, and as other individuals and groups get drawn into existing systems, either damping down the mad oscillations (Bion), or getting swept up in nonlinear amplification effects. Jaques (1955) claimed that such projections involve a social redistribution of internal objects where the recipients can either absorb or deflect them; but, as in the case of racism, it is rarely a 'free' choice.

> The effects of this dynamic on activists are multiple and variable as projected guilt interacts with individual psyches. One possibility is . . . [that] the negative stereotypes are accepted and embraced. The activist becomes a ferocious, moralising puritan, safe in the knowledge of her own salvation, unforgiving and condemnatory of all who fail to reach her standards. The advice she gives becomes deliberately unpalatable, the practices she advocates become hair-shirt, impossible extremes and . . . she takes satisfaction in others' failures. She finds like-minded people and together they separate themselves off from the rest of society and its desires.
>
> (Randall 2005: 175)

This perspective allows us to see that the problem of counterproductive campaigning is not only the 'fault' of activists, but is part of the wider social phantasy system involving complex interacting feedback loops on multiple scales, from affective to social, the resulting forms self-organizing in unpredictable ways and interacting with ecological networks. What other routes are there for dealing with these social projections? Randall (2005: 175) suggests that 'internalised guilt and burn-out' are common to many people 'working in the voluntary sector as well as in political movements.'

> Enthusiasm and idealism give way to exhaustion and disillusion. The young person . . . driven by an unexamined history of their own guilt takes on the burdens of the world . . . The needs of the other . . . become paramount. The person's sense of agency and effectiveness diminish in the face of the enormity of the injury they are trying to heal. Driving themselves to do more, often in the face of opposition, indifference or hatred, they eventually collapse.
>
> (Randall 2005: 175–176)

A third route is that of the idealized 'eco-warrior', who seeks narcissistic protection 'against the destructiveness of an over-active super-ego' (ibid.: 176). This role feeds back on the wider social system through its 'iconography and meaning for a wider audience' allowing people 'to ease the sense of guilt that not enough is being done and to counter the sense of being shamed by public perceptions of the environmental movement. Like good news from the front during a war, these adventures keep up the morale of the population at home' (ibid.).

Finally, there is the Romantic retreat from the world, an attempt to return to Eden where: 'Culture is opposed to nature, technology is opposed to environment, the country is valued more highly than the city and the primitive or indigenous is often idealised' (ibid.). In this black and white binary world, 'guilt is assuaged by the purity of one's own existence . . . At its extreme lie the paranoid fantasies of American survivalists and the nightmare of eco-fascism' (ibid.). However, despite these dangers, Randall emphasizes that there is much sanity and beauty in the ecological movement and that the problems she identifies are aggravated by the wider social situation, the wider ecology in which the individual and collective actors are constituted, in ways which echo Bion's discussion of group oscillations.

> Only as collective guilt is shared can it become . . . less persecutory and destructive and be managed in more creative ways. This only becomes possible when the issues become truly mainstream and the possibility of reparative action on an appropriate scale starts to seem realistic . . . [creating] a more comfortable climate for activists. As the arguments are taken more seriously, the projections onto activists are reduced and a bigger space is created for sanity and creativity. Although conscious levels of collective anxiety may be raised in the short term, if real action follows then there is a chance that both this and the collective guilt can be relieved.
>
> (Randall 2005: 176–177)

This pattern embodies a system of multi-stability, with complex shifts between basins of attraction as internal objects and affects flow through the network. We should also not suppose that such a gradual sharing of collective guilt would have a linear effect on the minds of activists and the public. In fact, we might rather expect to see major shifts and phase transitions between states, sometimes after long periods when the system seems stuck despite the best efforts to destabilize it by pushing it towards a bifurcation.

As Deleuze and Guattari (2003a: 216) write, 'a society is defined by its lines of flight, which are molecular. There is always something that flows or flees, that escapes the binary organizations, the resonance apparatus, and the overcoding machine.' Using complexity theory, we can understand our current period as one involving disorder and instability in some areas, while appearing stuck and frozen in others (when it stays within the basin of an attractor). The first often feels frightening while the second can be deadening and demoralizing. From an edge of chaos perspective, periods of instability are 'natural and necessary stages on the path toward greater self-organization' (Eidelson 1997: 68–69), but there are no guarantees that what will emerge will be more adaptive. We have already seen how this works on the individual psychodynamic level, including the anxieties involved during stages of disorder.

Moving up to the social level, this is likely to include 'frequent detours and shifting terrain as other individuals or groups struggle to adapt on the same landscape' (Eidelson 1997: 68–69) – a landscape which keeps deforming depending on each individual and collective action in ways which are impossible to predict with certainty. These dynamics are 'self-similar' and can be observed on all scales. Paradoxically, therefore, according to Eidelson (1997: 69), the complexity approach 'may actually provide simpler explanations for a variety of phenomena' and illuminate 'the interplay between the fragility and stability that characterizes many of the phenomena explored by behavioral and social scientists.'

Crucial for an ecopsychoanalytic conception of change is that for all of Guattari's three ecologies, 'under certain conditions even a small change in a system's parameters can produce dramatic effects' (Eidelson 1997: 69). The task then becomes experimental, as Deleuze and Guattari (2003a: 161) state. This includes the search for the 'lever points' (Holland 1995) necessary to produce a major shift in the system, whether these are psychological, social or ecological, helping to overcome resistances and inertia, and opening up the possibility of more radical transformation, as we work experimentally to move the system towards a phase transition.

> This is how it should be done: Lodge yourself on a stratum, experiment with the opportunities it offers, find an advantageous place on it, find potential movements of deterritorialization, possible lines of flight, experience them, produce flow conjunctions here and there, try out continuums of intensities segment by segment, have a small plot of new land at all times. It is through a meticulous relation with the strata that one succeeds in freeing lines of flight . . .
>
> (Deleuze & Guattari 2003a: 161)

Chapter 13

Deleuze|Guattari and the ecology of mind

Subject and object give a poor approximation of thought . . . Rather, thinking takes place in the relationship of territory and the earth . . . the earth constantly carries out a movement of deterritorialization . . . crayfish that set off walking in file at the bottom of the water . . . knights who ride a celestial line of flight. The earth is not one element among others but rather brings together all the elements within a single embrace while using one or another of them to deterritorialize territory.

(Deleuze & Guattari 2003b: 85)

Every abstract machine is linked to other abstract machines, not only because they are inseparably political, economic, scientific, artistic, ecological, cosmic – perceptive, affective, active, thinking, physical, and semiotic – but because their various types are as intertwined as their operations are convergent.

(Deleuze & Guattari 2003a: 514)

Intensive science and geophilosophy

Nomads have no history; they only have a geography.

(Deleuze & Guattari 2003a: 93)

We now reach the penultimate chapter of this book. After assessing the seriousness of the crisis we face and the various psychoanalytic approaches open to dealing with it, we concluded that, as Bateson tells us, we need a new way of thinking. Climate change, 'the greatest failure of thought in human history' (Doppelt 2008), represents a failure to fully engage with the interweaving complexities of the 'three ecologies' of mind, nature and society (Guattari 2000). The new nomadic sciences of complexity, combined with the philosophy of Deleuze and Guattari, help to provide a framework, or rather a 'meshwork' (DeLanda 2006), for thinking our way out of extinction.

In their book *Geophilosophy*, Bonta and Protevi (2004: 9) explore Deleuze and Guattari's rich use of terms usually applied only to the morphological processes of the Earth. *Plateau*, for example, is used to describe 'a self-ordering set of productive connections between forces without reference to an external governing source of order.' In terms of complexity theory this describes the structure-generating processes of self-organization. Similarly, Bonta and Protevi (2004: 9) write that: '*A Thousand Plateaus* likens the spatial effect of the State to the all-powerful suffocation and almost irre-versible landscape modification of the continental glacier' so that we should 'think through the glacial effects of the State and perhaps vice versa . . . Deleuze and Guattari's political version of complexity theory is unique and badly needed.'

Drawing on the new sciences, Deleuze and Guattari argue that structures are not limited to homeostatic equilibrium states (*stratas*) but also non-equilibrium nonlinear networks (*consistencies, rhizomes* or *war machines*). According to Bonta and Protevi (2004: 4): 'Consistencies have found their "reterritorialization" precisely in their capacity for "deterritorialization", or, in other words, they most feel at home when they are creatively changing.' With this combination of feeling at home precisely while wan-dering, Deleuze and Guattari's 'nomadology' enters what we could call the uncanny ecology, or strange ecology, of ecopsychoanalysis.

In *A Thousand Plateaus*, Deleuze and Guattari (2003a) describe two kinds of science: *axiomatics* (royal science) and *problematics* (minor science). *Axiomatics* approaches matter through the linear stratified forms of equi-librium which can be studied through the 'molarizing' process of averaging (this must be distinguished from the rhizome where 'The middle is by no means an average; on the contrary, it is where things pick up speed' [Deleuze & Guattari 2003a: 25]). As systems move away from equilibrium, 'individual, non-average, rare trajectories can trigger either a shift in system from one attractor to another or even the creation of a new set of attractors and bifurcators' (Bonta & Protevi 2004: 192). Minor (nonlinear) science concerns 'intense' morphogenetic processes operating far from equilibrium. They involve lines of flight, bifurcations or becomings, which open the system's creativity through 'the capacity for meshing into consistencies' (ibid.). The latter are defined as 'networks of bodies that preserve the heterogeneity of the members even while enabling systematic emergent behavior' (ibid.).

The distinction between minor and royal science is closely related to the difference between the terms *actual*, *virtual*, and *intensive*. The 'actual' is the physically existing state of a system locked into a basin of attraction, a state which 'hides' the intensive morphogenetic processes from which it was formed. It can thus be understood as 'the congealing of the intensive and the burying of the virtual' (Bonta & Protevi 2004: 49), the virtual being the phase space of all possible, not currently actualized, states. Bateson (2000: 250) makes a similar distinction when he writes that the 'Newtonian world ascribes reality to objects and achieves its simplicity by excluding the context or metarelationship' while the cyberneticist's world 'insists upon examining the metarelationships while achieving its simplicity by excluding all objects.'

The distinction between 'actual' and 'virtual' provides a new way to think about Žižek and Morton's (2007) 'ecology without nature'. If we take the physical structure of the Earth, which our 'life-world' experience tells us is a fixed, impenetrable background, literally our 'rock', geophilosophy creates a radical shift in perspective. As DeLanda writes, it is

> the self-organized activity of lava flows that is at the origin of many geological forms . . . the oceanic crust on which the continents are embedded is constantly being created and destroyed . . . [The] continental crust is under constant erosion so that its materials are recycled into the ocean, the rocks and mountains that define the most stable and durable traits of our reality . . . merely represent a local slowing down of this flowing reality . . . very slow for rocks, faster for lava.
>
> (DeLanda 2005: 258)

Similarly, our own bodies and minds represent temporary 'coagulations or decelerations in the flows of biomass, genes, memes, and norms' (ibid.). In this perspective, 'it is the flow . . . that matters, not the bodies and species that emerge from these flows' (ibid.: 258–259). Languages, institutions and indeed every other aspect of our reality merely represent a 'transitory hardening' in the vast flow of becoming. A similar 'slowing down' occurs in Deleuze and Guattari's (2003b: 118) critique of royal science which 'in order to gain *a reference able to actualize the virtual* operates as a freeze-frame . . . a fantastic *slowing down*.'

A related distinction here is between what they call *striated* and *smooth* space. As with their description of the 'glacial', stratification, a term also drawn from the geological sciences of the Earth, has equally valid applications to other domains without functioning as a metaphor. Bonta and Protevi (2004: 14) write that '*science that uses linear models to deal with stratified systems does so by means of a "striated space"*' and that the fact that 'stratifying' processes were first discovered in geology can be understood as merely a '*historical accident by the demonstration that the same (virtual) "abstract machine" lies behind the geological, biological, and social strata.*'

From this perspective, nonlinear and ecological sciences are distinguished by their emphasis on the non-striating, or what Deleuze and Guattari call, in a term which is apt to cause a certain amount of confusion, the 'smoothing' forces in a given system. Bonta and Protevi (2004) describe the interaction of these forces in the case of ecological systems:

> Emergent properties, intensive becomings, occur only in smooth space. The possibility for symbiosis, for mutualism, for a food web and eco-

system . . . is predicated on smoothing, not striating forces. When viewed as isolated entities, organisms can themselves be seen as stratified and located in striated space, but not the complex webs of forces known as ecosystems that have no centralized organization, no climax or end point, but only continuous variation and rhizomes.

(Bonta & Protevi 2004: 144)

The relation between smooth and striated space can be fractal, with 'patches of smooth space enclosed by striated space' (Bonta & Protevi 2004: 145). Furthermore, unlike some more naive readings of Deleuze and Guattari, we can't assume that a smooth space, or a schizophrenic molecularization, will save us; indeed, smooth space has now 'become the provenance of the State security forces that can descend on the land at any point after gathering surveillance information and are not bounded by territories or by segmented lines in general' (ibid.). Striated States have 'given way, via capitalism and military might, to a worldwide space of Empire that operates through a smooth space to achieve ever-more-homogeneous striated space' (ibid.: 155. See also Hardt & Negri 2000).

Within this opposition, Bonta and Protevi (2004: 95) suggest we look into *holey space*, a third 'underground space that can connect with smooth space and be conjugated by striated space', a fractal space which bypasses 'both the ground [*sol*] of nomadic smooth space and the land [*tern*] of sedentary striated space.' In our current situation holey spaces 'have flourished, for the only way to escape the spying eyes of State intelligence is to go underground' (ibid.). For example, while Deleuze and Guattari seem to view forests as striated by 'gravitational verticals', Bonta and Protevi see them as a classic example of this 'third' space:

> The tree, far from being the standard for the forest, is rather deterritorialized by it, though perhaps not in the types of European wood-lot forests that Deleuze and Guattari imagined . . . [T]hey exclude the dynamics of tropical rain forests where the tree is but part of a vast rhizome with no center, no sense of perspective, no organizing principle, no ground [*sol*] (the soil itself is infertile, because nutrients are in constant cyclic motion throughout the system, and are not stored there), where plants can grow from top to bottom and then back (the strangler fig) or defy gravity altogether (epiphytes). The rain forest contains a high ratio of flow to order, and its complexity is engendered by this far-from-equilibrium crisis state.
>
> (Bonta & Protevi 2004: 88–89)

Nonlinear temporalities

These ideas have the potential to open up new ways of viewing time, a theme we have already discussed briefly in the section on Freud's 'On

Transience' (see p. 72). Here we will see how the concepts of the virtual and the actual provide a new way to approach temporality, in particular the strange nonlinear temporalities which characterize psychoanalytic practice, if not always its theory. According to the post-Kleinian psychoanalyst Donald Meltzer:

> Time is not, in psychic reality, the necessarily linear, directional, and irreversible dimension that the physical sciences describe in the outside world. The idea of time is bound up with sequence, motion, distance, and ageing in a most complicated manner that lends itself very well to reversal, oscillation, circularity, discontinuity, and arrest. In its essence the idea of reparation is closely linked to these qualities of the idea of time.
>
> (Meltzer 1994: 214)

As is well known, Freud (cited in Matte-Blanco 1984: 459) mysteriously claimed that: '*The processes of the system Ucs. are timeless; i.e. they are not ordered temporally, are not altered by the passage of time; they have no reference to time at all.*' What does this mean? One innovative approach has been that of Matte-Blanco (1998) who understands the distinctions between Freud's Cs. and Ucs. systems in terms of the 'bi-logic' of symmetry (Ucs.) and asymmetry (Cs.). Matte-Blanco (1998: 104) suggests that 'without symmetry there could not be asymmetrical functioning in man. Asymmetrical relations . . . emerge from and come out of the sea of symmetry.' These emerging asymmetric forms can thus be understood as 'limited "incarnations" of a vast reality, just as an individual is, if viewed from a certain angle, a small "incarnation" of a propositional function' (ibid.).

We find here both an interesting potential connection with complexity theory which understands bifurcations as symmetry-breaking events (such as those involved in the morphogenesis of an egg or the unfolding of the universe), and Deleuze and Guattari's vision of the actual emerging from the sea of the virtual. Although he does not refer to Matte-Blanco, DeLanda's (2004: 127) writing shows striking parallels, for example when he writes that 'unlike actual time which is asymmetric relative to the direction of relative pasts and futures, a pure becoming would imply a temporality which is perfectly symmetric in this respect, the direction of the arrow of time emerging as a broken symmetry only as the virtual is actualized.'

Assemblage theory

> What is an assemblage? It is a multiplicity which is made up of heterogenous terms and which establishes liaisons, relations between . . . different natures . . . it is a symbiosis, a 'sympathy'.
>
> (Deleuze, cited in DeLanda 2006: 121)

Perhaps DeLanda's most important contribution in his complexity-theory-influenced take on Deleuze and Guattari is *assemblage theory*. Assemblage theory studies how structures at all scales emerge through their interacting components. To take one example: '*States are made up not only of people but also of wood, fields, gardens, animals and commodities*' (Deleuze & Guattari 2003a: 333). Applied to social processes it offers a method which, 'starting at the personal (and even subpersonal) scale, climbs up one scale at a time all the way to territorial states and beyond' (DeLanda 2006: 6). For DeLanda, assemblage theory offers social theory a 'solution to the micro-macro problem in terms of a multiplicity of social entities operating at intermediate levels of scale' (ibid.). This also helps to plug a gap in Deleuze and Guattari's own work, as they move too rapidly, in DeLanda's view, between the molecular and the macro.

In some ways this parallels a similar necessity in psychoanalytic social theory when engaging with the work of Freud, who notoriously jumped in one 'bold' leap between findings derived from clinical work with individual patients to diagnosing the whole of civilization. Freud rightly pointed to the need for those 'who have the courage to think new things before they can demonstrate them' (Freud 1895, cited in Gay 1995: 76). But while this move initiated a revolution in theories and methods for the social sciences, it necessarily also led to a particular form of psychological reductionism and the loss of a certain amount of the complexity of psychosocial phenomena.

So what is an assemblage? In keeping with the models of SO described in Chapters 10 and 11, 'assemblages always exist in populations however small' (DeLanda 2006: 16). In addition, unlike totalities 'in which parts are linked by relations of interiority', assemblages 'are made up of parts which are self-subsistent and articulated by relations of exteriority, so that a part may be detached and made a component of another assemblage' (ibid.). Assemblages are to be understood through the complex morphogenetic process through which they arise, the processes studied with such richness by complexity theory.

DeLanda's micro-study of building up assemblage on assemblage recalls Holland's (1995) work, which used complexity theory to study how agents self-organize into higher-level '*metaagents*', and on into '*meta-metaagents*', and so on. These include how an 'aggregation of business firms forms an economy, the combination of antibodies creates an immune system, and a network of neurons forms the nervous system' (Eidelson 1997: 34). Of course, in reality the story is more complex than this Russian doll image, as an agent from one level can join an assemblage at a hierarchically different level. This is especially true where human social processes are concerned.

For DeLanda (2006: 28), the ontological status of all assemblages of whatever size 'is always that of unique singular individuals' because 'unlike taxonomic essentialism in which genus, species and individual are separate ontological categories, the ontology of assemblages is flat since it contains nothing but differently scaled individual singularities (or hacceities).' Timothy Morton (2010b) has described the relation of this 'flat' ontology to the ecological thought with reference to the u-bend of Žižek's toilet – the u-bend which phenomenologically takes our shit away, out from our reality. However, ecology shows us that there is no outside, there is no ontological u-bend. It is not just that with the 'hyperobject' of climate change it has disappeared, it actually never existed. The ecological crisis just shows us this truth that was always staring us in the face, or perhaps another opening of our bodies.

This flat ontology has two sides: actual entities, which include 'all the differently scaled social assemblages [that] are individual singularities', and their associated phase spaces, described 'by a distribution of universal singularities' (Bonta & Protevi 2004: 40). According to DeLanda:

> Preserving the ontological independence of each scale not only blocks attempts at micro-reductionism (as in neoclassical economics) and macro-reductionism (as in world-systems analysis) but also allows the integration of the valuable insights that different social scientists have developed while working at a specific spatiotemporal scale, from the extremely short duration of the small entities studied by Erving Goffman to the extremely long duration of the large entities studied by Fernand Braudel. Assemblage theory supplies the framework where the voices . . . can come together to form a chorus that does not harmonize its different components but interlocks them while respecting their heterogeneity.
>
> (DeLanda 2006: 119)

Of course DeLanda does not restrict assemblages to social structures, as assemblage theory offers not only a 'new philosophy of society' (DeLanda 2006) but also a way to approach all three of Guattari's 'ecologies' in a dense heterarchy of connectivity where, as Deleuze and Guattari (2003a: 549) put it, 'territorial assemblage opens onto a social assemblage' which is also 'connected to cosmic forces' and to 'pulsations of the earth.'

Meshworks and strata

> There is no question, however, of establishing a dualist opposition between the two types of multiplicities, molecular machines and molar machines; that would be no better than the dualism between the One and the multiple. There are only multiplicities of multiplicities forming a single assemblage . . . In Kafka, it is impossible to separate the erection of a great paranoid bureaucratic machine from the installation of little schizo machines of becoming-dog or becoming-beetle.
>
> (Deleuze & Guattari 2003a: 34)

In DeLanda's (2006: 11) reading, the distinction between assemblages and strata found in Deleuze and Guattari collapses into the distinction between two forms of assemblages, or two potentials present in all systems, which he labels *meshworks* and *hierarchies*. He finds support in *A Thousand Plateaus*, where Deleuze and Guattari (2003a: 337) write that when they 'oppose the consistency of assemblages to the stratification of milieus . . . this opposition is only relative, entirely relative.'

> Just as milieus swing between a stratum state and a movement of destratification, assemblages swing between a territorial closure that tends to restratify them and a deterritorializing movement that connects them to the Cosmos. Thus it is not surprising that the distinction we were seeking is not between assemblage and something else, but between two limits of any possible assemblage.
>
> (Deleuze & Guattari 2003a: 337)

Drawing on complexity theory, DeLanda (2005: 62) argues that *stratified systems*, including, for example, 'sedimentary rocks, species, and social classes', are 'the product of definite structure-generating processes that take as their starting point a heterogeneous collection of raw materials (pebbles, genes, roles), homogenize them through a sorting operation, and then consolidate the resulting uniform groupings into a more permanent state.' This means that all these structures (bureaucracies, species, sedimentary rocks) can be said to belong to a wider class of stratified systems or *hierarchies*. The same 'virtual diagram' applies.

Meshworks, on the other hand, are formed differently. Igneous rocks are formed by cooling magma, a heterogeneous intense flow formed from multiple components with different crystallization thresholds. As magma cools 'its different elements separate as they crystallize in sequence . . . those that solidify earlier serve as containers for those that acquire a crystal form later' which results in 'a complex set of heterogeneous crystals that interlock with one another, and this is what gives granite its superior strength' (DeLanda 2005: 64). The next element in this 'diagram' involves 'intercalary elements' including events such as 'reactions between liquid magma and the walls of an already crystallized component, nucleation events within the liquid which initiate the next crystallization', and also the defects ('dislocations') inside the crystals 'which promote growth from within . . . Finally, some chemical reactions within the magma may also generate endogenous stable states . . . forming beautiful spiral and concentric-circle patterns' (ibid.).

These two diagrams, the two processes underlying meshworks and strata-formation, can be found in all registers. Ecosystems and the internet are good examples of meshworks, while a species' gene pool represents a 'hierarchy of homogeneous elements' (ibid.: 112). A given ecosystem is also part of 'a far more complex assemblage or "problem" involving processes and products . . . in the multiple interacting dimensions of the geomorphological, climatological, economic, political, social, and cultural registers' (Bonta & Protevi 2004: 15). However, the distinction is not absolute and, like the length of the fractal coastline, it is completely dependent on scale.

> Even animals in total reproductive isolation may exchange genetic materials via inheritable viruses . . . [T]he evolutionary process . . . [is] more a meshwork than a strict hierarchy, a . . . rhizome . . . than a neatly branching tree . . . [O]n the time-scale of evolution the whole of the gene pool of the biosphere is available to all organisms . . . the more dramatic steps and apparent discontinuities in evolution are in fact attributable to very rare events involving the adoption of part or all of a foreign genome.
>
> (DeLanda 2005: 38)

Thus the meshwork/hierarchy distinction is better viewed as the 'molarizing' and 'molecularizing' potentials of any given system. As DeLanda (2005: 260) writes, 'meshworks give rise to hierarchies and hierarchies to meshworks . . . undergoing processes of destratification as well as restratification, as its proportions of homogeneous and heterogeneous components change.'

Body without organs

> You don't do it with a sledgehammer, you use a very fine file . . . Dismantling the organism has never meant killing yourself, but rather opening the body to connections that presuppose an entire assemblage, circuits, conjunctions, levels and thresholds, passages and distributions of intensity, and territories and deterritorializations . . . You have to keep enough of the organism for it to reform each dawn . . . you have to keep small rations of subjectivity in sufficient quantity to enable you to respond to the dominant reality. Mimic the strata. You don't reach the BwO [body without organs], and its plane of consistency, by wildly destratifying.
>
> (Deleuze & Guattari 2003a: 160–161)

What is the 'body without organs' (BwO)? After having briefly introduced this concept in Chapter 9, it is time to explore it in more detail. On the surface this is one of the strangest of Deleuze & Guattari ideas, and it is seemingly defined differently at different points in their writing. The BwO 'is not an empty body stripped of organs, but a body upon which that which serves as organs . . . is distributed according to crowd phenomena . . . in the form of molecular multiplicities' (Deleuze & Guattari 2003a: 30). One way of approaching the BwO is to view it as the virtual diagram constituting the limits of destratification of a system, or what Deleuze and Guattari sometimes call the 'plane of consistency'. The Earth, for example, 'is a body without organs . . . permeated by unformed, unstable matters, by flows in all directions, by free intensities or nomadic singularities, by mad or transitory particles' (Deleuze & Guattari 2003a: 40).

DeLanda distinguishes between the absolute and the relative BwO, the latter being the limit of destratification of any particular system. Therefore, 'what counts as destratified at any given time and in any given space is entirely relative' (DeLanda 2005: 261). Thus, if we take 'a cosmic viewpoint, our entire planet would itself be a mere provisional hardening in the vast flows of plasma which permeate the universe' (ibid.). This (plasma) would be perhaps the absolute BwO for matter. However, for the flow of biomass the BwO might be viewed as an egg, while the transversal flow of genes via viruses would be the BwO for replicators.

DeLanda (2005: 267) argues that Deleuze and Guattari's concept of the BwO creates a vision of a world where 'geology, biology, and linguistics are not seen as three separate spheres' but as 'coexisting and interacting flows' where 'one stratum can serve directly as a substratum for another.' This is crucial for the perspective of this book and the interaction of the three ecologies on which it is based. As Deleuze and Guattari write:

> A semiotic fragment rubs shoulders with a chemical interaction, an electron crashes into a language, a black hole captures a genetic message, a crystallization produces a passion, the wasp and the orchid cross a letter . . . *The plane of consistency knows nothing of differences in level, orders of magnitude, or distances. It knows nothing of the difference between the artificial and the natural. It knows nothing of the distinction between contents and expressions.*
>
> (Deleuze and Guattari 2003a: 69)

As we saw in Chapter 12, Deleuze and Guattari (2003a: 161) call for an experimental approach to draw out the virtual potentialities of the BwO. However, despite the at times one-dimensional celebration of 'schizoid destratification' by many of their followers (without the experience of the clinical psychoanalysis of Guattari), Deleuze and Guattari (2003a: 161) emphasize that in this process caution is required because: 'Staying stratified . . . is not the worst that can happen; the worst that can happen is if you throw the strata into demented or suicidal collapse.'

Memetics and the ecology of mind

> Every concept always has a *history* . . . In any concept there are usually bits or components that come from other concepts, which corresponded

to other problems and presupposed other planes . . . a concept also has a *becoming* that involves its relationship with concepts situated on the same plane. Here concepts link up with each other, support one another, coordinate their contours, articulate their respective problems, and belong to the same philosophy, even if they have different histories.

(Deleuze & Guattari 2003b: 18)

How do ideas interact? Is there some sort of natural selection which determines the survival of some ideas and the extinction or death of others? What sort of economics limits the multiplicity of ideas in a given region of mind? What are the necessary conditions for stability (or survival) of such a system or subsystem?

(Bateson 2000: xxiii)

Deleuze and Guattari, and also Bateson, point us towards a new ecological way of thinking about mind. Bateson's (2000) *Steps Towards the Ecology of Mind*, which partly inspired Guattari's (2000) *Three Ecologies*, provides a way to understand extinction as not only referring to biological organisms, but also to social and psychological forms, in ways which are deeply connected. Fallacies in the ecology of ideas can have direct and catastrophic results on the social and ecological registers (Bateson 2000: 297). As Bateson (2000: 492) writes: 'There is an ecology of bad ideas, just as there is an ecology of weeds, and it is characteristic of the system that basic error propagates itself. It branches out like a rooted parasite through the tissues of life.'

Bateson's ecology of mind shares similarities with the neo-Darwinian concept of *memes*, or cultural replicators (Dawkins 1989; Blackmore 2000).

We see an ant laboriously climbing up a stalk of grass . . . No good at all accrues to the ant. Is it just a fluke, then? . . . that's exactly what it is . . . The ant's brain has been invaded by a lancet fluke . . . tiny parasitic worms that need to get themselves into the intestines of a sheep or cow in order to reproduce . . . [M]emes . . . use human brains (instead of sheep stomachs) as their temporary homes, and jump from brain to brain to reproduce . . . they have been getting better and better at negotiating this elaborate cycle (because of all the competition between memes for limited places in brains) and, also like the lancet flukes, they don't need to have a clue about how or why they do this . . . They don't have nervous systems; they don't even have bodies . . . They are actually more like a simple virus . . . a virus is just a string of nucleic acid (a gene) with attitude . . . a meme is an information-packet with attitude – a recipe or instruction manual for doing something cultural . . . What is a meme made of? It is made of information which can be carried in *any* physical medium.

(Dennett 2003: 174–175)

Like the fluke or a virus, a meme does not necessarily benefit its host because if 'it can be horizontally transmitted at a greater rate than its bearer can reproduce, that bearer's fitness becomes largely irrelevant . . . cigarette smoking leaves a trail of corpses no less dead than those felled by a clone of spirochetes' (Dennett 2003: 178). Richard Dawkins, who is credited with first suggesting the concept of memes, explains that examples of memes include 'tunes, ideas, catch-phrases, clothes fashions, ways of making pots or of building arches' (Dawkins 1989: 192).

> Just as genes propagate themselves in the gene pool by leaping from body to body via sperms or eggs, so memes propagate themselves in the meme pool by leaping from brain to brain via a process which, in the broad sense, can be called imitation . . . If the idea catches on, it can be said to propagate itself, spreading from brain to brain . . . memes should be regarded as living structures, not just metaphorically but technically . . . When you plant a fertile meme in my mind you literally parasitize my brain, turning it into a vehicle for the meme's propagation in just the way that a virus may parasitize the genetic mechanism of a host cell. And this isn't just a way of talking – the meme for, say, 'belief in life after death' is actually realized physically, millions of times over, as a structure in the nervous systems of individual men the world over.
>
> (ibid.)

Thus what Dennett (2003: 188) calls 'universal Darwinism' refers to an abstract machine or algorithm which is *substrate-neutral*. One meme that Bateson (2000: 467) describes is 'Socrates', who 'as a bioenergetic individual is dead. But much of him still lives as a component in the contemporary ecology of ideas.' The same could be said of Bateson, Freud, and that strange assemblage we call Deleuze|Guattari, who continue to morph into strange new fractal patterns in the rhizosphere (Deleuze & Guattari 2003a: 238).

Partial objects, larval subjects, and the ecological self

> Mental characteristics of the system are immanent, not in some part, but in the system as a whole.
>
> (Bateson 2000: 274)

> The plane of immanence has two facets as Thought and as Nature . . . That is why there are always many infinite movements caught within each other, each folded in the others, so that the return of one instantaneously relaunches another in such a way that the plane of immanence is ceaselessly being woven, like a gigantic shuttle . . . they constitute its variable curvature, its concavities and convexities, its fractal nature.
>
> (Deleuze & Guattari 2003b: 38)

Bateson (2000: 318) claims that 'there are multiple differences between the thinking system and the 'self' as popularly conceived.' First, the mind he describes is not transcendent but 'immanent in a network of causal pathways' (ibid.). Following psychoanalysis, it is also 'not bounded with consciousness but extends to include the pathways of all unconscious mentation' (ibid.). But Bateson takes a further leap, claiming that the 'network is not bounded by the skin but includes all external pathways along which information can travel' so that '*any* ongoing ensemble of events and objects which has the appropriate complexity of causal circuits and the appropriate energy relations will surely show mental characteristics' (ibid.). Bateson thus initiates a neoSpinozist philosophy of mind within a purely materialist framework.

For Bateson, the communication system 'is not the physical individual but a wide network of pathways of messages' (ibid.: 251).

> Some of these pathways *happen* to be located outside the physical individual, others inside . . . the characteristics of the *system* are in no way dependent upon any boundary lines which we may superpose upon the communicational map. It is not communicationally meaningful to ask whether the blind man's stick or the scientist's microscope are 'parts' of the man who uses them . . . no boundary line – e.g. halfway up the stick – can be relevant in a description of the topology of this net.
>
> (ibid.)

We can find certain echoes of this in recent neuroscientific approaches to mind and consciousness. In particular, Dennett (2003: 127) writes that: 'If you make yourself really small, you can externalize virtually everything', by which he means that if you limit mind to consciousness and ignore unconscious processing you are left with the paradox discovered by Libet (2004) that the 'brain' makes decisions before 'you' do. For Dennett (2003: 127), '[t]his retreat of the Self into a walled enclave within which all the serious work of authorship has to be done parallels another retreat into the center of the brain . . . the Cartesian Theater', the idea of a central HQ within the brain where 'you' sit, responding to information and making decisions. Instead Dennett is emphatic: '*There is no such place*' (ibid.). 'Free will' should therefore not be understood as a causeless point of agency, but is rather something that 'has to be smeared out over time, not measured at instants . . . You are not out of the loop; you *are* the loop . . . You are not an extensionless point' (ibid.).

The mind/brain itself in this model functions rather like an ant colony or a pack, exhibiting 'swarm intelligence'. While Dennett (2003: 62) does not use these precise terms, he is describing a process of self-organization and emergence, a process which needs 'no ego or judge or . . . philosopher-king, no organ of unity or continuity' (ibid.). For Dennett (2003: 212), the recursive loops we have already studied in various forms, from stigmergy onwards, can, like the trail-laying activity of ants, include our own past choices so that consciousness becomes a crucial part of a system allowing an infinite process of recursivity. According to Dennett, this 'makes decision making a crowd phenomena' (ibid.).

This fits remarkably well with Deleuze's (2004: 78) theory of 'larval subjects': 'We speak of our "self" only in virtue of these thousands of little witnesses . . . [or] prepersonal singularities.' Deleuze and Guattari (2003a: 64) describe these as emerging from the 'cerebral-nervous milieu . . . the prehuman soup immersing us' and argue that 'the brain is a population.' Larval subjects and partial objects ('wild thoughts without a thinker' [Bion 1997]) self-organize into larger assemblages with emergent properties, which Varela, Thompson and Rosch (1991) call a 'society of mind'. Deleuze and Guattari include in this 'society' emergent assemblages below (larval subjects) and above (social machines) the traditionally conceived human subject. In the latter we could include the redistribution of internal objects through the social phantasy systems described by Elliott Jaques (1955) that was discussed in Chapter 12.

Furthermore, Deleuze and Guattari distinguish between the *subject of enunciation* (the 'I' or ego) and the *subject of the statement* (that which is named or 'bound to statements in conformity with a dominant reality') (Bonta & Protevi 2004: 155). The self is thus precariously balanced between forces both above (the 'collective assemblages of enunciation' which constrain but also enable it) and below (the larval subjects out of which it forms through emergent processes of self-organization). Thus the schizo-analytic unconscious is 'an acentered system . . . a machinic network of finite automata' (Deleuze & Guattari 2003a: 18), a self-organizing swarm or pack.

Deleuze and Guattari's approach to human subjectivity has many parallels with Bateson (2000: 315), who argues that while 'mind' can be described as 'immanent in those circuits of the brain which are complete within the brain' it is also immanent to pathways 'complete within the system, brain *plus* body . . . [or] man *plus* environment . . . the mental world . . . is not limited by the skin.' Bateson (2000: 467) suggests that just as 'Freudian psychology expanded the concept of mind inwards to include the whole communication system within the body – the autonomic, the habitual, and the vast range of unconscious process', we need a similar expansion outward. Both moves reduce 'the scope of the conscious self' and thereby demand a certain humility. Internal/external distinctions still retain some relevance, however, as 'coding and transmission of differences outside the body is very different from the coding and transmission inside'. However, these distinctions remain relative because '[e]xceptions occur on both sides of the line' (ibid.: 460).

This framework leads to a truly ecological conception of a mind 'immanent in the large biological system: the ecosystem. Or, if I draw the system boundaries at a different level . . . the total evolutionary structure' (ibid.: 466). However, Bateson (ibid.: 493) warns that this should not be confused with the 'Supreme Mind of Aristotle . . . incapable of error and incapable of insanity.' Rather, what he calls immanent mind 'is only too capable of insanity' (ibid.). As Bateson writes, 'the eco-mental system called Lake Erie is a part of *your* wider eco-mental system . . . if Lake Erie is driven insane, its insanity is incorporated in the larger system of *your* thought and experience' (ibid.: 492).

This brings us to the problem of consciousness in the modern world, and to how fallacies in the ecology of ideas impact on natural ecologies:

> On the one hand, we have the systemic nature of the individual human being, the systemic nature of the culture in which he lives, and the systemic nature of the biological, ecological system around him; and, on the other hand . . . consciousness is, almost of necessity, blinded to the systemic nature of the man himself . . . the systems are nonetheless punishing of any species unwise enough to quarrel with its ecology.
>
> (Bateson 2000: 440)

The dangers of the anthropocentrism which is so distrusted by eco-psychology are connected here to the system blindness of consciousness. For Bateson, while 'life depends upon interlocking *circuits* of contingency', unaided consciousness 'must always tend toward hate' because 'seeing only arcs of circuits, the individual is continually surprised and necessarily angered when his hardheaded policies return to plague the inventor' (ibid.: 146). We therefore need to open ourselves up to the wider arcs that make up immanent mind.

Here we return to the concept of the ecological self introduced in Chapter 7. Even Daniel Dennett (2003: 180), as 'hard-nosed' a scientist-philosopher as any, entertains the possibility of this leap, arguing that the 'self-as-ultimate-beneficiary can in principle be indefinitely distributed . . . extending the domain of the self.' The alternative, given our current ecological crisis, is bleak. In our current precarious situation, Bateson's words of warning are more cogent now than ever:

> [A]s you arrogate all mind to yourself, you will see the world around you as mindless and therefore not entitled to moral or ethical consideration. The environment will seem to be yours to exploit . . . If this is your estimate of your relation to nature *and you have an advanced technology*, your likelihood of survival will be that of a snowball in hell. You will die either of the toxic by-products of your own hate, or, simply, of over-population and overgrazing . . . If I am right, the whole of our thinking about what we are and what other people are has got to be restructured. This is not funny, and I do not know how long we have to do it in.
>
> (Bateson 2000: 468)

Chapter 14

Ecopsychoanalysis and the future of the three ecologies

> The last three or four centuries have witnessed an intense homogeniza-
> tion of the world (biologically, linguistically, economically) . . . Changing
> our way of thinking . . . is a necessary first step, but . . . we will need to
> destratify reality itself . . . without the guarantee of a golden age ahead,
> knowing full well the dangers . . . [T]hese new theories offer a . . . joyful
> conception of reality.
>
> (DeLanda 2005: 271–274)

> A healthy ecology of human civilization would be defined . . . [as a]
> system of environment combined with high human civilization in which
> the flexibility of the civilization shall match that of the environment to
> create an ongoing complex system, open-ended for slow change of even
> basic (hard-programmed) characteristics.
>
> (Bateson 2000: 502)

Dreaming at the precipice

The metaphor of an acrobat on a high wire referred to by Bateson (2000:
506) is particularly apt for us now. The acrobat, in order not to fall,
requires maximum freedom to 'move from one position of instability to
another.' This is the paradox of order and disorder that we discussed in
Chapter 11. In our current ecological crisis we must face the possibility that
achieving the freedom and flexibility that we need to survive requires a
fundamental re-examination of many of the basic coordinates of our lives,
and some of our most cherished theories. In analyzing the rise and fall of
past civilizations, we find that a 'new technology for the exploitation of
nature or a new technique for the exploitation of other men . . . gives elbow
room or flexibility' but that 'the using up of that flexibility is death'
(Bateson 2000: 503).

Like the patient stuck on a local optima that we discussed in Chapter 12,
unable or unwilling to cross the threshold to a more adaptive peak, entire

species, and civilizations, have in the past found themselves in dangerous dead ends and unable to change. These dead ends include those within the ecology of mind, ways of thinking and being that become pathological if they fail to evolve along with the constantly shifting relations in the constitution of natural and social ecosystems. Ecopsychoanalysis, which draws on the tools and ideas of nonlinear science, understands that our world is governed by nonlinear dynamics, to the extent that the prediction and control promised by Enlightenment rationality will always remain to some degree illusory. Instead, we need to engage with the creativity of the Earth, and follow the lines of flight we uncover, exploring 'the potential for self-organization inherent in even the humblest forms of matter-energy' (DeLanda 2005: 273).

Our species has experienced such severe existential threats before. One of the most extreme examples was an evolutionary bottleneck which molecular biology shows us occurred approximately 70,000 years ago, when the human species was down to the last few thousand individuals or even less. Geological evidence suggests that this near extinction may have been linked to the Toba supervolcano in Indonesia, whose eruption triggered sudden climate change with major environmental impacts (Dawkins 2004). We do not know how we emerged from that particular crisis, or how close we may have come to extinction at various other times in our history.

We might reflect on these experiences as applying to the whole species an idea that Winnicott (1974: 104) once discussed in terms of the fear of breakdown in individual psychoanalysis. For Winnicott, this fear refers to a breakdown that has already occurred, but it was a catastrophe which took place before there was yet a subject to fully experience it with a reflective consciousness. At the risk of anthropocentrism, we might do well to consider Dennett's (2003: 267) point that in many ways we do occupy a unique position in the history of the Earth, as 'wherever lineages found themselves on local peaks of the adaptive landscape, their members had no way of so much as wondering whether or not there might be higher, better summits on the far side of this valley or that.'

Despite all the defensive reasons to *not* know which we explored in Chapters 4–7, we are, to some extent at least, becoming conscious of the enormity of the danger which confronts us. Today we are forced to think in these complex terms, to wonder about other valleys and other peaks on the plane of immanence, our virtual realm of possibility, to find a path through the current deadlock. As we saw in Part I of this book, these are difficult times. As Bateson (2000: 495) writes, the 'massive aggregation of threats to man and his ecological systems arises out of errors in our habits of thought at deep and partly unconscious levels.'

The contribution of psychoanalysis is precisely to help us to overcome such errors through investigating their unconscious roots. Ecopsychoanalysis recognizes the need for a radical questioning of our theories, whether psychoanalytic, philosophical, scientific or political, and the corresponding ways of living individually and collectively that they make possible and reflect. However, it does so through a respectful engagement with the best that our various traditions have to offer, entering into uncanny new symbioses, making these disciplines strange to themselves not in order to destroy them but to make them more vital and alive.

Despite the gravity of our situation, there are 'patches of sanity still surviving in the world' (Bateson 2000: 495), ideas in the ecology of mind worth exploring, helping us to construct a new alpha function we can only hope is capable of dreaming at the precipice. This book has sought to uncover what some of the components of this might be, focusing in particular on the constructive synergy between psychoanalysis, complexity theory, ecology, and the philosophy of Deleuze and Guattari. Ecopsychoanalysis wonders whether it is precisely in the very severity of the desperate ecological situation we face that a great opportunity lies for re-imagining the human, our societies, and our place in the world. It is in the ecopsychological spirit of nurturing hope while facing despair that this book was written.

However, there is no 'big Other' (Žižek 2007) to guarantee our success, or even our future existence. In a chaotic world without certainty, ecopsychoanalysis can turn to the experimental pragmatics of Deleuze and Guattari (2003a: 161): 'Lodge yourself on a stratum, experiment with the opportunities it offers . . . find potential movements of deterritorialization, possible lines of flight, experience them, produce flow conjunctions here and there, try out continuums of intensities segment by segment, have a small plot of new land at all times.'

Assumptions according to which we have long lived our lives collapse as we begin to feel the disturbing effects of the hyperobject of climate change on the ecology of mind. Ecopsychoanalysis itself can be viewed as a hyperobject in that it does not yet fully exist. It should not be seen as an end state but a process of becoming, a work in progress, a meshwork emerging at the interstices of the three ecologies, and the elaboration of an alpha function that is able to think and dwell in our new uncanny home. As Bateson (2000: 512) writes, 'we are not outside the ecology for which we plan – we are always and inevitably a part of it. Herein lies the charm and the terror of ecology.' Ecopsychoanalysis can never occupy an outside from which to explore and engage with the new strange ecology(s), but is always already *extimate* with it (Lacan 1992: 139).

For all its chaos, *because* of all its chaos, the world is still a place of wonder, and we can only hope that we find ways of staying in it at least a little while longer. The nonlinearity and chaos of nature, and the forms of thinking required to sustain our relationship to it beyond the limited horizons of our experience, are both frightening and liberating. Yet, despite the anxiety, guilt and terror that climate change forces us to face, this moment of crisis can also offer us an opportunity for a more open vision of ourselves, as subjects, as societies, and as a species among the inter-connected life systems of the Earth.

References

Abraham, D. (1995). A postscript on language, modeling, and metaphor. In D. Abraham & A. Giligen (eds), *Chaos Theory in Psychology: Contributions in Psychology*. Greenwood (pp. 311–336).

Adorno, T. & Horkheimer, M. (2002). *Dialectic of Enlightenment*. Stanford University Press.

Aizenstat, S. (1995). Jungian psychology and the world unconscious. In T. Roszak, M. Gomes & A. Kanner (eds) (1995), *Ecopsychology: Restoring the Earth, Healing the Mind*. Sierra Club Books (pp. 92–100).

American Psychological Association (2010). Global Climate Change Psychology: Addressing a Multifaceted Phenomenon and Set of Challenges. Report of the APA Task Force on the Interface Between Psychology & Global Climate Change.

Anisimov, O. (2007). Potential feedback of thawing permafrost to the global climate system through methane emission. *Environmental Research Letters*, *2*(4), 1–7.

Aron, L. (1996). *A Meeting of Minds: Mutuality in Psychoanalysis*. The Analytic Press.

Axelrod, R. A. (1984). *The Evolution of Cooperation*. Basic Books.

Baiocchi, G. & Minx, J. (2010). Understanding changes in the UK's CO_2 emissions: A global perspective. *Environmental Science and Technology*, *44*(4), 1177–1184.

Bak, P. (1994). Self-organized criticality: A holistic view of nature. In G. Cowan, D. Pines & D. Meltzer (eds), *Santa Fe Institute Studies In the Sciences of Complexity, Proceedings Volume XIX. Complexity: Metaphors, models, and reality*. Addison Wesley (pp. 477–496).

Bak, P. & Chen, K. (1991). Self-organized criticality. *Scientific American*, *264*(1), 46–53.

Bakhtin, M. (1984). *Rabelais and His World*. Indiana University Press.

Bamberg, S. & Schmidt, P. (1999). Regulating transport: Behavioral intervention in the field. *Journal of Consumer Policy*, *22*, 479–509.

Bandura, A. (1986). *Social Foundations of Thought and Action: A Social Cognitive Theory*. Prentice Hall.

—— (2002). Environmental sustainability by sociocognitive deceleration of population growth. In P. Schmuck & W. Schultz (eds), *Psychology of Sustainable Development*. Kluwer (pp. 209–238).

Barbosa, P. & Castellanos, I. (eds) (2004). *Ecology of Predator-Prey Interactions.* Oxford University Press.

Barkow, J. (2006). *Missing the Revolution: Darwinism for Social Scientists.* Oxford University Press.

Barrows, A. (1995). The ecopsychology of child development. In T. Roszak, M. Gomes & A. Kanner (1995). *Ecopsychology: Restoring the Earth, Healing the Mind.* Sierra Club Books (pp. 101–110).

Bateson, G. (2000). *Steps Towards an Ecology of Mind.* University of Chicago Press.

—— (2002). *Mind and Nature: A Necessary Unity.* Hampton Press.

Baum, W. (2005). *Understanding Behaviorism: Behavior, Culture and Evolution.* Blackwell.

BBC (2009). Green spaces 'improve health'. Retrieved from: http://news.bbc.co.uk/2/hi/8307024.stm

—— (2010a). Climate scepticism 'on the rise'. Retrieved from: http://news.bbc.co.uk/2/hi/science/nature/8500443.stm

—— (2010b). BBC Climate Poll. Retrieved from: http://news.bbc.co.uk/nol/shared/bsp/hi/pdfs/05_02_10climatechange.pdf

—— (2010c). Climate science must be more open, say MPs. Retrieved from: http://news.bbc.co.uk/2/hi/science/nature/8595483.stm

Becker, E. (1973). *The Denial of Death.* Collier-Mac.

Bell, D. (2007). 'Anything is Possible and Everything is Permitted': Psychoanalytic Reflections on Hannah Arendt's Elements of Totalitarianism. 45th Congress of the International Psychoanalytical Association, Berlin 2007. Retrieved from: http://www.ipa.org.uk/docs/Fipa-200701-381287-1-Totalit13.doc

Bell, J. (2006). *Philosophy at the Edge of Chaos: Gilles Deleuze and the Philosophy of Difference.* University of Toronto.

Bertalanffy, L. (1968). *General System Theory: Foundations, Development, Applications.* George Braziller.

Bertens, H. (1995). *The Idea of the Postmodern: A History.* Routledge.

Beyer, W. (2003). Mandelbrot Set. Retrieved from: http://commons.wikimedia.org/wiki/User:Wolfgangbeyer and http://www.wolfgangbeyer.de/

Bigda-Peyton, F. (2004). When drives are dangerous: Drive theory and resource over-consumption. *Modern Psychoanalysis, 29*, 251–270.

Bion, W. (1957). The differentiation of the psychotic from the non-psychotic personalities. *International Journal of Psycho-Analysis, 38*, 266–275. Reprinted in *Second Thoughts* (1984).

—— (1958). On hallucination. *International Journal of Psycho-Analysis, 39*(5), 341–349. Reprinted in *Second Thoughts* (1984).

—— (1959). Attacks on linking. *International Journal of Psycho-Analysis, 40*(5–6), 308–315.

—— (1961). *Experiences in Groups And Other Papers.* Tavistock.

—— (1962a). The psychoanalytic study of thinking. *International Journal of Psycho-Analysis, 43*, 306–310.

—— (1962b). *Learning from Experience.* Heinemann.

—— (1965). *Transformations.* William Heinemann.

Bion, W. R. (1967). Notes on memory and desire. *Psycho-Analytic Forum, 1*(3), 271–280. Reprinted in E. Bott Spillius (ed.) (1988), *Melanie Klein Today Vol. 2: Mainly Practice.* Routledge (pp. 17–21).

—— (1984). *Second Thoughts: Selected Papers on Psychoanalysis*. Karnac.

—— (1989). *Elements of Psychoanalysis*. Karnac.

—— (1997). *Taming Wild Thoughts*. Karnac.

—— (2007). *Attention and Interpretation*. Karnac.

Bird, W. (2007). *Natural Thinking: Investigating the Links Between the Natural Environment, Biodiversity and Mental Health*. Royal Society for the Protection of Birds.

Black, J., Stern, P. & Elworth, J. (1985). Personal and contextual influences on household energy adaptations. *Journal of Applied Psychology, 70*(1), 3–21.

Blackmore, S. (2000). *The Meme Machine*. Oxford University Press.

Bodnar, S. (2008). Wasted and bombed: Clinical enactments of a changing relationship to the Earth. *Psychoanalytic Dialogues, 18*, 484–512.

Bonabeau, E., Dorigo, M. & Theraulaz, G. (1999). *Swarm Intelligence: From Natural To Artificial Systems*. Oxford University Press.

Bonaparte, M. (1971). *The Life and Works of Edgar Allan Poe*. Humanities Press.

Bondi, L. & Fewell, J. (2003). 'Unlocking the cage door': The spatiality of counselling. *Social and Cultural Geography, 4*(4), 527–547.

Bonta, M. & Protevi, J. (2004). *Deleuze and Geophilosophy: A Guide and Glossary*. Edinburgh University Press.

Boston Change Process Study Group & Nahum, J. (2008). Forms of relational meaning: Issues in the relations between the implicit and reflective-verbal domains. *Psychoanalytic Dialogues, 18*(2), 125–148.

Bowlby, J. (1988). *A Secure Base: Parent–Child Attachment and Healthy Human Development*. Tavistock professional book. Routledge.

Boyer, A. (2008). Extinction patterns in the avifauna of the Hawaiian islands. *Diversity and Distributions: A Journal of Conservation Biogeography, 14*(3), 509–517.

Bradshaw, G. (2009). Transformation through service: Trans-species psychology and its implications for ecotherapy. In L. Buzzell & C. Chalquist (eds), *Ecotherapy: Healing with Nature in Mind*. Sierra Club Books (pp. 157–165).

Brody, E. (1962). *Review of The Non-human Environment in Normal Development and Schizophrenia*, by Harold Searles. *Psychoanalytic Quarterly, 31*, 104–106.

Brohan, P., Kennedy, J. J., Harris, I., Tett, S. F. B. & Jones, P. D. (2006). Uncertainty estimates in regional and global observed temperature changes: A new dataset from 1850. *Journal of Geophysical Research, 111*, 1–26.

Broughton, J. & Siegel, L. (2006). Early California: A killing field – Research shatters utopian myth, finds Indians decimated birds. *Continuum* (magazine of the University of Utah), Spring Issue. Retrieved from: http://www.eurekalert.org/pub_releases/2006-02/uou-eca021006.php

Brower, M. & Leon, W. (1999). *The Consumer's Guide to Effective Environmental Choices: Practical Advice From the Union of Concerned Scientists*. Random House.

Brown, S. & Stenner, P. (2009). *Psychology without Foundations: History, Philosophy and Psychosocial Theory: Constructionism, Mediation and Critical Psychology*. Sage Publications.

Brownsell, A. (2009, June 23). United Nations launches Hopenhagen climate change campaign. *Marketing*. Retrieved from: http://www.marketingmagazine.co.uk/news/915337/United-Nations-launches-Hopenhagen-climate-change-campaign/

Büntgen, U., Tegel, W., Nicolussi, K., McCormick, M., Frank, D., Trouet, V., Esper, J. *et al.* (2011, January 13). 2500 Years of European Climate Variability and Human Susceptibility. *Science.* doi: 10.1126/*science.1197175*

Busch, F. (2007). 'I Noticed': The emergence of self-observation in relationship to pathological attractor sites. *International Journal of Psycho-Analysis, 88*, 423–441.

Buss, D. (2004). *Evolutionary Psychology: The New Science of the Mind.* Pearson/A & B

—— (ed.) (2005). *The Handbook of Evolutionary Psychology.* Wiley (pp. 5–67).

Butler, J. (2006). *Gender Trouble: Feminism and the Subversion of Identity.* Routledge.

Butler, R. (2008, Spring issue). A climatologist walks into a bar: An inconvenient joke. *Intelligent Life Magazine.* Retrieved from: http://www.moreintelligentlife.com/story/a-climatologist-walks-into-a-bar

Buzzell, L. (2009). Asking different questions: Therapy for the human animal. In L. Buzzell & C. Chalquist (eds) (2009), *Ecotherapy: Healing with Nature in Mind.* Sierra Club Books (pp. 46–54).

Buzzell, L. & Chalquist, C. (eds) (2009a). *Ecotherapy: Healing with Nature in Mind.* Sierra Club Books.

Buzzell, L. & Chalquist, C. (2009b). Psyche and nature in a circle of healing. In L. Buzzell & C. Chalquist (eds), *Ecotherapy: Healing with Nature in Mind.* Sierra Club Books (pp. 17–21).

Camazine, S., Deneubourg, J.-L., Franks, N., Sneyd, J., Theraulaz, G. & Bonabeau, E. (2001). *Self Organization In Biological Systems.* Princeton University Press.

Cameron, J. (2010, February 17). Interview by Charlie Rose [Television recording]. Retrieved from: www.charlierose.com/view/interview/10866#frame_top

Canavan, G. (2008). Thoughts on Zizecology. *Culture Monkey.* Retrieved from: http://culturemonkey.blogspot.com/2008/06/thoughts-on-zizecology-1.html

Carter, N. (ed.) (2010). Minding the animal psyche. *Spring: A Journal of Archetype and Culture 83*, spring edition.

Cess, R. (2005). Atmospheric science: Water vapor feedback in climate models. *Science, 310*(5749), 795–796.

Chalquist, C. (2009). A look at the ecotherapy research evidence. *Ecopsychology, 1*(2), 1–11.

Chodorow, N. (1991). *Feminism and Psychoanalytic Theory.* Yale University Press.

Clarke, S. (2003). *Social Theory, Psychoanalysis and Racism.* Palgrave Macmillan.

Clarke, S. & Hoggett, P. (eds) (2008). *Object Relations and Social Relations: The Implications of the Relational Turn in Psychoanalysis.* Karnac.

Climate Action Network (2010). *Think globally sabotage locally: How and why European companies are funding climate change deniers in the 2010 US Senate race.* Climate Action Network (Europe, October 2010). Retrieved from: http://www.climnet.org/component/docman/doc_download/1719-caught-eu-companies-funding-climate-legislation-blockers-in-us-senate

Clover, C. (1993). *Men, Women and Chain Saws: Gender in the Horror Film.* Princeton University Press.

Cohen, M. (1997). *Reconnecting With Nature: Finding Wellness Through Restoring Your Bond With the Earth.* Ecopress.

Cohen, P. & Cohen, J. (2001). Life values and adolescents' mental health. In

P. Schmuck & K. Sheldon (eds), *Life Goals and Well-Being. Towards a Positive Psychology of Human Striving*. Hogrefe & Huber (pp. 167–181).

Cohen, S. (2001). *States of Denial: Knowing about Atrocities and Suffering*. Polity.

Cooper, J. (2007). *Cognitive Dissonance: 50 Years of a Classic Theory*. Sage Publications.

Coren, G. (2010, January 9). If I hear another global warming joke, I'll . . . *The Times*. Retrieved from: http://www.timesonline.co.uk/tol/comment/columnists/giles_coren/article6981487.ece

Creed, B. (1993). *The Monstrous Feminine*. Routledge.

—— (2005). *Phallic Panic: Film, Horror and the Primal Uncanny*. Melbourne University Press.

—— (2009). Freud's worst nightmare: Dining with Dr. Hannibal Lecter. In S. Schneider (ed.), *Horror Film and Psychoanalysis: Freud's Worst Nightmare*. Cambridge University Press.

Crompton, T. (2010). Common cause: The case for working with our cultural values. WWF, Oxfam, Friends of the Earth, CPRE, Climate Outreach Information Network. Retrieved from: http://assets.wwf.org.uk/downloads/common_cause_report.pdf

Crutzen, P. & Stoermer, E. (2000). The 'Anthropocene'. *Global Change Newsletter*, *41*, 17–18.

Csikszentmihalyi, M. (1999). If we are so rich, why aren't we happy? *American Psychologist*, *54*(10), 821–827.

Dalal, F. (2002). *Race, Colour and the Process of Racialization: New Perspectives from Group Analysis, Psychoanalysis and Sociology*. Routledge.

Darley, J. & Latané, B. (1968). Bystander intervention in emergencies: Diffusion of responsibility. *Journal of Personality and Social Psychology*, *8*, 377–383.

Dawes, R. (1980). Social dilemmas. *Annual Review of Psychology*, *31*, 169–193.

Dawes, R. & Messick, D. (2000). Social dilemmas. *International Journal of Psychology*, *35*(2), 111–116.

Dawkins, R. (1989). *The Selfish Gene*. Oxford University Press.

—— (1996). *The Blind Watchmaker: Why the Evidence for Evolution Reveals a Universe without Design*. W. W. Norton & Company.

—— (1997). *Climbing Mount Improbable*. W. W. Norton & Co.

—— (2004). *The Ancestors Tale: A Pilgrimage to the Dawn of Life*. Weidenfeld & Nicolson.

Day, W. (1985). *In the Circles of Fear and Desire: A Study of Gothic Fantasy*. Chicago University Press.

DeLanda, M. (2004). *Intensive Science and Virtual Philosophy*. Continuum.

—— (2005). *A Thousand Years of Nonlinear History*. Swerve.

—— (2006). *A New Philosophy of Society: Assemblage Theory and Social Complexity*. Continuum.

Deleuze, G. (1986). *Cinema 1: The Movement-Image*. University of Minnesota Press.

—— (1989). *Cinema 2: The Time-Image*. University of Minnesota Press.

Deleuze, G. & Guattari, F. (2000). *Anti-Oedipus: Capitalism and Schizophrenia*. Viking.

—— (2003a). *A Thousand Plateaus: Capitalism and Schizophrenia*. University of Minnesota Press.

—— (2003b). *What is Philosophy?* Verso.

DeMayo, N. (2009). Horses, humans, and healing. In L. Buzzell & C. Chalquist (eds), *Ecotherapy: Healing with Nature in Mind*. Sierra Club Books (pp. 149–156).

De Mijolla-Mellor, S. (2005). On Transience. *International Dictionary of Psycho-analysis*. Retrieved from: http://www.encyclopedia.com/doc/1G2-3435301016.html

Dennett, D. (2003). *Freedom Evolves*. Viking.

Derrida, J. (1998). *Resistances of Psychoanalysis*. Stanford University Press.

Desslet, A., Zhang, Z. & Yang, P. (2008). Water-vapor climate feedback inferred from climate fluctuations, 2003–2008. Geophysical Research Letters, 35, L20704.doi: 10.1029/2008GL035333

Dewey, J. (2005). *Art as Experience*. Penguin Perigree.

Diamond, J. (2006). *Collapse: How Societies Choose to Fail or Survive*. Penguin.

Dietrich, D., Fodor, G., Zucker, G. & Bruckner, D. (eds) (2008). *Simulating the Mind: A Technical Neuropsychoanalytical Approach*. Springer.

Dodds, J. (2008). Artificial group psychodynamics: Emergence of the collective. In D. Dietrich, G. Fodor, G. Zucker & D. Bruckner, *Simulating the Mind: A Technical Neuropsychoanalytical Approach*. Springer.

—— (2010). Psychoanalysis and Ecology at the Edge of Chaos. MPhil Thesis, Sheffield University's School for Health and Related Research (ScHARR).

—— (2011a). The monstrous brain: A neuropsychoanalytic aesthetics of horror? *Psyart Journal for the Psychological Study of the Arts*. Retrieved from: http://www.psyartjournal.com/article/show/dodds-the_monstrous_brain_a_neuropsychoanalyti

—— (2011b). From psychoanalysis to schizoanalysis? On Anna Powell's 'Deleuze and Horror Film'. *Deleuze Studies* (forthcoming).

—— (2011c). The ecology of phantasy. In M.-J. Rust & N. Totton, *Vital Signs: Psychological Responses to Ecological Crisis*. Karnac.

Dooley, K. (1997). A complex adaptive systems model of organization change. *Nonlinear Dynamics, Psychology, and Life Sciences*, *1*(1), 69–97. doi: 10.1023/A:1022375910940

Doppelt, R. (2008). The greatest failure of thought in human history. *Christian Science Monitor*. Retrieved from: http://www.csmonitor.com/Commentary/Opinion/2008/0827/p09s01-coop.html

Dore, M. (2010). Modelling sustainable development: A nonlinear approach. *Society for Chaos Theory in Psychology and Life Sciences Newsletter*, *18*(1), 14–19. (Special theme article collection on nonlinearity & sustainability).

Dujisin, Z. (2007). Environmentalism as bad as communism. Interpress Sevice News Agency. Retrieved from: http://ipsnews.net/news.asp?idnews=37133

Durning, A. (1995). Are we happy yet? In T. Roszak, M. Gomes & A. Kanner (eds), *Ecopsychology*. Sierra Club Books (pp. 68–76).

Edelman, G. (2006). *Second Nature: Brain Science and Human Knowledge*. Yale University Press.

Eidelson, R. (1997). Complex adaptive systems in the behavioral and social sciences. *Review of General Psychology*, *1*(1), 42–71.

Elgin, D. (1993). *Voluntary Simplicity: Toward a Way of Life that is Outwardly Simple, Inwardly Rich* (rev. ed.). Quill.

Elkins, J. (1994). The failed and the inadvertent: Art history and the concept of the unconscious. *International Journal of Psychoanalysis*, *75*, 119–132.

Elliot, A. (1999). *Social Theory and Psychoanalysis in Transition: Self and Society from Freud to Kristeva*. Free Association Books.

Fairbairn, R. (1992). *Psychoanalytic Studies of the Personality*. Routledge.

Felman, S. & Laub, D. (1991). *Testimony: Crises of Witnessing in Literature, Psychoanalysis, and History*. Routledge.

Ferenczi, S. (1952). First contributions to psycho-analysis. *Internatinal Psycho-Analysis Library*, *45*, 1–331. Hogarth Press and the Institute of Psycho-Analysis.

Finckenauer, J. (1982). *Scared Straight! and the Panacea Phenomenon*. Prentice-Hall.

Finucane, M., Alhakami, A., Slovic, P. & Johnson, S. (2000). The affect heuristic in judgments of risks and benefits. *Journal of Behavioral Decision Making*, *13*(1), 1–17.

Fisher, A. (2009). Ecopsychology as radical praxis. In L. Buzzel & C. Chalquist, *Ecotherapy: Healing with Nature in Mind*. Sierra Club Books.

Fonagy, P., Gergely, G., Jurist, E. & Target, M. (2002). *Affect Regulation, Mentalization, and the Development of the Self*. Other Press.

Foucault, M. (1988). *Madness and Civilization: A History of Insanity in the Age of Reason*. Vintage.

Foulkes, S. (1990). *Selected Papers of S.H. Foulkes: Psychoanalysis and Group Analysis*. Karnac.

Fraha, A. (2004). Systems psychodynamics: The formative years of an interdisciplinary field at the Tavistock Institute. *History of Psychology*, *7*(1), 65–84.

Francois, C. (1999). Systemics and cybernetics in a historical perspective. *Systems Research and Behavioral Science*, *16*, 203–219.

Freud, A. (1936). *The Ego and the Mechanisms of Defence*. Hogarth.

Freud, S. (1900a). The interpretation of dreams. *SE IV* (pp. ix–627).

—— (1900b). Letter from Freud to Fliess, February 1, 1900. *The Complete Letters of Sigmund Freud to Wilhelm Fliess, 1887–1904*, 397–398. Belknap Press.

—— (1905). Jokes and their relation to the unconscious. *SE VIII* (pp. 1–247).

—— (1909). Analysis of a phobia in a five-year-old boy. Pelican Freud Library, Vol. 8 (1977).

—— (1910). 'Wild' psycho-analysis. *SE XI* (pp. 219–228).

—— (1911). Formulations on the two principles of mental functioning. *SE XII* (pp. 213–226).

—— (1913a). Totem and taboo. *SE XIII* (pp. vii–162).

—— (1913b). The theme of the three caskets. *SE XII* (pp. 289–302).

—— (1915). Thoughts for the times on war and death. *SE XIV* (pp. 273–300).

—— (1916). On transience. *SE XIV* (pp. 303–307).

—— (1918). From the history of an infantile neurosis. *SE XVII* (pp. 1–124).

—— (1919). The 'Uncanny'. *SE XVII* (pp. 217–256).

—— (1920). Beyond the pleasure principle. *SE XVIII* (pp. 7–66).

—— (1921). Group psychology and the analysis of the ego. *SE XVIII* (pp. 65–144).

—— (1925). Some psychical consequences of the anatomical distinction between the sexes. *SE XIX* (pp. 241–258).

—— (1927). The Future of an Illusion. *SE XXI* (pp. 1–56).

—— (1930). Civilization and its Discontents. *SE XXI* (pp. 57–146).

—— (1933). New Introductory Lectures On Psycho-Analysis. *SE XXII* (pp. 1–182).

—— (1938). An outline of psycho-analysis. *SE XXIII* (pp. 139–208).

—— (1991). A seventeenth-century demonological neurosis. In *Civilization, Society and Religion*. Penguin (pp. 377–433).

Freud, S. & Einstein, A. (1933). Why War. In S. Freud, New Introductory Lectures on Psycho-Analysis. *SE XXII* (pp. 1–182).

Friedländer, S. (1978). *History and Psychoanalysis: An Inquiry into the Possibilities and Limits of Psychohistory*. Holmes & Meier.

Friedlingstein, P., Bopp, L., Ciais, P., Dufresne, J.-L., Fairhead, L., LeTrent, H., Orr, J. et al. (2001). Positive feedback between future climate change and the carbon cycle. *Geophysical Research Letters, 28*(8), 1543–1546.

Fromm, E. (1964). *The Heart of Man*. Harper & Row.

—— (1992). *The Anatomy of Human Destructiveness*. Holt.

—— (2001). *The Fear of Freedom*. Routledge.

—— (2006). *Beyond the Chains of Illusion: My Encounter with Marx and Freud*. Continuum.

Frosh, S. (2010). *Psychoanalysis Outside the Clinic: Interventions in Psychosocial Studies*. Palgrave Macmillan.

Frumkin, H. (2001). Beyond toxicity: The greening of environmental health. *American Journal of Preventative Medicine, 20*(3), 234–240.

Frumkin, H. & Louv, R. (2007). The powerful link between conserving land and preserving health. For the Land Trust Alliance Special Anniversary Report 2007. Retrieved from: http://atfiles.org/files/pdf/FrumkinLouv.pdf

Fuery, P. (2003). *Madness and Cinema: Psychoanalysis, Spectatorship and Culture*. Palgrave Macmillan.

Galatzer-Levy, R. (1995). Psychoanalysis and dynamical systems theory: Prediction and self similarity. *Journal of the American Psychoanalytic Association, 43*, 1085–1113.

Gardiner, M. (ed.) (1972). *The Wolf-Man and Sigmund Freud*. Hogarth.

Gardner, G. & Stern, P. C. (1996). *Environmental Problems and Human Behavior*. Allyn & Bacon.

Gay, P. (1995). Freud: A Life for Our Time. Papermac.

Genosko, G. (1993). Freud's bestiary: How does psychoanalysis treat animals? *Psychoanalytic Review, 80*, 603–632.

—— (2002). *Felix Guattari: An Aberrant Introduction*. Continuum.

Gifford, R. (2007). *Environmental Psychology: Principles and Practice* (4th ed.). Optimal Books.

Gillett, N. (2007). Greenhouse gases and water vapour: When 'positive feedback' is a bad thing. Retrieved from: http://www.scientificblogging.com/news_account/greenhouse_gases_and_water_vapor_when_positive_feedback_is_a_bad_thing

Gillett, N., Arora, V., Zickfeld, K., Marshall, S. & Merryfield, W. (2011). Ongoing climate change following a complete cessation of carbon dioxide emissions. *Nature Geoscience*. doi:10.1038/ngeo1047. Retrieved from: http://dx.doi.org/10.1038/ngeo1047

Glance, N. & Huberman, B. (1994). The dynamics of social dilemmas. *Scientific American, 270*, 76–81.

Glikson, A. (2010). CO_2 mass extinction of species and climate change. Australian National University. Retrieved from: www.countercurrents.org/glikson220210.htm

Glover, N. (2009). *Psychoanalytic Aesthetics: An Introduction to the British School*.

Karnac. See also: http://www.psychoanalysis-and-therapy.com/human_nature/glover/index.html

Goggin, J. & Goggin, E. (2002). *Death of a 'Jewish Science': Psychoanalysis in the Third Reich*. Purdue University Press.

Goldberger, A., Peng, C. & Lipsitz, L. (2002). What is physiologic complexity and how does it change with aging and disease? *Neurobiology of Aging, 23*, 23–26.

Goldenberg, S. (2010, October 24). Tea Party climate change deniers funded by BP and other major polluters: Midterm election campaigns of Tea Party favourites DeMint and Inhofe have received over $240,000. *The Guardian*. Retrieved from: http://www.guardian.co.uk/world/2010/oct/24/tea-party-climate-change-deniers

Goldstein, J. (1995). Unbalancing psychoanalytic theory: Moving beyond the equilibrium model of Freud's thought. In R. Robertson & A. Combs (eds), *Chaos Theory in Psychology and the Life Sciences*. Lawrence Erlbaum (pp. 239–251).

Gomes, M. & Kanner, A. (1995a). The rape of the well-maidens: Feminist psychology and the environmental crisis. In T. Roszak, M. Gomes & A. Kanner (1995), *Ecopsychology: Restoring the Earth, Healing the Mind*. Sierra Club Books (pp. 111–121).

—— (1995b). The all consuming self. In T. Roszak, M. Gomes & A. Kanner, *Ecopsychology: Restoring the Earth, Healing the Mind*. Sierra Club Books. (pp. 77–91).

Gordon, D. (1999). *Ants and Work: How an Insect Society is Organized*. Springer-Verlag.

Gottman, J., Murray, J., Swanson, C., Tyson, R. & Swanson, K. (2003). *The Mathematics of Marriage: Dynamic Nonlinear Models*. MIT Press.

Goujon, P. (2006). From logic to self-organization: Learning about complexity. In B. Feltz, M. Crommelinck & P. Goujon (2006), *Self-Organization and Emergence in Life Sciences*. Springer.

Gould, L. (1997). Correspondences between Bion's basic assumption theory and Klein's developmental positions: An outline. *Free Associations*. Retrieved from: http://www.human-nature.com/free-associations/bion.html

Gould, L., Stapley, R. & Stein, M. (eds) (2006). *The Systems Psychodynamics of Organizations: Integrating Group Relations, Psychoanalytic, and Open Systems Perspectives*. Karnac.

Gould, S. & Eldredge, N. (1993). Punctuated equilibrium comes of age. *Nature, 366*(6452), 223–227.

Grasse, P.-P. (1982–1986). *Termitologia*. Vol. I: *Anatomie Physilogie Reproduction*; Vol. II: *Fondation des Sociétés Construction*; Vol. III: *Comportement Socialité Écologie Évolution Systématique*. Masson.

Green, V. (2004). *Emotional Development in Psychoanalysis, Attachment Theory and Neuroscience*. Brunner-Routledge.

Greenberg, J., Arndt, J., Simon, L., Pyszczynski, T. & Solomon, S. (2000). Proximal and distal defenses in response to reminders of one's mortality: Evidence of a temporal sequence. *Personality and Social Psychology Bulletin, 26*(1), 91–99.

Greenson, R. (1967). *The Technique and Practice of Psychoanalysis*. International Universities Press.

Griffin, S. (2000). *Woman and Nature: The Roaring Inside Her*. Sierra Club Books.

Grigaby, J. & Stevens, D. (2000). *Neurodynamics of Personality*. Guilford Press.

Grotstein, J. (1990). Nothingness, meaninglessness, chaos, and the "Black Hole" I:

The importance of nothingness, meaninglessness, and chaos in psychoanalysis. *Contemporary Psychoanalysis*, *26*, 257–290.

Guastello, S. (2004). Progress in applied nonlinear dynamics. *Nonlinear Dynamics, Psychology and Life Sciences*, *8*(1), 1–15.

—— (2001). Nonlinear dynamics in psychology. *Discrete Dynamics in Nature and Society*, *6*(1), 11–29.

Guattari, F. (1995). *Chaosmosis: An Ethico-aesthetic Paradigm*. Indiana University Press.

—— (2000). *The Three Ecologies*. Athlone.

Guntrip, H. (1995). *Personality Structure and Human Interaction: The Developing Synthesis of Psychodynamic Theory*. Karnac.

Haken, H. (1995). Some basic concepts of synergetics with respect to multistability in perception, phase transitions and formation of meaning. In P. Kruse & M. Stadler (eds), *Ambiguity in Mind and Nature*. Springer Verlag.

Hall, A. & Manabe, S. (1999). The role of water vapor feedback in unperturbed climate variability and global warming. *Journal of Climate*, *12*, 2327–2346.

—— (2000). Effect of water vapor feedback on internal and anthropogenic variations of the global hydrologic cycle. *Journal of Geophysical Research*, *105*(D5), 6935–6944.

Hansen, J. (2008). Climate threat to the planet: Implications for energy policy and intergenerational justice. Bjerknes Lecture, American Geophysical Union, San Francisco, California. December 17, 2008.

Hardin, G. (1968). The tragedy of the commons. *Science*, *162*(3859), 1243–1248.

Hardt, M. & Negri, A. (2000). *Empire*. Harvard University Press.

Haselton, M., Nettle, D. & Andrews, P. (2005). The evolution of cognitive bias. In D. Buss (ed.), *Handbook of Evolutionary Psychology*. Wiley (pp. 724–746).

Hayles, K. (ed.) (1991). *Chaos and Order: Complex Dynamics in Literature and Science*. University of Chicago Press.

Heinberg, R. (2009). The psychology of peak oil and climate change. In L. Buzzell & C. Chalquist (eds), *Ecotherapy: Healing with Nature in Mind*. Sierra Club Books (pp. 197–204).

Heinemann, E. (2000). *Witches: A Psychoanalytic Exploration of the Killing of Women*. Free Association Books.

Herzogenrath, B. (ed.) (2008). *An [Un]Likely Alliance: Thinking Environment[s] with Deleuze|Guattari*. Cambridge Scholars.

—— (ed.) (2009). *Deleuze|Guattari & Ecology*. Palgrave Macmillan.

Hickman, L. (2008). Can you joke about climate change? *Guardian Environment Blog*. Retrieved from: http://www.guardian.co.uk/environment/blog/2008/may/08/whyclimatechangeisnojoke

Higbee, K. (1969). Fifteen years of fear arousal: Research on threat appeals. *Psychological Bulletin*, *72*(6), 426–444.

Hinshelwood, R. (1989). *What Happens in Groups: Psychoanalysis, the Individual and the Community*. Free Association Books.

—— (1991). *Dictionary of Kleinian Thought*. Free Association Books.

Hoggett, P. (2009). The Psychological and Political Challenge of Facing Climate Change. The Politics and Emotions of Climate Change Denial. Conference at the University of the West of England, Bristol, March 2009 [Audio]. Retrieved from: http://real.uwe.ac.uk/download/hlss/climatechangeconference/hoggett.mp4

Holdaway, R. & Jacomb, C. (2000). Rapid Extinction of the Moas (Aves: Dinor-nithiformes): Model, Test, and Implications. *Science, 287*(5461), 2250–2254.

Holland, J. (1995). *Hidden Order: How Adaptation Builds Complexity.* Addison Wesley.

Holland, N. (2003). The willing suspension of disbelief: A neuro-psychoanalytic view. *PsyArt.* Retrieved from: http://www.psyartjournal.com/article/show/n_holland-the_willing_suspension_of_disbelief_9_ne

—— (2007). Tickled rats and human laughter. *Neuro-Psychoanalysis, 9*(1), 41–57.

Holleran, S. (2004). Ecozilla: The Day After Tomorrow. Retrieved from: http://boxofficemojo.com/reviews/?id=1339&p=.htm

Hopper, E. (2002). *Traumatic Experience in the Unconscious Life of Groups: The Fourth Basic Assumption: Incohesion: Aggregation/Massification or (ba) I:A/M.* Jessica Kingsley.

Hornero, R., Jimeno, N., Sanchez, C., Poza, J. & Aboy, M. (2006). Variability, regularity, and complexity of time series generated by schizophrenic patients and control subjects. *IEEE Transactions on Biomedical Engineering, 53*(2), 216–218.

Houzel, D. (2005). Selected Fact. In A. de Mijolla & G. Cengage (eds), *International Dictionary of Psychoanalysis.* Also available from http://www.enotes.com/psychoanalysis-encyclopedia/selected-fact

Hudson, J. & Bruckman, A. (2004). The bystander effect: A lens for understanding patterns of participation. *Journal of the Learning Sciences, 13*(2), 165–195.

Hyde, L. (1998). *Trickster Makes This World: Mischief, Myth, and Art.* Farrar Straus & Giroux.

IPCC (2007). *Climate Change 2007: Synthesis Report.* Cambridge University Press.

—— (2009). Thirty-First Session of the Intergovernmental Panel on Climate Change: Scoping of the IPCC 5th Assessment Report: Cross Cutting Issues. Retrieved from: http://www.ipcc.ch/meetings/session31/inf3.pdf

Irigaray, L. (1985). *This Sex Which Is Not One.* Cornell University Press.

Iwakabe, S. (1994). Psychotherapy and chaos theory: The metaphoric relationship between psychodynamic therapy and chaps theory. *Psychoanalytic Psychology, 11*(1), 1–19.

Jacobsen, J. (2010). Some basic concepts from sustainability. *Society for Chaos Theory in Psychology and Life Sciences Newsletter* (Special Theme Article Collection on Nonlinearity and Sustainability), *18*(1), 7–11.

James, W. (1911). The moral equivalent of war. In W. James, *Memories and Studies.* Longmans, Green & Co. (pp. 265–296).

Jaques, E. (1955). Social systems as a defence against persecutory and depressive anxiety. In M. Klein, P. Heimann & R. Money-Kyrle (eds), *New Directions in Psychoanalysis.* Karnac (pp. 478–498).

Johnson, E. & Tver, A. (1983). Affect, generalization, and the perception of risk. *Journal of Personality and Social Psychology, 45*(1), 20–31.

Jones, E. (1957). *Sigmund Freud: Life and Work, Vol. 3.* Hogarth.

—— (2008). *On the Nightmare.* Meisel Press.

Jones, R. (1990). Understanding paper recycling in an institutionally supportive setting: An application of the theory of reasoned action. *Journal of Environmental Systems, 19*(4), 307–321.

Jonsson, P. (2010). Climate scientists exonerated in 'climategate' but public trust damaged. *Christian Science Monitor.* Retrieved from: http://www.csmonitor.com/

Environment/2010/0707/Climate-scientists-exonerated-in-climategate-but-public-trust-damaged

Jordan, M. (2009). Nature and self: An ambivalent attachment? *Ecopsychology*, *1*(1), 26–41.

Jordan, M. & Marshall, H. (2010). Taking counselling and psychotherapy outside: Destruction or enrichment of the therapeutic frame? *European Journal of Psychotherapy & Counselling*, *12*(4), 345–359.

Jung, C. (1961). *Memories, Dreams, Reflections*. Random House.

Kaes, R. (2007). *Linking, Alliances, and Shared Space: Groups and the Psychoanalyst*. IPA Publications.

Kahneman, D., Slovic, P. & Tver, A. (eds) (1982). *Judgment Under Uncertainty: Heuristics and Biases*. Cambridge University Press.

Kaku, M. (1995). *Hyperspace: A Scientific Odyssey Through Parallel Universes, Time Warps, and the 10th Dimension*. Anchor.

Kaplan, R. & Kaplan, S. (1989). *The Experience of Nature: A Psychological Perspective*. Cambridge University Press.

Kaplan-Solms, K. & Solms, M. (2000). *Clinical Studies in Neuropsychoanalysis: Introduction to a Depth Neuropsychology*. Karnac.

Kasting, J. (1988). Runaway and moist greenhouse atmospheres and the evolution of Earth and Venus. *Icarus*, *74*(3), 472–494.

Katzev, R. & Johnson, T. (1983). A social-psychological analysis of residential electricity consumption: The impact of minimal justification techniques. *Journal of Economic Psychology*, *3*(3–4), 267–284.

—— (1987). *Promoting Energy Conservation: An Analysis of Behavioral Techniques*. Westview.

Kauffman, L. & Sabelli, H. (1999). BIOS: Creative Organization Beyond Chaos. Presentation given at the *International Society for Systems Sciences*, 1998. Retrieved from: http://www.ceptualinstitute.com/genre/sabelli-kauffman/bios.htm

Kauffman, S. (1993). *The Origins of Order*. Oxford University Press.

Kellert, S. & Wilson, E. (eds) (1993). *The Biophilia Hypothesis*. Island Press.

Kelly, K. (1994). *Out of Control: The Rise of Neo-Biological Civilization*. Addison Wesley.

Kelso, J. (1995). *Dynamic Patterns: The Self-Organization of Brain and Behavior*. MIT Press.

Kerr, R. & Kintisch, E. (2010). Climatologists feel the heat as science meets politics. *Science*, *330*(6011), 1623. doi: 10.1126/science.330.6011.1623

Kieffer, C. (2007). Emergence and the analytic third: Working at the edge of chaos. *Psychoanalytic Dialogues*, *17*(5), 683–703.

King, S. (1981). *Dance Macabre*. Vintage.

Klein, M. (1987). *The Selected Melanie Klein*. (J. Mitchell, Ed.). Free Press.

Klein, M., Heimann, P. & Money-Kyrle (eds) (1955). *New Directions in Psycho-Analysis: The Significance of Infant Conflict in the Pattern of Adult Behaviour*. Maresfield.

Klein, N. (2009). *No Logo*. Picador.

Kluckhohn, F. & Strodtbeck, F. (1961). *Variations in Value Orientations*. Row, Peterson & Co.

Kohut, H. (1985). *The Analysis of the Self*. International Universities Press.

Koopmans, M. (1998). Chaos theory and the problem of change in family systems. *Nonlinear Dynamics, Psychology, and Life Sciences*, 2(2), 133–148.

Kristeva, J. (1982). *Powers of Horror: An Essay on Abjection*. Columbia University Press.

Kübler-Ross, E. (1973). *On Death and Dying*. Routledge.

—— (2005). *On Grief and Grieving: Finding the Meaning of Grief Through the Five Stages of Loss*. Simon & Schuster Ltd.

Kuhn, T. (1996). *The Structure of Scientific Revolutions*. University of Chicago Press.

Kurtzman, D. (2010). Global warming jokes: Late-night jokes about global warming. Retrieved from: http://politicalhumor.about.com/od/environment/a/globalwarming.htm

Lacan, J. (1974). *Le Seminaire. Livre XX. Encore, 1972–1973*. Seuil.

—— (1977). *Ecrits: A Selection*. London Tavistock Publications.

—— (1992). *The Seminar. Book VII. The Ethics of Psychoanalysis, 1959–1960*. Routledge.

—— (1998). *The Four Fundamental Concepts of Psycho-analysis*. Vintage.

Langs, R. (1979). *The Therapeutic Environment*. Jason Aronson.

—— (1982). *Psychotherapy: A Basic Text*. Jason Aronson.

Lasch, C. (1991). *The Culture of Narcissism: American Life in an Age of Diminishing Expectations*. W. W. Norton.

Lashof, D. & DeAngelo, B. (1997). Terrestrial ecosystem feedbacks to global climate change. *Annual Review of Energy and the Environment*, *22*, 75–118.

Lawrence Berkeley National Laboratory (2006, May 22). Feedback loops in global climate change point to a very hot 21st century. *Science Daily*. Retrieved from: http://www.sciencedaily.com/releases/2006/05/060522151248.htm

Lawrence, G. (1997). Totalitarian states of mind in institutions. In D. Armstrong, G. Lawrence & R. M. Young, *Group Relations: An Introduction*. Process Press. Available from: http://human-nature.com/rmyoung/papers/paper99.html

Lee, A. (1997). Process contracts. In C. Sills (ed.), *Contracts in Counselling* Sage (pp. 194–212).

Lemieux, P. (1994). *Chaos and the Social Sciences: An Introductory Overview*. Liberty.

Lertzman, R. (2008). Environmental anxiety: Moving from 'flight' to 'fight'. Retrieved from: http://www.greenawards.co.uk/about/blog?item=environmental_anxiety:_moving_from_flight_to_fight

—— (2009). The ability to split. Retrieved from: http://www.rennlertzman.org/blog/?p=145

Levi, P. (2010). Beyond judgement. Retrieved from: http://connexions.org/CxLibrary/Docs/CX5018-BeyondJudgement.htm

Ley, W. (2008). The ecological dimension of psychoanalysis and the concept of inner sustainability. *Journal of the American Psychoanalytic Association*, *56*(4), 1279–1307.

Libet, B. (2004). *Mind Time: The Temporal Factor in Consciousness*. Harvard University Press.

Lifton, R. (1968). *Death in Life: Survivors of Hiroshima*. Random House.

Linde, H. (2010). Is *Avatar* radical environmental propaganda? *Mother Nature*

Network. Retrieved from: http://www.mnn.com/technology/research-innovations/blogs/is-avatar-radical-environmental-propaganda

Long, S. (2008). *The Perverse Organization and its Deadly Sins*. Karnac.

Lonie, I. (1995). The princess and the swineherd: Applications of chaos theory to psychodynamics. In R. Robertson & A. Combs (eds), *Chaos Theory in Psychology and the Life Sciences*. Lawrence Erlbaum (pp. 285–294).

Lovelock, J. (2000). *Gaia: A New Look at Life on Earth*. Oxford University Press.

Lynas, M. (2008). *Six Degrees: Our Future on a Hotter Planet*. National Geographic.

Lyotard, J.-F. (1997). *The Postmodern Condition: A Report on Knowledge*. University of Minnesota Press.

Macfarlane, R. (2007). *The Wild places*. Granta.

Mack, J. (1995). The politics of species arrogance. In T. Roszak, M. Gomes & A. Kanner (eds) (1995), *Ecopsychology: Restoring the Earth, Healing the Mind*. Sierra Club Books (pp. 279–287).

Mackay, A. L. (1991). *A Dictionary of Scientific Quotations*. Taylor & Francis.

Macy, J. (1995). Working through environmental despair. In T. Roszak, M. Gomes & A. Kanner (eds), *Ecopsychology: Restoring the Earth, Healing the Mind*. Sierra Club Books (pp. 240–251).

Mahler, S., Pine, F. & Bergman, A. (2000). *The Psychological Birth of the Human Infant: Symbiosis and Individuation*. Basic Books.

Manchester Metropolitan Unversity (MMU) (2005). *Becoming for Beginners*. Retrieved from: www.hssr.mmu.ac.uk/deleuze-studies/on-deleuze

Mandelbrot, B. (1983). *The Fractal Geometry of Nature*. W. H. Freeman.

Manica, A., Amos, W., Balloux, F. & Hanihara, T. (2007). The effect of ancient population bottlenecks on human phenotypic variation. *Nature*, *448*(7151), 346–348.

Marcuse, H. (1998). *Eros and Civilization: A Philosophical Inquiry into Freud*. Routledge.

Marks-Tarlow, T. (2004). The self as a dynamical system. *Nonlinear Dynamics, Psychology, and Life Sciences*, *3*(4), 311–345.

—— (2008). *Psyche's Veil: Psychotherapy, Fractals and Complexity*. Routledge.

Marshall, G. (2001, September 22). The psychology of denial: Our failure to act against climate change. *The Ecologist*. Retrieved from: http://ecoglobe.ch/motivation/e/clim2922.htm

—— (2005). Sleepwalking into disaster: Are we in a state of denial about climate change? *Perspectives on Climate Change No. 4*. Climate Outreach and Information Network (COIN). Retrieved from: http://www.networkforclimateaction.org.uk/toolkit/positive_alternatives/people_and_society/COIN_Are_we_in_a_State_of_Denial_about_Climate_Change.pdf

—— (2009, March 7). Strategies of evasion and denial in social attitudes to climate change. Lecture given at the University of the West of England 'The Psychological and Political Challenge of Facing Climate Change' Conference. Co-sponsored by Psychotherapists and Counsellors for Social Responsibility.

Matte-Blanco, I. (1984). Reply to Ross Skelton's Paper 'Understanding Matte-Blanco'. *International Journal of Psycho-Analysis*, *65*, 457–460.

—— (1998). *The Unconscious as Infinite Sets: As Essay in Biologic*. Karnac.

Mayes, L. C. (2005). Something is different but what or why is unclear:

Commentary on the Boston Change Process Study Group. *Journal of the American Psychoanalytical Association*, *53*, 745–750.

Meltzer, D. (1967). *Psychoanalytical process*. Clunie Press.

—— (1992). *The Claustrum: An Investigation of Claustrophobic Phenomena*. Clunie Press.

—— (1994). *Sincerity and Other Works: Collected Papers of Donald Meltzer*. Karnac.

Menzies-Lyth, I. (1988). *Containing Anxiety in Institutions: Selected Essays, Vol. 1*. Free Association Books.

Metzner, R. (1993). The psychopathology of the human–nature relationship. In *Spirit, Self and Nature: Essays in Green Psychology*. Four Trees Books (pp. 55–69).

Miller, M. (1999). Chaos, complexity, psychoanalysis. *Psychoanalytic Psychology*, *16*(3), 355–379.

Milner, M. (2010). *On Not Being Able to Paint*. Routledge.

Mind (2007). The green agenda for mental health. Retrieved from: http://www.mind.org.uk/assets/0000/2138/ecotherapy_report.pdf

Mishan, J. (1996). Psychoanalysis and environmentalism: First thoughts. *Psychoanalytic Psychotherapy*, *10*(1), 59–70.

Mitchell, S. (1988). *Relational Concepts within Psychoanalysis: An Integration*. Harvard University Press.

—— (ed.) (2007). *Relational Psychoanalysis*. Analytic Press.

Monbiot, G. (2005). Climate change: A crisis of collective denial? Retrieved from: http://www.valuesineducation.org.au/pdf/monbiot050504.pdf

—— (2010, October 11). The values of everything: Progressive causes are failing: here's how they could be turned around. Retrieved from: http://www.monbiot.com/2010/10/11/the_values_of_everything/

Moran, M. (1991). Chaos and psychoanalysis: The fluidic nature of mind. *International Review of Psychoanalysis*, *18*(2), 211–221.

Morell, V. & Lanting, F. (1999, February). The Sixth Extinction. *National Geographic*, pp. 42–59.

Morton, T. (2007). *Ecology Without Nature: Rethinking Environmental Aesthetics*. Harvard University Press.

—— (2010a). *The Ecological Thought*. Harvard University Press.

—— (2010b). Presentation as part of the Panel Discussion 'Promiscuous Ontologies', RMMLA Convention, Albuquerque, New Mexico, 15 October 2010 [Audio]. Available from: http://ecologywithoutnature.blogspot.com/2010/10/promiscuous-ontologies-mp3.html

—— (2010c, November 9). Hyperobjects are Nonlocal [Blog post]. Retrieved from: http://ecologywithoutnature.blogspot.com/2010/11/hyperobjects-are-nonlocal.html

Naess, A. (1988). *Self Realization: An Ecological Approach to Being in the World*. Murdoch University.

Nelson, M. (1961). Review of *The Nonhuman Environment in Normal Development and in Schizophrenia* by Harold F. Searles. *The Psychoanalytic Review*, *48C*, 121–123.

Newitz, A. (2008). What's causing the "Earth without us" craze in new Sci-fi movies? Retrieved from: http://io9.com/360623/whats-causing-the-earth-without-us-craze-in-new-scifi-movies

Nicholsen, S. (2003). *The Love of Nature and the End of the World: The Unspoken Dimensions of Environmental Concern*. MIT Press.

Nicolis, G. & Prigogine, I. (1989). *Exploring Complexity: An Introduction*. W.H. Freeman.

Norberg-Hodge, H. (2009). *Ancient Futures: Lessons from Ladakh for a Globalizing World*. Sierra Club Books.

Norgaard, R. & Randers, J. (2002). Tracking the ecological overshoot of the human economy. Proceedings of the National Academy of Sciences, July 9 (pp. 9266–9271). Retrieved from: www.pnas.org/cgi/doi/10.1073/pnas.142033699

Oechel, W., Hastings, S., Vourlrtis, G., Jenkins, M., Reichers, G. & Grulke, N. (1993). Recent change of Arctic tundra ecosystems from a net carbon dioxide sink to a source. *Nature*, *361*(6412), 520–523.

Ogden, T. (1983). The concept of internal object relations. *International Journal of Psycho-Analysis*, *64*, 227–242.

—— (1992). *Projective Identification and Psychotherapeutic Technique*. Karnac.

Olson, R. (1995). Sustainability as a social vision. *Journal of Social Issues*, *51*(4), 15–35.

Oppenheim, L. (2005). *A Curious Intimacy: Art and Neuro-Psychoanalysis*. Routledge.

Oppenheimer, M. & Todorov, A. (2006). Global warming: The psychology of long-term risk. In M. Oppenheimer & A. Todorov (eds), *The Psychology of Long-Term Risk*. Special issue of *Climatic Change*, *77*(1–2), 1–6.

Orr, D. (1994). *Earth in Mind: On Education, Environment, and the Human Prospect*. Island Press.

Osbaldiston, R. & Sheldon, K. M. (2002). Social dilemmas and sustainability: Promoting people's motivation to "cooperate with the future." In P. Schmuck & W. Schultz (eds), *Psychology of Sustainable Development*. Kluwer (pp. 37–49).

Oskamp, S. (1995a). Applying social psychology to avoid ecological disaster. *Journal of Social Issues*, *51*(4), 217–238.

—— (1995b). Resource conservation and recycling: Behavior and policy. *Journal of Social Issues*, *51*(4), 157–177.

—— (2000). A Sustainable Future for Humanity?: How Can Psychology Help? *American Psychologist*, *55*(5), 496–508.

Ostrom, E. (1990). *Governing the Commons: The Evolution of Institutions for Collective Action*. Cambridge University Press.

Palombo, S. (1999). *The Emergent Ego: Complexity and Coevolution in the Psycho-analytic Process*. International Universities Press.

—— (2007). Complexity theory as the parent science of psychoanalysis. In C. Piers, P. Muller & J. Brent (eds), *Self-Organizing Complexity in Psychological Systems*. Jason Aronson.

Panksepp, J. (2004). *Affective Neuroscience: The Foundations of Human and Animal Emotions*. Oxford University Press.

Parker, I. (2010, January 14). *Avatar*: Visions of the eco-blues. *Socialist Resistance*. Retrieved from: http://socialistresistance.org/?p=806

Parsons, M. (2000). *The Dove that Returns, the Dove that Vanishes*. Routledge.

Patrzalek, E. (2010). Fractals: Useful beauty (General introduction to fractal

geometry). Retrieved from: http://www.fractal.org/Bewustzijns-Besturings-Model/
Fractals-Useful-Beauty.htm

Pawlik, K. (1991). The psychology of global environmental change: Some basic data
and an agenda for cooperative international research. *International Journal of
Psychology*, *26*(5), 547–563.

Perna, P. (1997). Regression as evolutionary process: A view from dialectics and
chaos theory. In F. Masterpasqua & P. Perna (eds), *The Psychological Meaning of
Chaos*. American Psychological Association (pp. 97–116).

Piers, C., Muller, P. & Brent, J. (eds) (2007). *Self-Organizing Complexity in Psychological Systems*. Jason Aronson.

Pincus, D. (2001). A framework and methodology for the study of nonlinear, self-
organizing family systems. *Nonlinear Dynamics, Psychology, and Life Sciences*,
5(2), 139–173.

Poe, E. (1998). *The Tell-Tale Heart: And, the Premature Burial*. Harper-Collins.

Poorie, K. (2010, March 20). SRK means India for Cameron. *The Times of India*.
Retrieved from: http://timesofindia.indiatimes.com/entertainment/bollywood/
news-interviews/SRK-means-India-for-Cameron/articleshow/5702067.cms

Postel, S. (1992). Denial in the Decisive Decade. In *State of The World 1992: A
Worldwatch Institute Report on Progress Toward a Sustainable Society*. W. W.
Norton & Co.

Powell, A. (2006). *Deleuze and Horror Film*. Edinburgh University Press.

Prigogine, I. & Stengers, I. (1984). *Order Out Of Chaos: Man's New Dialogue With
Nature*. Bantam Books.

Qvortrup, L. (2006). Understanding new digital media: Medium theory or complexity theory. *European Journal of Communication*, *21*(3), 345–356.

Rabelais, F. (1965). *Gargantua and Pantagruel*. Penguin.

Randall, R. (2005). A new climate for psychotherapy? *Psychotherapy and Politics
International*, *3*(3), 165–179.

Rank, O. (1989). *The Double: A Psychoanalytic Study*. Karnac.

Rasool, C. I. & De Bergh, C. (1970). The Runaway Greenhouse and the Accumu-
lation of CO_2 in the Venus Atmosphere. *Nature*, *226*(5250), 1037–1039.

Read, R. (2010). *Avatar*: A call to save the future. *Radical Anthropology*, 35–40.
Retrieved from: http://www.radicalanthropologygroup.org/old/journal_04.pdf

Reser, J. (2007). Psychology and the Natural Environment: A Position Statement
Prepared for the Australian Psychological Society. The Australian Psychological
Society Ltd.

Revkin, A. (1992). *Global Warming: Understanding the Forecast*. Abbeville Press.

Ricoeur, P. (1970). *Freud and Philosophy: An Essay on Interpretation*. Yale University Press.

Ridley, M. (1997). *Origins of Virtue*. Penguin Classics.

Robbins, B. & Goicoechea, J. (1996). The paranoid-schizoid and depressive positions in the psychogenesis of the self: A phenomenological investigation into the
ontological foundations of object relations theory. *Mythos and Logos*. Retrieved
from: http://mythosandlogos.com/objectrelations.html

Robinson, K. S. (ed.) (1997). *Future Primitive: The New Ecotopias*. Tor Books.

Rodman, F. R. (2002). The holding environment after September 11 – Psychoanalysis in the twenty-first century: A moment of reflection. *Free Associations*,
9(4), 487–499.

Rohrer, F. (2008). Why the fascination with the end of the world? *BBC News Magazine*. Retrieved from: http://news.bbc.co.uk/2/hi/uk_news/magazine/7600966.stm

Roper, L. (1994). *Oedipus and the Devil: Witchcraft, Religion and Sexuality in Early Modern Europe*. Routledge.

Rosenfeld, H. (1971). A clinical approach to the psychoanalytic theory of the life and death instincts: An investigation into the aggressive aspects of narcissism. *International Journal of Psycho-Analysis, 52*(2), 169–178.

Roszak, T. (1995). Where psyche meets Gaia. In T. Roszak, M. Gomes & A. Kanner (eds), *Ecopsychology: Restoring the Earth, Healing the Mind*. Sierra Club Books (pp. 1–17).

—— (2002). *Voice of the Earth: An Exploration in Ecopsychology*. Phanes Press.

—— (2009). A psyche as big as the Earth. In L. Buzzell & C. Chalquist (2009), *Ecotherapy: Healing with Nature in Mind*. Sierra Club Books (pp. 30–36).

Roszak, T., Gomes, M. & Kanner, A. (eds) (1995). *Ecopsychology: Restoring the Earth, Healing the Mind*. Sierra Club Books.

Royle, N. (2003). *The Uncanny: An Introduction*. Manchester University Press.

Rust, M.-J. (2004). Creating psychotherapy for a sustainable future. *Psychotherapy and Politics International, 2*(1), 50–63.

—— (2008). Climate on the couch: Unconscious processes in relation to our environmental crisis. *Psychotherapy and Politics International, 6*(3), 157–170. Also available from: http://www.chinadialogue.net/article/show/single/en/2912-Climate-on-the-couch-2-

Sander, L. (1983). To begin with: Reflections of ontogeny. In J. Lichetenberg & S. Kaplan (eds), *Reflections on Self-Psychology*. Analytic Press (pp. 85–104).

Santostefano, S. (2004). *Child Therapy in the Great Outdoors: A Relational View*. Hillside Press.

Sawaya, R. (2010). The runaway effects that could accelerate global warming. Retrieved from: http://climate-change.suite101.com/article.cfm/positive_feed back_ mechanisms_and_climate_change

Scalzone, F. & Zontini, G. (2001). The dream's navel between chaos and thought. *International Journal of Psycho-Analysis, 82*(2), 263–282.

Scharff, D. (2000). Fairbairn and the self as an organized system: Chaos theory as a new paradigm. *Canadian Journal of Psychoanalysis, 8*(2), 181–195.

Scheinkman, J. & Woodford, M. (1994). Self-organized criticality and economic fluctuations. *American Economic Review, 84*(2), 417–421.

Schmuck, P. & Sheldon, K. (eds) (2001). *Life Goals and Well-Being. Towards a Positive Psychology of Human Striving*. Hogrefe & Huber (pp. 167–181).

Schmuck, P. & Vlek, C. (2003). Psychologists can do much to support sustainable development. *European Psychologist, 8*(2), 66–76. Also available from: http://psycnet.apa.org/journals/epp/8/2/66.pdf

Schneider, S. (2009). *Horror Film and Psychoanalysis: Freud's Worst Nightmare*. Cambridge University Press.

Schor, J. (1998). *The Overspent American*. Basic Books.

Schur, M. (1972). *Freud: Living and Dying*. International Universities Press.

Schwab, G. (ed.) (2008). *Derrida, Deleuze, Psychoanalysis*. Columbia University Press.

Science Daily (2011, January 10). Species loss tied to ecosystem collapse and recovery. Retrieved from: http://www.sciencedaily.com/releases/2011/01/110110103834.htm

Scott, G. (ed.) (2002). *Selected Letters of John Keats*. Harvard University Press.

Scull, J. (1999). Ecopsychology: Where does it fit in psychology? Retrieved from: http://members.shaw.ca/jscull/ecointro.htm

Searles, H. (1960). *The Nonhuman Environment in Normal Development and in Schizophrenia*. International Universities Press.

—— (1972). Unconscious processes in relation to the environmental crisis. *Psychoanalytic Review*, *59*(3), 361–374.

Sendak, M. (1988). *Where the Wild Things Are*. Harper-Collins.

Segal, H. (1988). Silence is the real crime. In H. Levine, D. Jacobs & L. Rubin (eds) (1988), *Psychoanalysts and the Nuclear Threat*. Analytic Press (pp. 35–58).

Seshadri-Crooks, K. (2000). *Desiring Whiteness: A Lacanian Analysis of Race*. Routledge.

Shapiro, E. (1995). Restoring habitats, communities, and souls. In T. Roszak, M. Gomes & A. Kanner (eds), *Ecopsychology: Restoring the Earth, Healing the Mind*. Sierra Club Books (pp. 224–239).

Shepard, P. (1995). Nature and madness. In T. Roszak, M. Gomes & A. Kanner (eds), *Ecopsychology: Restoring the Earth, Healing the Mind*. Sierra Club Books (pp. 21–40).

Sherif, M., Harvey, O. J., White, B. J., Hood, W. E. & Sherif, C. W. (1961). *Intergroup Conflict and Cooperation: The Robber's Cave Experiment*. University of Oklahoma Book Exchange.

Shermer, M. (1995). Exorcising Laplace's demon: Chaos and antichaos, history and metahistory. *History and Theory*, *34*, 59–83.

—— (2008, December 11). Reel life: *The Day the Earth Stood Still*. *Scientific American*. Retrieved from: http://www.scientificamerican.com/article.cfm?id=review-day-the-earth-stood-still

Shevrin, H. (1996). *Conscious and Unconscious Processes: Psychodynamic, Cognitive, and Neurophysiological Convergences*. Guilford Press.

Shimojo, S., Kamitani, Y. & Nishida, S. (2001). Afterimage of perceptually filled-in surface. *Science*, *293*(5535), 1677–1680.

Shipman, P. (2010). The animal connection and human evolution. *Current Anthropology*, *51*(4), 519–538.

Silberstein, M. (1998). Emergence and the Mind-Body Problem. *Journal of Consciousness Studies*, *5*(4), 464–482.

Skarda, C. & Freeman, W. (1987). How brains make chaos in order to make sense of the world. *Behavioural and Brain Sciences*, *10*, 161–195.

Skinner, B. F. (1969). *Contingencies of Reinforcement: A Theoretical Analysis*. Appleton-Century-Crofts.

—— (1981). Selection by consequences. *Science*, *213*(4507), 501–504.

Small, P. (2010). Retrieved from: http://www.stigmergicsystems.com/stig_v1/index.html

Smelik, A. (2007). Review of *Phallic Panic: Film, Horror and the Primal Uncanny* by Barbara Creed. *Senses of Cinema*, Retrieved from: http://archive.sensesofcinema.com/contents/books/07/43/phallic-panic.html

Smith, W. J. (2008a). *The Day the Earth Stood Still*: Hollywood goes deep ecology.

Retrieved from: http://stanford.wellsphere.com/bioethics-article/the-day-the-earth-stood-still-hollywood-goes-deep-ecology/540609

—— (2008b). Anti humanism comes to the movies. Retrieved from: http://www.firstthings.com/blogs/secondhandsmoke/2008/12/12/anti-humanism-comes-to-the-movies/

Sobel, D. (2001). *Children's Special Places: Exploring the Role of Forts, Dens, and Bush Houses in Middle Childhood* (The Child in the City Series). Wayne State University Press.

Soden, B. & Held, I. (2006). An assessment of climate feedbacks in coupled ocean-atmosphere models. *Journal of Climate*, *19*, 3354–3360.

Sole, R. & Goodwin, B. (2000). *Signs of Life: How Complexity Pervades Biology*. Basic Books.

Solms, M. & Turnbull, O. (2003). *The Brain and the Inner World: An Introduction to the Neuroscience of the Subjective Experience*. Other Press.

Spitzform, M. (2000). The ecological self: Metaphor and developmental experience? *Journal of Applied Psychoanalytic Studies*, *2*, 265–285.

Spruiell, V. (1993). Deterministic chaos and the sciences of complexity: Psychoanalysis in the midst of a general scientific revolution, *Journal of the American Psychoanalytic Association*, *41*(1), 3–44. Also available from: http://www.analysis.com/vs/vs93a.html

Stacey, R. (2003). *Complexity and Group Processes: A Radically Social Understanding of Individuals*. Brunner-Routledge.

—— (2006). Complexity at the edge of the basic-assumption group. In L. Gould, R. Stapley & M. Stein (eds), *The Systems Psychodynamics of Organizations: Integrating Group Relations, Psychoanalytic, and Open Systems Perspectives*. Karnac (pp. 91–114).

Steiner, J. (1985). Turning a blind eye: The cover up for Oedipus. *International Review of Psycho-Analysis*, *12*(11), 161–172.

Steiner, R. (1989). 'It's a new kind of diaspora . . .' *International Review of Psycho-Analysis*, *16*, 35–78.

Stern, P. (2000). Psychology and the science of human–environment interactions. *American Psychologist*, *55*(5), 523–530.

—— (2004, April). Understanding global change: What psychology can contribute. *International Human Dimensions on Global Climate Change Newsletter*, pp. 4–5.

—— (2005). Understanding Individuals' Environmentally Significant Behavior. *Environmental Law Reporter*, *35*(10785), 1–6.

Stern, P. & Gardner, G. (1981). Psychological research and energy policy. *American Psychologist*, *36*(4), 329–342.

Stern, P., Dietz, T., Abel, T., Guagnano, G. & Kalof, L. (1999). A social-psychological theory of support for social movements: The case of environmentalism. *Human Ecology Review*, *6*, 81–97.

Stewart, I. (1989). *Does God Play Dice? The New Mathematics of Chaos*. Blackwell.

Stora, J. B. (2007). *When the Body Displaces the Mind*. Karnac.

Tallis, R. C. (2009). Burying Freud. Retrieved from: www.human-nature.com/freud/tallis.html

Thompson, J. N. (1994). *The Coevolutionary Process*. University of Chicago Press.

Tobais, M. (ed.) (1985). *Deep Ecology*. Avant Books.

Tooby, J. & Cosmides, L. (2005). Conceptual foundations of evolutionary psychology. In D. Buss (ed.), *The Handbook of Evolutionary Psychology*. Wiley (pp. 5–67).

Topia (2010). Retrieved from: http://www.topia.com/project/fractal/mandelbulb. html

Totton, N. (2011). *Wild Therapy: Undomesticating Inner and Outer Worlds* (draft version). PCCS Books.

Trezise, T. (2008). Between history and psychoanalysis: A case study in the reception of holocaust survivor testimony. *History & Memory*, *20*(1), 7–47.

Tschacher, W. & Scheier, C. (1997). Complex psychological systems: Synergetics and chaos. In F. Masterpasqua & P. Perna (eds), *The Psychological Meaning of Chaos*. American Psychological Association (pp. 273–299).

Tudor, A. (1997). Why horror? The peculiar pleasures of a popular genre. *Cultural Studies*, *11*(3), 446–463.

Twitchell, J. (1988). *Dreadful Pleasures: An Anatomy of Modern Horror*. Oxford University Press.

UK Met Office (2009). Retrieved from: http://www.metoffice.gov.uk/news/releases/archive/2009/warmest-decade

Ulrich, R. (1984). View through a window may influence recovery from surgery. *Science*, *224*(4647), 420–421.

—— (1991). Effects of health facility interior design on wellness: Theory and recent scientific research. *Journal of Health Care Design*, *3*, 97–109.

—— (1999). Effects of gardens on health outcomes: Theory and research. In C. Marcus & M. Barnes (eds), *Healing Gardens: Therapeutic Benefits and Design Recommendations*. John Wiley (pp. 27–86).

—— (2000). Environmental research and critical care. In D. K. Hamilton (ed.), *ICU 2010: Design for the Future*. Center for Innovation in Health Facilities (pp. 195–207).

Ulrich, R., Simons, R., Losito, B., Fiorito, E., Miles, M. & Zelson, M. (1991). Stress recovery during exposure to natural and urban environments. *Journal of Environmental Psychology*, *11*(3), 201–230.

Ulrich, R., Lunden, O. & Eltinge, J. (1993). Effects of exposure to nature and abstract pictures on patients recovering from heart surgery. Paper presented at the 33rd Meetings of the Society for Psychophysiological Research, Rottach-Egern, Germany. Abstract published in *Psychophysiology*, *30*(Supplement 1), 7.

Uzzell, D. (2010). Collective solutions to a global problem. *The Psychologist*, *23*(11), 880–883.

Van Vugt, M. (2009). Averting the tragedy of the commons: Using social psychological science to protect the environment. *Current Directions in Psychological Science*, *18*(3), 169–173.

Varela, F., Thompson, E. & Rosch, E. (1991). *The Embodied Mind: Cognitive Science and Human Experience*. MIT Press.

Verderber, S. & Reuman, D. (1987). Windows, views, and health status in hospital therapeutic environments. *The Journal of Architectural and Planning Research*, *4*(2), 120–133.

Vidal, J. (2009, December 19). Rich and poor counties blame each other for failure of Copenhagen deal. *The Guardian*. Retrieved from: http://www.guardian.co.uk/environment/2009/dec/19/copenhagen-blame-game

—— (2010, March 30). US oil company donated millions to climate sceptic groups, says Greenpeace. *The Guardian*. Retrieved from: http://www.guardian.co.uk/environment/2010/mar/30/us-oil-donated-millions-climate-sceptics

Vital-Brazil, H. (2001). An ethics for the psychoanalyst in the postmodern age. *International Forum of Psychoanalysis*, *10*(2), 151–162.

Vlek, C. (1996). Collective risk generation and risk management: The unexploited potential of the social dilemmas paradigm. In W. Liebrand & D. Messick (eds), *Frontiers in Social Dilemmas Research*. Springer-Verlag (pp. 11–38).

Voiland, A. (2010, January 21). 2009: Second warmest year on record: End of warmest decade. NASA Goddard Institute for Space Studies. Retrieved from: http://www.giss.nasa.gov/research/news/20100121/

Wachtel, P. (2003). Full pockets, empty lives: A psychoanalytic exploration of the contemporary culture of greed. *American Journal of Psychotherapy*, *63*, 103–120.

Wackernagel, M., Schulz, N. B., Deumling, D., Linares, A., Jenkins, M., Kapos, V., Monfreda, C., Loh, J., Myers, N., Norgard, R., Randers, J. & Monfreda, C. (2002). Tracking the ecological overshoot of the human economy. *Proceedings of the National Academy of Sciences*, *99*(14), 9266–9271.

Waffle, V. (2003). Introduction to ecology. Retrieved from: http://www.suite101.com/article.cfm/ecology/104867

Walker, J. (2009). Intersubjectivity and the human encounter with nature. CAPA Counseling and Psychotherapy Outdoors Newsletter Edition 2, Summer 2009. Retrieved from: http://www.outdoortherapy.org.uk/files/outdoortherapy/home/CAPO_newsletter_no_2.pdf

Ward, P. (2007). *Under a Green: Global Warming, the Mass Extinctions of the Past, and What They Can Tell Us About Our Future*. Harper Collins.

Watson, J. B. (1970). *Behaviorism*. W.W. Norton.

Weinstein, N., Grubb, P. & Vautier, S. (1986). Increasing automobile seat belt use: An intervention emphasizing risk susceptibility. *Journal of Applied Psychology*, *71*(2), 285–290.

Weintrobe, S. (2011a). On healing split internal landscapes. 'Engaging with Climate Change: Psychoanalytic Perspectives' Conference, October 2011. *The Institute of Psychoanalysis News & Events* Annual Issue.

—— (ed.) (2011b). *Engaging with Climate Change: Psychoanalytic Perspectives*. Routledge.

Weisman, A. (2007). *The World Without Us*. Thomas Dunne Books.

Wenshou, W. (2008). Respondence and feedback of modern sand deserts to climate change: A case study in Gurbantunggut Desert. *Chinese Science Bulletin*, *45*(12), 1137–1142.

White, J. R., Shannon, R. D., Weltzin, J. F., Pastor, J. & Bridgham, S. D. (2008). Effects of soil warming and drying on methane cycling in a northern peatland mesocosm study. *Journal of Geophysical Research*, *113*, G00A06. doi: 10.1029/2007JG000609

Whiteside, J. & Ward, P. (2011). Ammonoid diversity and disparity track episodes of chaotic carbon cycling during the early Mesozoic. *Geology*, *39*(2), 99–102.

Widegren, O. (1998). The new environmental paradigm and personal norms. *Environment and Behavior*, *30*(1), 75–100.

Wilson, E. (1984). *Biophilia*. Harvard University Press.

Wilson, E. O. (2003). *The Future of Life*. Abacus.

Wilson, E. O. & Holldobler, B. (1988). Dense heterarchies and mass communication as the basis of organization in ant colonies. *Trends in Ecology and Evolution*, *3*(3), 65–68.

Winnicott, D. (1945). Primitive Emotional Development. *International Journal of Psycho-Analysis*, *26*(3–4), 137–143.

—— (1963). Dependence in Infant Care, in Child Care, and in the Psycho-Analytic Setting. *International Journal of Psycho-Analysis*, *44*, 339–344.

—— (1965). *The Maturational Process and the Facilitating Environment*. International Universities Press.

—— (1974). Fear of Breakdown. *Internaitonal Review of Psycho-Analysis*, *1*, 103–107.

—— (1987). *Through Pediatrics to Psychoanalysis: Collected Papers*. Karnac.

—— (1989). Metapsychological and clinical aspects of regression within the psycho-analytical set-up. In *Through Paediatrics to Psychoanalysis*. Tavistock.

—— (1999). *Playing and Reality*. Routledge.

Winter, D. D. (1996). *Ecological Psychology: Healing the Split Between Planet and Self*. Harper Collins.

Winter, D. & Koger, S. (2004). *The Psychology of Environmental Problems*. Lawrence Erlbaum Associates.

World Bank (2010). World development report 2010: Development and climate change. Retrieved from: http://go.worldbank.org/BKLQ9DSDU0

World Meteorological Organization (2011). 2010 in the top three warmest years; 2001–2010 warmest 10-year period. Press Release No. 905, United Nations. Retrieved from: http://www.wmo.int/pages/mediacentre/press_releases/pr_905_en.html

Young, R. (1994). Ambiguous space: Projective identification. In *Mental Space*. Process Press. Also available from: http://www.human-nature.com/mental/chap7.html

—— (2002). Psychoanalysis, fundamentalism and terrorism. Retrieved from: http://human-nature.com/rmyoung/papers/pap139.html

Yudkow, E. (2006). Cognitive biases potentially affecting judgment of global risks. In M. J. Rees, N. Bostron & M. M. Cirkovic (eds), *Global Catastrophic Risks*. Oxford University Press.

Zalasiewicz, J., Kapp, P., Pelletier, J., Rohrmann, A., Heermance, R., Russell, J. & Ding, L. (2008). Are we now living in the Anthropocene? *GSA Today*, *18*(2), 4–8.

Zetzel, E. (1965). The theory of therapy in relation to a developmental model of the psychic apparatus. *International Journal of Psycho-Analysis*, *46*, 39–52.

Zimmerman, M. (2007). Intrinsic versus extrinsic value. *Stanford Encyclopedia of Philosophy*. Retrieved from: http://plato.stanford.edu/entries/value-intrinsic-extrinsic/

Zita, J. (1998). *Body Talk: Philosophical Reflections on Sex and Gender*. Columbia University Press.

Žižek, S. (1991). *Looking Awry: An Introduction to Jacques Lacan through Popular Culture*. MIT Press.

—— (2003). *Organs without Bodies: Deleuze and Consequences*. Routledge.

—— (2007). Censorship today: Violence, or ecology as a new opium for the masses. Retrieved from: http://www.lacan.com/zizecology1.htm

—— (2009). *The Sublime Object of Ideology* (2nd ed.) (The Essential Žižek). Verso.

—— (2010, March 4). Return of the natives. *New Statesman*. Retrieved from: http://www.newstatesman.com/film/2010/03/avatar-reality-love-couple-sex

Zom-B (2010). Mandelbrot sequence. Retrieved from: http://en.wikipedia.org/wiki/File:Mandelbrot_sequence_new.gif

Index

abjection theory 118, 131
Aborigines, Australian 98
abstract machine 150, 157–8, 176, 183, 194
acceptance 89
accomplices 68
actual (def.) 184–5
adaptive peaks 171–2, 198, 199
addictive/compulsive consumerism 36–7, 54, 62–5, 87
advertising 8, 37, 63
aesthetic ecology 137, 146
affect regulation 85. *see also* emotionality; feelings
affective contamination 126
The Age of Stupid: (Armstrong) 37, 39
aggressor, identification with 71–2
Alien (horror film) 117
Alien Resurrection (horror film) 130, 131
alienation 62, 70, 80–1, 103, 104
alpha function 14–16, 49, 200
ambivalent attachment 84
American Psychological Association task force on climate change 11
An American Werewolf in London (horror film) 117
analytic third 172
Anasazi people 20, 163–4
animal: human bonds 94; phobias. *see* phobias; self 71, 80, 121. *see also* becoming-animal
annihilation, desire for 36. *see also* death
Antarctic ice sheets 21
anthropocene 4
anthropocentrism 36, 62, 81, 197
anthropology, radical 39
anthropomorphism 143, 152–3

anticipatory mourning 70, 72–3, 89
ants/termites 153–63, 193, 195
anxiety 5, 46–8, *66*; and classical psychoanalysis 30–1; climate crisis 40, 93; and consumption 64–5, 87; Freud on 31–5; and humour 45; nuclear disaster 92; persecutory 67; and relationship to nature 90; responses to 9. *see also* eco-anxiety; fear
apathy 70, 92
apocalypticism 40, 67, 70, 71
arborescent system 34, 133–4
art, nature representations in 106–8, 137, 139, 145–6
assemblage theory 153, 187–9, 196
asymmetric logic 42, 187
atmospheric water vapour 21
attachment theory 58, 84, 85
attacks on linking 15
attractors 16, 19, 105, 149; basin of 19, 20, 177, 179, 181; edge of chaos 173; geophilosophy 184; landscapes 160; and psychoanalysis 168, 173–5; strange 150, 160, 174. *see also* chaos/ chaos theory
Australian Aborigines 98
authoritarianism 34
automata 122
automaton-conformity 34
Avatar (horror film) 37, 38–9, 132–3
'Averting the Tragedy of the Commons' (Van Vugt) 7
avoidant attachment 84
axiomatics 184

bad object 69
Bakhtin, M. 119–23